CREATED *for* RELATIONSHIP WITH GOD

*Created For Relationship with God*
*Meditations on Accessing and Dwelling in a Vibrant Relationship with God.*

Copyright © 2024 Andrey Boynetskiy

All rights reserved. No part of this publication may be reproduced in a retrieval system, or transmitted in any form or by any means—electronic, mechanical, photocopying, recording, or otherwise—without the prior written permission of the publisher.

Unless otherwise noted, all scripture taken from the New King James Version®. Copyright © 1982 by Thomas Nelson. Used by permission. All rights reserved. | Scriptures taken from the Holy Bible, New International Version®, NIV®. Copyright © 1973, 1978, 1984, 2011 by Biblica, Inc.™ Used by permission of Zondervan. All rights reserved worldwide. www.zondervan.com The "NIV" and "New International Version" are trademarks registered in the United States Patent and Trademark Office by Biblica, Inc.™| Scripture quotations marked (NLT) are taken from the Holy Bible, New Living Translation, copyright ©1996, 2004, 2015 by Tyndale House Foundation. Used by permission of Tyndale House Publishers, Carol Stream, Illinois 60188. All rights reserved.

This manuscript has undergone viable editorial work and proofreading, yet human limitations may have resulted in minor grammatical or syntax-related errors remaining in the finished book. The understanding of the reader is requested in these cases. While precaution has been taken in the preparation of this book, the publisher and author assume no responsibility for errors or omissions, or for damages resulting from the use of the information contained herein.

This book is set in the typeface *Athelas* designed by Veronika Burian and Jose Scaglione.

Paperback ISBN: 979-8-8711-5862-3
Hardcover ISBN: 979-8-3305-1835-7

A Publication of *Tall Pine Books*
119 E Center Street, Suite B4A | Warsaw, Indiana 46580
*www.tallpinebooks.com*

| 1 24 24 20 16 02 |

Published in the United States of America

# CREATED *for* RELATIONSHIP WITH GOD

ANDREY BOYNETSKIY

*Inspired by God's love, I give glory to Him for granting me the opportunity to share His heart, His will, and His desire through this book.*

*A special thanks goes to my wife, Elena, for her unwavering support, her assistance in proofreading, and her encouraging words that kept me motivated when the writing process proved challenging and the progress seemed slow.*

# Contents

Introduction .................................................................. 9

1. The Ultimate Meaning of Life ................................. 11
2. Getting Born Again ................................................ 29
3. The Sin Issue .......................................................... 51
4. Indicator of Relationship ....................................... 71
5. Created to Love and Be Loved .............................. 87
6. The Hindrances..................................................... 111
7. What Leads to Success?........................................ 127
8. The Secret Place ................................................... 147
9. The Types of Prayer ............................................. 165
10. Our Authority ...................................................... 191
11. Unresolved and Unhealed Past............................ 209
12. The Outside Influence ......................................... 229
13. Evangelizing......................................................... 239
14. Relationship vs. Religion ..................................... 245

Appendix ................................................................... 271
Author Bio ................................................................. 275
Follow Up .................................................................. 277
Citations .................................................................... 279
Chapter Study Questions .......................................... 281
Keyword Index .......................................................... 287

# Introduction

HAVE YOU EVER felt lost, adrift in a sea of uncertainty? Longing for a life filled with purpose, tired of feeling stuck and yearning for something more? *Created for a Relationship with God* unlocks the secrets to a purpose-driven, victorious life in a relationship with our Creator—the life we were created for.

This book delves into the heart of a loving heavenly Father, revealing His desires for His creation through biblical truth. It equips you with specific steps to overcome obstacles that hinder a deep and personal relationship with God. By exploring how our choices impact both our lives and our connection with Him, *Created for a Relationship with God* offers practical solutions for reconciliation with God and unveils the true purpose and meaning of life, extending far beyond this earthly life into eternity.

During street evangelism, I recognized the challenge of effectively conveying the full message of salvation due to limited time and short attention spans. To address this, I committed myself to creating concise written explanations of core gospel concepts in about 20 pages. These explanations covered essential topics like the nature of God, the concept of sin, Jesus' sacrifice on the cross, redemption, salvation, reconciliation with God, and establishing a personal relationship with Him.

The plan was to distribute these written handouts to those who expressed interest during street evangelism. This approach inspired me to write a more comprehensive book titled *Sharing the Gospel*. This book would delve deeper into three key areas: how to be born again, how to cultivate a relationship with God, and how to get involved in ministry and discover God's calling for one's life.

After completing two sections of *Sharing the Gospel*, I revisited the notes and insights I had accumulated over the years regarding my personal relationship with Jesus. As I compiled these thoughts into a single chapter, it became clear that the depth and richness of the material wouldn't fit within a single chapter. The content deserved a dedicated book to explore the profound nature of a relationship with God.

CHAPTER ONE

# The Ultimate Meaning of Life

*You will seek me and find me when you seek me with all your heart.* (Jeremiah 29:13)

MANKIND WAS CREATED in the right relationship with God at the start of creation. As Genesis 3:8 tells us, "And they heard the sound of the Lord God walking in the garden in the cool of the day, and Adam and his wife hid themselves from the presence of the Lord God among the trees of the garden." However, through Adam and Eve's disobedience, we were doomed to die due to sin, becoming burdened with guilt, shame, and condemnation and separated from God.

Instead of enjoying God like they used to, Adam and Eve became filled with fear and sin. And sin created a chasm between a holy God and sinful humanity. This separation has echoed through generations, marking human existence with a longing for fulfillment amidst the weight of guilt, fear, and angst. You and I were also born into this state. Yet God, in His mercy, made a way for us to be redeemed and restored to the original relationship He had with mankind before the fall. He did so by sending His Son, Jesus Christ.

God is our Creator, and He created us for a specific purpose. This purpose begins with reconciling with Him, knowing Him intimately, loving Him deeply, and entering into a vibrant relationship with Him. This entails getting right with God, continually pursuing Him, glorifying Him in our actions, serving Him wholeheartedly, and sharing His love with others. God created us for His own plan, not for ourselves. We weren't meant to chase our own desires; God created us for His glory. We can't glorify Him without serving Him and we can't serve Him without loving Him, which comes from being in a relationship with Him. The way to establish a relationship is through getting born again (this will be explained in greater details in the next chapter) and being adopted into His family. Through this adoption, we start to get to know who God is and discover God's character. We find out His divine plan for our lives, which can include ministries and acts of service that bring Him glory.

By design, we are created with a void in our hearts, a void that has a specific shape. What is that shape? It's the shape of God. God created us with a God-shaped void that only He can fill. To place *anything* else in the spot where God belongs is to try to place a square peg in a round hole, as they say. This will only lead to frustration and lack. God is bigger and better than anything we can imagine. To put something else in His place is to put something that is smaller and worse than Him in that spot. It will never satisfy.

The God-shaped hole in our hearts can only be filled by God Himself—our Creator. If you have ever felt like something was missing or that there was more to your existence, it's because of an internal awareness of the God-shaped hole in your heart. We often attempt to fill that void and bring ourselves ultimate satisfaction with the wrong things. We pursue fleeting pleasures, temporary gratification, relationships, vices, and substances that leave us lacking at the end of the day. We've all heard these types of stories before. Apart from Him, this God-shaped void within us remains, leaving us restless and searching for meaning in all the wrong places.

A large number of people around the world are searching for something more to satisfy their souls. They remain unfulfilled, experiencing emptiness in their hearts and a deep sense of longing—a recognition that something essential is missing at the core of their being. They attempt to fill this 'God-shaped void' with temporary, unfulfilling alternatives that ultimately fail to satisfy, leaving them with even more emptiness in their hearts. God does not want us to be miserable, though, which is why He offers us a solution. God has not only told us that He is the One who can fill the void, but He has provided a path to make it simple. In other words, He has not only shown us the piece of the puzzle we need, He has also shown us exactly how and where to place it.

We will never be truly happy apart from God. He doesn't want us to be lost in this pursuit of empty substitutes. Instead, He offers us the embrace of His perfect love, a love that surpasses anything the world can offer. He invites us into a loving relationship, tugging at our hearts to experience the captivating beauty of His grace. Open your heart and give Him a chance to reveal His love to you.

> *He has made from one blood every nation of men to dwell on all the face of the earth, and has determined their preappointed times and the boundaries of their dwellings, so that they should seek the Lord, in the hope that they might grope for Him and find Him, though He is not far from each one of us.* (Acts 17:26-27)

Our quest for fulfillment becomes a constant search for happiness, in pursuit of fleeting pleasures, leaving us tied to temporary gratification that can't satisfy us completely. We're left with a void that can only be filled with the eternal love which flows from the heart of our Creator. Without God, without a relationship with Him, we won't feel complete; we will always feel that something is missing in our lives. Nothing will ever satisfy our soul like He can, and we won't be able to experience the true meaning of life for which God has created us. God is saying to each one of us, "I want you to be complete, and I created you to find wholeness only in connection with Me, in a loving relationship with Me. That's why I draw you close, so you can experience the fullness of life in My presence."

The Bible states, "God looks down from heaven upon the children of men, to see if there are any who understand, who seek God" (Psalm 53:2). God's desire is to have a unique, personal, and loving relationship with you. From the very beginning, when we were still sinners and enemies of God, He extended His love to us through the sacrifice of Jesus Christ so that we could have a relationship with Him. John reminds us, "And we know that the Son of God has come and has given us an understanding, that we may know Him who is true; and we are in Him who is true, in His Son Jesus Christ. This is the true God and eternal life" (1 John 5:20).

In His justice, God laid out a path for us to bridge the gap and enter into a relationship with Him. He provided the solution to fill the void with His love, enabling us to live the purposeful life He intended for us. This reconciliation, this filling of the void, hinges on one thing: returning to Him and repenting of our sins.

God has already provided a solution to sin; the question remains, will we embrace it? Though sinless Himself, Jesus Christ died for our sins, opening the door to reconciliation with God, a priceless gift offered through His sacrifice on the cross. Now we have an amazing opportunity to enter into a loving relationship with God. We have all strayed from Him, yet He longs to extend His loving embrace if we simply allow Him. John reminds us of the gift of salvation. "Behold! The Lamb of God who takes away the sin of the world!" (John 1:29). And again, John mentions this: "He Himself is the propitiation for our sins, and not for ours only but also for the whole world" (1 John 2:2).

People argue that there are many paths to God. However, God has only outlined one singular way and that is through relationship with Jesus Christ. Only through the sacrifice of Jesus Christ can we find forgiveness for our sins and forge a relationship with God. Jesus' death on the cross reconciled us to God, bridging the gap that separated us from Him and reuniting us in a real relationship with the eternal Creator. Jesus is the means by which God has manifested His love toward us. The Scriptures beautifully express this love: "In this the love of God was manifested toward us, that God has sent His only begotten Son into the world, that we might live through Him. In this is love, not that we loved God, but that He loved us and sent His Son to be the propitiation for our sins" (1 John 4:9-10).

Some feel that God is distant and exists somewhere way out in the ether. The truth is, God left heaven to come to earth and traveled this vast distance to prove one point: that He longs to be close to us. He has already drawn closer to us through Jesus' sacrifice at Calvary. Now it's our turn to draw closer to God (see James 4:8).

Jesus desires for us to know Him personally and intimately. If we reject Jesus' sacrifice, then we're rejecting God's love. God is patiently waiting to get back together with His rebellious creation. He does so by giving us chance after chance to get to know Him and to experience His goodness. Notice, I used the word "experience."

We know God, not just by reading about Him in the Bible, but through *experience*. The Scriptures are more than mere text on a page; it gives us an opportunity to know the heart of God. Through His Word, we become familiar with Him by both *personal revelation* and *experience*. It is living in the daily reality that God is with you and longs to speak to you.

This journey begins with being born again, opening the door to an everlasting relationship. Agreeing to embrace God's love is revealed by the action of accepting the sacrifice of Jesus Christ. That's the only way we can start having a loving relationship with God. Jesus is personal, and He desires a personal, intimate relationship with each one of us so much that He went to the cross for that purpose. As we read in Paul's letter to Timothy, "For this is good and acceptable in the sight of God our Savior, who desires all men to be saved and to come to the knowledge of the truth" (1 Timothy 2:3-4).

To reject His sacrifice is to turn away from the outstretched arms of God's love. Jesus yearns for a deep, personal relationship with each of us. Will we open our hearts to His love?

**Worth and Value**

Driven by immense love, Jesus chose to take upon Himself the judgment for our sins, to bear the consequences of our sinful lives and die in our place. By this action, He demonstrated His love and showed us that we are so valuable in His eyes. Our inherent worth is demonstrated in our bearing the image and likeness of God. If people were not extremely precious and valuable in His eyes, Jesus would have never done what He did at the cross. We only pay high prices for things that are very valuable and precious. The innocent blood of the Son of God is the highest price imaginable. This means, we collectively and individually are unthinkably valuable for God!

To put it simply, our worth and significance cannot be *earned*; it has to be *discovered*. You have value because God doesn't create worthless things, and there are no mistakes or accidents in God's work. Once you understand this, it will radically change your life. Our worth is declared by God; we can't take credit for it based on our achievements, but rather on God's love. All God wants is for us to recognize our value through His eyes and love Him with everything we have. When you doubt your value, you overlook the extent of value God has placed on you through His love. Your value is determined by God's love for you. We spend so much time trying to demonstrate to society and God our worth in order to gain recognition. Why? So that God and people will value us and act favorably toward us. But at the end of the day, our value is inherent and given by the free gift of God. All God wants is for us to recognize Him in our lives and love Him with everything we have. In this, others will recognize God's love in our lives, as well.

If Jesus hadn't proved His love to us on the cross, then it may be harder to trust His love for us. Because Jesus proved His love and our worth, we have no reason to doubt His goodness and our own value. Jesus cares for you so much that He died to know you personally and have fellowship with you as His beloved bride. We cannot diminish God's love offered to us through the sacrifice of Jesus Christ; we can only respond to it by accepting it or rejecting it. Recognizing our significance in the eyes of God should pull our hearts toward accepting His grace. It's not by our merit, but by His grace, that He revealed Himself and offered us restoration.

God doesn't want us to have low self-esteem, to feel down about our problems, to remain ashamed and guilty of the past or present. He wants to remove anything that sin has damaged and corrupted in our lives. When He removes these things, we are able to see our true worth which He reveals.

Though we wandered away, God is patiently waiting to get back together with His rebellious creation. He holds open the door to reconciliation by giving us countless opportunities to experience His love. This is an intimate and personal pursuit. When God wanted to win mankind back to Himself, He did not use a written contract or business negotiation. Instead, He shed His blood and gave us the love letter of the Scriptures to demonstrate His desire for personal relationship. It was so important for God to reconcile with us that He sent Jesus to be a mediator. It was so important to *Jesus* that we reconcile with the Father that He was willing to die to give us a chance at re-establishing our connection with Him. It was so important to the Holy Spirit that He is actively working to draw in the hearts of men day and night. Knowing God's deep desire in this way will help you to properly value your relationship with Him. Note that this invitation is not just for a few, but for all. Paul wrote, "[God] desires all men to be saved and to come to the knowledge of the truth" (1 Timothy 2:4).

### Perception and Reception

God can talk to anyone, and He does so from time to time, but He has *true* relationships with His children. His children are those who have been born of Him through getting born again. The reason many don't find a relationship with God is because they simply aren't looking for it. It's not God's fault that we haven't reached out to Him to establish union with Him. He has made Himself ever available, with arms wide open on the cross. Our role is to remove our false perceptions of who He is and embrace the authentic Jesus.

There exists a common misconception that Jesus did it *all*. Yes, He did it *all* in terms of making salvation available to you and me. However, Christ's death and resurrection do not automatically restore our relationship with God. Just because Jesus died for all doesn't mean that everyone accepts and receives His sacrifice and embraces His love in return. Our reception of Jesus makes all the difference. The ultimate act of love was demonstrated to everyone on the cross. It is crucial to recognize that Jesus died for our sins and desires to become our personal Savior. In reality, only some decide to accept salvation by repenting from their sins and being born again.

By believing in Him, repenting of our sins, and being born again, we can establish a relationship with God. We must respond personally, sincerely, and with a commitment to turn away from our sin through repentance, knowing that only Christ can save us from our fallen state. The only way to have a relationship with God is to go through the process of being born again, which consists of four parts: belief in the divine nature of Jesus, repentance, water baptism, and receiving the Holy Spirit.

> *Repent, and let every one of you be baptized in the name of Jesus Christ for the remission of sins; and you shall receive the gift of the Holy Spirit.* (Acts 2:38)

The truth is, He has already laid out the criteria for us to be born again and become adopted into His family. We do not have to make up our own criteria of how to be reconciled with God; He has already laid out the steps for us. The issue is not on God's part but ours. He has always wanted to be best friends. Yet through our bad perception and lack of reception, we hinder that connection from ever being established. Whether it's our past, our flesh, our love of sin, or other worldly things, we must let go of all that prevents us from embracing Jesus.

God is saying to each one of us, "Find connection with Me and a loving relationship with Me. That's why I draw you to Me, so you will experience the fullness of life in My presence."

## Unique Union

> *And we know that the Son of God has come and has given us an understanding, that we may know Him who is true; and we are in Him who is true, in His Son Jesus Christ. This is the true God and eternal life.* (1 John 5:20)

This "understanding" of Jesus is key to living a successful life. What is success? To love and be loved! God created us with the purpose of knowing Him, loving Him, and receiving His love. God created us uniquely with our distinguished character and personality. He longs to have a unique relationship with us which is unrepeatable with anyone else. God does not create cookie cutter people and copy/paste relationships with His children.

The truth is, our soul longs for this unique connection with

God. We have been wired to pine for His love. We desire to pour out love, as well. Yet, because of our free will, we have chosen to avoid God's love toward us, which means we have no love to give back to Him or others. Substitutes for God's love prove to only harm us in the long run. To put it simply, if we're not experiencing God, it doesn't matter how successful we think our life is. We're missing the most important thing in this life, the ultimate purpose for which we were created. To acknowledge God is to acknowledge the real reason for our existence. Without God, life loses its primary purpose, and its meaning is obscured.

Every aspect of our lives is influenced by our unique relationship with God, or lack thereof. We are spiritual beings, and we were created to have spiritual experiences with God through our relationships with Him. These experiences are unique for all believers. As you journey in your Christian walk, you will find the way you talk to God and the way God talks to you is unique and custom. We all enter the same door of salvation, if we choose it, yet the relationship with God on the other side is unique for everyone. It is all thanks to His love.

God not only gives His love but wants His love to be reciprocated back to Him. God is self-sufficient. He doesn't need us to be fulfilled and complete, but He made a decision to create us and be with us in a close bond.

Do we really desire to know the God who created us? In theory, we can understand that God loves us, but if we have never experienced His love in our lives, we will never fully understand. Experiencing His love intimately can only be possible by first establishing a connection with Him.

God is not only our mighty Creator but also a loving heavenly Father. He wants us to be His sons and daughters. God invites each of us to join His family in order to have fellowship. He has already shown us the way to be born again in order to join His family, becoming His children and beginning a loving relationship with Him. All we have to do is come to God and approach

Him on His terms. If we don't make a commitment and follow through to repent and be born again, then with our actions we show that we reject God and don't intend to accept His love. We have a choice to make and we will never be forced into a relationship with our Creator. God is not going to barge into our lives. He does not force Himself on anyone. We must willingly ask and invite Him in. He desires for us to be part of His family. This life is God-given, and we only have that chance while we are still alive, here on earth, to reconcile with God and have our relationship with Him restored. He created us for a relationship and a union with Him, and this should come before all other goals and plans. True happiness comes from knowing God and living in connection with Him, and the key to happiness is experiencing God's love and finding contentment in spending time with Him. We can't be happy apart from the source of life, the source of our existence, and the ultimate love, which is God.

Throughout the Bible, God's constant call echoes: "I have done everything possible to be in relationship with you. Are you doing everything possible on your end?" God longs for us to go beyond hearing of His love and reading about His love and invites us into a journey of discovery, where His nature and presence is revealed in personal encounters with Him in our everyday lives.

What has God not yet proven? What has He not yet done in order for us to say "yes" to Him? The problem is that we can fail to recognize this and continue to ignore or reject His attempts. We need to make a decision to repent of our sins in order to establish our connection with God.

It's mind-boggling that God decides to dwell in us in order to have a relationship. Just consider this: the Creator of the universe—who is an all-powerful and all-knowing being, perfectly good—desires a relationship with humankind. How can we reject His love? God loves us, you and me, but we will never experience His love completely if we don't accept it.

## An Eternal Viewpoint

The book of Jeremiah starts with an interesting revelation from God: "Before I formed you in the womb I knew you" (Jeremiah 1:5). In other words, God's plan for our life was created in eternity long before we were conceived.

How does this impact us today? As believers, our focus should be on that which is eternal. Knowing that God crafted plans for us from eternity can be a stabilizing, comforting force in our lives, especially during challenging times. It reminds us that our lives have purpose and meaning, even when we can't see it. Paul said, "While we do not look at the things which are seen, but at the things which are not seen. For the things which are seen are temporary, but the things which are not seen are eternal" (2 Corinthians 4:18). We were created for the eternal purpose of living and dwelling in His presence for eternal fellowship with Him and to pursue and draw close to God. It is not just a temporary pursuit for the here and now. It is an eternal one.

In the busyness of everyday life, caught up in the daily grind, it's easy to forget about the reality of eternity. However, pausing to consider life from an eternal perspective helps us remember who God is and our standing before Him. We put in a lot of effort into sustaining our physical lives, but how do we treat our spiritual lives? How much importance do we put in our eternal walk with God, as opposed to temporary things? Are we making sure that our spiritual life is healthy?

If we would see how our businesses, jobs, families, and interactions affect us spiritually, we would be more vigilant in how we go about life. We would change things and continuously adapt our lives and choices in order for our relationship with Jesus to prosper. By walking with God, we will see things for what they really are in the spiritual world.

Can we prove with our actions that we want to spend eternity in His presence? Many people don't want to put in enough effort in order to change their lives in favor of eternity because it's uncomfortable to them. They lack the necessary motivation because they are carnal-minded, self-focused, and care about the well-being of their physical lives rather than the well-being of their spiritual lives. The truth is, we're truly spiritual beings. We are eternal souls encased in a temporary, physical body. The physical body is temporary, but the spiritual body is eternal. Those who are only concerned with this life are concerned with their physical well-being and self-gratification, whereas God is more concerned with the well-being of our spiritual souls, which is eternal. So, which do you think is more important?

> *For I know the thoughts that I think toward you, says the Lord, thoughts of peace and not of evil, to give you a future and a hope.* (Jeremiah 29:11)

If you really love someone, your real genuine love for them entails wanting the very best and greatest good for them as a whole. God cares for our well-being. He desires us and keeps our best interests in mind. This is exactly why He calls us to turn away from sin. He knows that sin distances us from Him in this life and in eternity. People defend their flesh like it's their best friend, but in reality, the flesh is the enemy of our spirit. Paul wrote to the Galatians:

> *For the flesh lusts against the Spirit, and the Spirit against the flesh; and these are contrary to one another, so that you do not do the things that you wish.* (Galatians 5:17)

God is deeply interested in our spiritual upkeep. He gave us an entire book that aims to help us in that process. God doesn't just want us to merely struggle to *survive* spiritually but to *thrive* and flourish spiritually. This is abundant life (see John 10:10). And that's why, out of love for us, God is interested in our reconciliation with Him.

Not only are we focused on eternal things, but our union with God itself is eternal. Knowing God is not a temporary pursuit but one that we will enjoy forever. God is waiting patiently for us to partner with Him. We can ignore the call of the Holy

Spirit in our lives for a while, sometimes even years. But He is patiently waiting and, from time to time, He reminds us of Himself by knocking on the door of our hearts and gently calling us to respond to His call. What kind of love waits for so long?

## What's Guiding You?

If God is not guiding you through a personal relationship, then what is guiding your life?

None of us want to live out our lives in vain and miss the most important purpose for which we were created. The question is, are we experiencing God? And if not, then why aren't we? Many rush through life toward an eternal destination with their actions speaking on their behalf: "I don't have time for God now." This is a scary thought. We must realize, from the eternal standpoint, how important Jesus' sacrifice is and we'll agree that we do have time for Jesus. After all, He gave us more than His time, He gave us His all, He gave us His very life. As we experience encounters with Jesus, these personal experiences become our own and they cannot be taken away from us. We won't be able to doubt a real experience with the living God.

If God is not directing our lives, something else is. As we come close to Him, His voice directs our steps. His plan becomes transparent in our lives. Don't be obstinate and continue to resist His pull on your heart. Learn to yield to His leading.

Oftentimes people misunderstand God based on their experiences, their rejection, and the pain and suffering they have received from others, and they deny His existence before they can even establish a relationship with Him. They never allowed God's love to be revealed in their lives and never gave themselves a chance to personally experience His love for them. Without the initial encounter with God through an established relationship, the person doesn't know what they're missing. The unfulfilled void due to the absence of God in our lives compels us to seek fulfillment in passing pleasures that leave us ever empty. But when we experience a glimpse of His presence, when He fills the emptiness of our void, only then will our hearts burn with an insatiable desire to relive that closeness, to yearn for an encounter with Him.

## All or Nothing

Can you fully explain to me your relationship with your parents? You can't fully explain the relationship you have with your family because it cannot be explained; it has to be experienced. In the same way, I can't fully explain a relationship with God. You must experience it for yourself. Once you have experienced it, no one can take that away from you.

We may understand that a relationship with Jesus is important in theory, but we will never truly understand the significance of a relationship with Him until we dive in. A person has to not just understand the importance of a relationship with Jesus but also desire to have it established. Once we encounter God and experience Him personally, we will quickly see that He is far more important than anything else in this world.

God's desire is to be the center of our lives, and He is the only one who deserves that place. When we come to Him, we surrender all. If the relationship is not there or it's lacking, this means we are not in the right stance with Him. Despite knowing that having a relationship with Jesus is very important, we can still make excuses as to why we can't find time, don't have enough energy, or why other people or circumstances prevent us from doing so. And by compromising, we try to downplay the importance of a relationship from an eternal standpoint. Excuses won't work before God. We're not going to say to Him one day, "I got born again, but I never really got to the point of knowing You because I didn't have enough time and motivation. I prioritized other things in my life over You." This won't fare before God's throne.

This life is a test of who is going to seek God. Who is going to reach out to God and grab on to Him when so many things want to take first place in our lives? There is an ongoing competition for your attention. We live in a time when things, events, and people are claiming our time continually. Many are not willing to put the effort into passing the test. And the question from Jesus remains for all of us, "Are you Mine? Do you belong to Me? Do you love Me?"

Real life begins when what we desire most in our lives matches what God desires most in our lives. You have likely tried many things in life, but have you tried Jesus? If you have never tried to encounter Jesus to establish a relationship with Him, now is the time to give Him a chance to change your life.

And if you want this relationship to start, you can simply tell Him, "I give up trying to run my life the way I want. I give my life completely to you, Jesus, and I want to live my life the way you want it to be lived, putting aside all my selfish ambitions! I don't want to value anything in this world more than You."

## The Conscience and Free Will

We all have a God-given moral compass within us and it's our conscience. God's laws are written in our hearts. Whether or not someone has read the Bible, they have a basic internal understanding of right and wrong. Paul wrote:

> *...who show the work of the law written in their hearts, their conscience also bearing witness, and between themselves their thoughts accusing or else excusing them in the day when God will judge the secrets of men by Jesus Christ, according to my gospel.* (Romans 2:15-16)

Our conscience is the innate ability to distinguish between what is right and what is wrong, between what is good and what is evil. It convicts us when we do wrong and gives us approval when we do right. God gave us a conscience so we could come to terms with the fact that we're sinners in need of a Savior. Our conscience lets us feel shame and guilt when we sin. It tells us to stop distancing ourselves from God's love and from the relationship we have with Him. We can defile or sear our conscience if we continue to ignore it. Don't ignore the conviction of your conscience; act upon it and turn away from your sins.

Our conscience also allows us to analyze our spiritual life and our relationship with God. Do we have a relationship with Him? Do we feel His presence alone in fellowship with Him? And if that's the case, what level is it at? Is it growing, or what prevents it from growing? Can it be improved? What are some of the things that hinder our relationship? What's standing in the way? Let's examine our lives and ask God, "Is there something that I overlook in my life that hinders my relationship with You? Is there anything that I think is acceptable but actually displeases You, Lord?" The conscience acts as a spiritual thermometer, taking our temperature and reminding us to get back to the things of God.

We have to obey our conscience, however, and sadly, many people do not. This is because God created us with a free will. This is the ability to choose. You have a free will to choose what to think, say, or do. Your free will is a wonderful gift from God. The main purpose for which God gives free will is to allow humanity to choose to love Him. You have a free will to love or reject God. In order for love to be real, it must be freely given. You were created with a free will because love requires freedom in order to be real. It isn't really love if you are controlled by someone or forced to love someone.

Love allows you to choose someone with your own free will. Love is a choice that we make. God doesn't want to manipulate and control our freedom; that's why we have the ability to choose to seek Him and reach out to Him or not. God gave you the ability to respond to His love by loving Him back. He wants you to choose Him freely, without force or coercion. He wants your love to be true to Him. Free will is essential in our relationship with God. It's what makes us unique as His creation and He wants us to exercise it to choose Him. God values your free will, so He will not force Himself on you. You need to ask Him to be in your life.

We can exercise our free will to accomplish our own agenda apart from God. We can use our free will to turn away from God and define our own purpose in life or we can choose to reconcile back to God through the sacrifice of Jesus on the cross. We are accountable for our autonomous actions. All our actions have consequences because of the choices we make, which is why we will all be held accountable for our choices, our actions, our words, and our thoughts.

With our conscience, we can perceive right from wrong and then, with our free will, choose good or evil. They work together. Instead of rebelling against God, we can choose to submit to Him and repent of our sins. We will find our purpose when we choose to be born again and become part of God's family.

This born-again process is only the beginning. It introduces us to the reason for our very creation: a vital relationship with the living God. From there God leads us into His plan for our lives.

Without implementing this necessary step, fulfillment is only a pipedream that we will never actually realize. But when we truly encounter God and abide in union with Him, the God-shaped hole is filled and our life finally *begins*.

## CHAPTER TWO

# Getting Born Again

*And you He made alive, who were dead in trespasses and sins... (Ephesians 2:1)*

BEING IN SIN is not just the difference between being good and bad, it's the difference between being *dead* and *alive*. Our sinful nature stands in the way of our ability to establish a relationship with God. It keeps us distant and keeps us dead. This is the one single separator between you and the Lord.

From the beginning, we live with a sinful nature and are spiritually dead, and it pulls us away from God and prevents us from having a loving relationship with Him. It was not God's intent to be separated from man, but man willingly separated himself from God through disobedience. We are spiritually dead before we are fully born again. Living with a sinful nature makes us sinners before God.

You might ask, why can't God have relationship with sinful mankind? The truth is, God is holy. He is untouched by sin and darkness. Therefore, in order for us to commune with Him, we must be washed clean of our sins by the blood of Jesus.

Our inherent sinful nature poses a significant barrier to cultivating a deep and meaningful relationship with God. It was never part of God's divine plan for us to be estranged from Him; rather, it was through mankind's willful disobedience that this separation came to pass.

As the Scripture that starts this chapter states, we are dead before the new birth. However, Paul goes on to write, "But God, who is rich in mercy, because of His great love with which He loved us, even when we were dead in trespasses, made us alive together with Christ" (Ephesians 2:4-5).

Until then, we were unable to receive the things of the Spirit. The natural man does not receive the things of the Spirit of God, because they are foolish and silly to him (see 1 Corinthians 2:14). We were in what Paul calls "the mind of the flesh," which is not able to submit to God or please God. Paul explained that the carnal mind is against God and not subject to the law of God, nor can be. He ultimately explains that those who are in the flesh *cannot* please God, no matter how hard they try (see Romans 8:7-8).

The gospel, however, takes us beyond being mere "natural men" and makes us spiritual through a born-again experience. This new birth leads to a new life. You cannot live your old life after a new birth. This process is a work of God, wherein God adopts us into His family. We are no longer sinners but saints created in Christ's righteousness.

Previously, we had lived for ourselves in sin, indulging in the flesh, loving what the world had to offer, and being spiritually dead the whole time. But now, through spiritual transformation, we live for God as our Father, belonging to His family.

### The Born Again Necessity

Some might think they can become a good person and be truly *alive* without being born again. This is not so. Being brought to life is a gift from God, and that gift only comes through the removal of sin, and the removal of sin only happens through the born-again experience.

> *For all have sinned and fall short of the glory of God.* (Romans 3:23)

The Old Testament affirms this same reality: "For there is not a just man on earth who does good and does not sin" (Ecclesiastes 7:20). Isaiah also wrote, "All we like sheep have gone astray; we have turned, every one, to his own way" (Isaiah 53:6).

If we fail to acknowledge our *need* for salvation, we will fail to *receive* salvation. We have to come to God on His terms. He already set the criteria by which we can be born again and become His child. God provides a solution to our sin problem through the sacrifice of Jesus Christ on the cross and His resurrection on the third day.

Sin has created a giant gap between man and God. Some pretend the gap does not exist and, as a result, live without union with God. You must see the *why* behind salvation to start with. Once we acknowledge *why* we need salvation, we can explore the steps involved in the process—which we will explore next.

## The Process

The complete process of becoming born again involves four steps, and all four steps need to happen for the process to be complete. According to the Word of God, these four steps are: belief, repentance, water baptism, and baptism in the Holy Spirit. Let's explore those in detail.

## Belief

It's important that we don't just have *belief* but that we have *belief* in the correct things. To be born again, one must believe in Jesus as the Son of God and that He was born of a virgin, Mary, was fully man and fully God here on earth. That He is part of the divine Godhead who lived a perfect, sinless life, was crucified and died for our sins and was resurrected on a third day, and is now seated at the right hand of the Father. Our belief means putting trust in Jesus as Savior.

In order for faith to be real, it requires a follow up action confirming the faith. Faith is shown through action to validate if we really believe what we believe. If we believe something, we will act upon it. The Bible teaches that, "Faith without works is dead" (James 2:26).

Obedience to God's Word demonstrates our faith. Obedient faith is also revealed in putting our trust in Jesus and obeying what He says in His Word. Having faith means realizing that what Jesus says in His Word is the truth and acting upon it by doing what it says. We keep on trusting Jesus no matter what situations are presented to us, and we continue on believing with unwavering faith in the face of difficult circumstances. This is the evidence of true belief. Belief that crumbles easily is not belief at all.

Genuine faith signifies agreement with God's truth and prompts us to seek reconciliation with Him. Faith always requires action to prove its authenticity and sincerity. It's characterized by trust in Jesus for salvation and is demonstrated through obedience to God by repenting of our sins. If we believe in God but don't repent of our sins and ask for forgiveness, then our faith will not do us any good and it will not help us in our reconciliation with God. Believing in and of itself is not enough. There needs to be repentance that backs up our faith.

There's a price to pay in life for our decision to continue in faith and keep on trusting Jesus. But knowing *what* we are paying the price for gives us strength to persevere.

### Repentance

As a person is becoming born again, the Holy Spirit speaks to his heart and mind to show him that he is a sinner and in need of salvation through the gospel. This person's belief in Jesus as Savior also comes with a conviction of sin. This leads us to repentance.

Repentance is not feeling regret or remorse. Regret is when a person feels sadness, disappointment, or sorrow over something that they have done or haven't done to themselves in the past. Remorse is when a person feels a sense of guilt and shame for the past wrongs of what they have done or haven't done to others in the past. Regret is self-directed while remorse is directed at others.

Repentance is different altogether. Repentance is the recognition of what our sins have done against God and realizing that by committing sin, we have offended God. We have broken God's laws and deserve God's righteous anger and His just judgment. Repentance realizes that there is a massive gap between us and God and we are 100% at fault.

Repentance requires a realization of one's true brokenness. A genuine recognition of our sinfulness and guilt will also lead to genuine sorrow, shame, and even hatred for the sins that we have committed. This acknowledgment leads to godly sorrow and forms a repentant heart before God by taking responsibility for our own actions and not blaming someone else for our sins.

A repentant mentality is accepting the truth that we are not holy, righteous, or just and that God is holy, righteous, and perfectly just. Repentance is acknowledging that we have sinned against a holy God and understanding the effect of our sin from God's perspective. It means seeing yourself and your life through God's eyes. It is a turning away from sin toward God.

Even our good deeds are often sins of self-righteousness and don't match up to God's perfect standard and, therefore, don't please God. The Greek word for repentance is called *metanoia* which means *to change the mind*. Repentance leads to turning away from your wicked ways and confessing sins by accepting Jesus' sacrifice on the cross. Repentance is not asking the Lord for forgiveness with the intent to sin again. Repentance doesn't mean saying sorry and continuing on with your sin.

The *sin, repent, repeat* cycle means you're not truly sorry for the sin you have committed. Repentance means you are rejecting your sin completely. Repentance is an honest, regretful acknowledgement of sin and taking personal responsibility for it, with a commitment to change. Repentance is a change of mind that leads to a change of heart, which in turn leads to a change in actions. Changed behavior is a product of true confession of sins. How do we demonstrate our repentance? By the deeds that follow. Know this: repentance is not a one time ordeal but an ongoing process in the lives of believers.

True repentance is followed up by acknowledging Him as our Master, surrendering to His perfect will, then following and obeying Him. We need to realize that we all fall short and need God's mercy to avoid His righteous judgment for our sins.

Belief and repentance are the first two aspects of man's response to God's offer of salvation. They go hand in hand. One of Christ's first sermons was, "The time is fulfilled, and the kingdom of God is at hand. *Repent*, and *believe* in the gospel" (Mark 1:15, emphasis added). We cannot repent without believing and we cannot believe without seeing the true need for repentance. Those who repent have also believed.

Repentance and belief precede by water baptism. In fact, they are necessary before the water baptism can take place. If one was water baptized but has no faith and/or hasn't repented of their sins, then they continue to remain under the power of sin and are still in bondage to darkness. Water baptism by itself will not resurrect their spiritual being to a new life.

### Water Baptism

Water baptism is a part of the salvation process and an essential component in becoming born again. According to Scripture, water baptism in conjunction with faith and repentance and in filling of the Holy Spirit is necessary to be saved. Mark wrote, "He who believes and is baptized will be saved; but he who does not believe will be condemned" (Mark 16:16). Water baptism can only come after true repentance and it is for the remission (forgiveness) of sins. Water baptism is a breaking away from the old life and becoming a new creation. Water baptism is an act of practical expression of obedience in faith to God.

A believer's faith is what makes water baptism real. Only after genuine repentance and a turning away from one's old life can one be baptized in order to die to their old sinful life in the water and be set free from the power of sin. Water baptism is a commandment, not a suggestion.

When a person is water baptized, with full submersion, the law of sin connected to their sinful nature is done away with by breaking away the chains of sin and the grip of the power of sin altogether. After baptism, we are not a slave of sin any longer.

Unbelievers are under a bondage to the law of sin. It rules over their flesh. In water baptism, Jesus takes us out of the dominion and kingdom of darkness and places us into the kingdom of light. In water baptism, we give up being a master of our own life and willingly submit to the lordship of Jesus Christ. After baptism, we receive a clean conscience before God.

The word *baptisto* is not translated from the original Greek to English but rather transliterated from Greek to English, so it's simply spelled in English letters. The definition of the word *baptisto* is *to dip repeatedly, to immerse, to submerge, to cleanse by dipping or submerging, to soak, to drench, to plunge, to wash, to make clean with water, to wash one's self and to bathe.*

So, water baptism means complete immersion and submersion in water. According to the Bible, water baptism is not sprinkling of water on the head. The biblical water baptism involves a full immersion of a believer. The word *baptism* in the New Testament has two meanings, one being a bath or cleansing. Just like in the physical world, the purpose of a bath is to remove dirt by washing it away in order to become clean. The same can be said of water baptism. We are baptized after we acknowledge that we are spiritually unclean in our sins.

> *Arise and be baptized, and wash away your sins.* (Acts 22:16)

> *Let us draw near with a true heart in full assurance of faith, having our hearts sprinkled from an evil conscience and our bodies washed with pure water.* (Hebrews 10:22)

> *...according to His mercy He saved us, through the washing of regeneration and renewing of the Holy Spirit.* (Titus 3:5)

The other meaning of *baptism* in the Scriptures is *a burial*. The purpose of burial is obviously to bury someone who is dead. Burial is a ceremony involving a method of final disposal of a dead body. Water baptism is the burial of an old life.

> *Or do you not know that as many of us as were baptized into Christ Jesus were baptized into His death?* (Romans 6:3)

> *...buried with Him in baptism, in which you also were raised with Him through faith in the working of God, who raised Him from the dead.* (Colossians 2:12)

The part of burial in water baptism represents the burial for the old man which is our carnal, rebellious nature (body of sin). The old spiritual man dies and a new person resurrects to life.

Water baptism is death, burial, and resurrection to a new life. Paul expounded on this in detail, writing, "Therefore we were buried with Him through baptism into death, that just as Christ was raised from the dead by the glory of the Father, even so we also should walk in newness of life. For if we have been united together in the likeness of His death, certainly we also shall be in the likeness of His resurrection, knowing this, that our old man was crucified with Him, that the body of sin might be done away with, that we should no longer be slaves of sin. For he who has died has been freed from sin. Now if we died with Christ, we believe that we shall also live with Him, knowing that Christ, having been raised from the dead, dies no more. Death no longer has dominion over Him" (Romans 6:4-9).

During the water baptism, our old nature that we used to have when we lived in sin dies with Christ on the cross. We've been buried with Christ in baptism, and sin has no more dominion over us.

> *Likewise you also, reckon yourselves to be dead indeed to sin, but alive to God in Christ Jesus our Lord.* (Romans 6:11)

Water baptism must be done in good conscience. A good conscience means a sincere one, and it comes into agreement with God on the importance and necessity of water baptism. It is not a half-hearted decision. We choose to follow God's commandment regarding water baptism by acting with a good conscience. Paul emphasized this, writing to Timothy, "Now the purpose of the commandment is love from a pure heart, *from* a good conscience, and *from* sincere faith" (1 Timothy 1:5). He also wrote, "Cleanse your conscience from dead works" (Hebrews 9:14).

Peter also covered the topic, "There is also an antitype which now saves us—baptism (not the removal of the filth of the flesh, but the answer of a good conscience toward God), through the resurrection of Jesus Christ" (1 Peter 3:21).

Water baptism is more than a cleansing and more than a burial. It is a resurrection and the putting on of Christ (see Galatians 3:27; Romans 13:14; Colossians 3:10; Ephesians 4:24; Romans 8:29).

Why is it important to "put on Christ"? Putting on Christ is a mandatory act, a necessity that must happen for us to be clothed in His righteousness. We can't get born again and not put on Christ. Those who clothe themselves with the Lord Jesus are believers who do not focus on gratifying the desires of the sinful nature. We put on Christ when our old ways are nailed to the cross and we wear the grace and forgiveness of Jesus as a glorious garment for all the world to see.

To put on Christ means to follow Him in discipleship, letting our lives be conformed to the image of Jesus rather than adapting ourselves to the pattern of this world. We are to be transformed by the renewing of our minds and the modification of our behavior into the model of Christ's life on earth. Putting on Christ means abiding in Jesus and living to please Him. Note the apostle Paul's thoughts on this critical issue:

> *I have been crucified with Christ; it is no longer I who live, but Christ lives in me; and the life which I now live in the flesh I live by faith in the Son of God, who loved me and gave Himself for me.* (Galatians 2:20)

> *...knowing this, that our old man was crucified with Him, that the body of sin might be done away with, that we should no longer be slaves of sin. For he who has died has been freed from sin. Now if we died with Christ, we believe that we shall also live with Him.* (Romans 6:6-8)

> *In Him you were also circumcised with the circumcision made without hands, by putting off the body of the sins of the flesh, by the circumcision of Christ, buried with Him in baptism, in which you also were raised with Him through faith in the working of God, who raised Him from the dead. And you, being dead in your trespasses and the uncircumcision of your flesh, He has made alive together with Him, having forgiven you all trespasses.* (Colossians 2:11-13)

## Baptism in the Holy Spirit

The Holy Spirit is a person. The Spirit of God is not an "it" but "Him." The Holy Spirit is the third person in the trinity of the

Godhead. Jesus had promised to send the Holy Spirit while He was still here on earth. God has given us the Holy Spirit as a helper, as an intercessor, as a counselor, as a comforter, and as a teacher.

The Holy Spirit's prayer language is expressed and spoken through tongues. When the person is baptized in the Holy Spirit, they begin to speak in tongues. The sign of speaking in tongues confirms the evidence of receiving the baptism of the Holy Spirit and the validation of the Holy Spirit's indwelling within the believer.

The Holy Spirit is critical to our salvation. Jesus said, "Most assuredly, I say to you, unless one is born of water and the Spirit, he cannot enter the kingdom of God" (John 3:5). Peter preached, "Therefore being exalted to the right hand of God, and having received from the Father the promise of the Holy Spirit, He poured out this which you now see and hear" (Acts 2:33). The same book of Acts later records, "...who, when they had come down, prayed for them that they might receive the Holy Spirit. For as yet He had fallen upon none of them. They had only been baptized in the name of the Lord Jesus. Then they laid hands on them, and they received the Holy Spirit" (Acts 8:15-17).

Receiving the Holy Spirit is an event that sometimes happens just before water baptism, but most of the time it happens after. For instance, the Spirit (as a dove) rested on the shoulder of Jesus just after His water baptism (see Matthew 3).

## Why We Need the Holy Spirit

Before His ascension, Jesus said, "Nevertheless I tell you the truth. It is to your advantage that I go away; for if I do not go away, the Helper will not come to you; but if I depart, I will send Him to you. And when He has come, He will convict the world of sin, and of righteousness, and of judgment" (John 16:7-8). Furthermore, He taught, "And I will pray the Father, and He will give you another Helper, that He may abide with you forever—

the Spirit of truth, whom the world cannot receive, because it neither sees Him nor knows Him; but you know Him, for He dwells with you and will be in you. I will not leave you orphans; I will come to you" (John 14:16-18). He continued in John 16, saying, "I still have many things to say to you, but you cannot bear them now. However, when He, the Spirit of truth, has come, He will guide you into all truth; for He will not speak on His own authority, but whatever He hears He will speak; and He will tell you things to come. He will glorify Me, for He will take of what is Mine and declare it to you. All things that the Father has are Mine. Therefore I said that He will take of Mine and declare it to you" (John 16:12-15).

He repeatedly makes the point that the Holy Spirit will come to teach us, in the place of Jesus, as though we were walking with Jesus directly. "These things I have spoken to you while being present with you. But the Helper, the Holy Spirit, whom the Father will send in My name, He will teach you all things, and bring to your remembrance all things that I said to you" (John 14:25-26).

After one receives the water baptism, God washes their sins away, removes the guilt and condemnation, and also breaks addiction to sin. He gives a new heart and a new conscience. The next and final step of the born again process involves receiving the baptism of the Holy Spirit with the sign of new tongues. At that point, the Holy Spirit indwells in us and guides us through life.

Being baptized in the Holy Spirit is a sign of getting fully born again. The baptism in the Holy Spirit is a spiritual baptism unlike the physical baptism in water. We must have the Holy Spirit within us. Paul wrote, "If anyone does not have the Spirit of Christ, he is not His" (Romans 8:9).

In the New Testament, aside from two exceptions, baptism in the Holy Spirit happened through the physical act with the laying on of hands. "And when Paul had laid hands on them, the Holy Spirit came upon them, and they spoke with tongues and prophesied" (Acts 19:6). Also with Peter we see, "While Peter was still speaking these words, the Holy Spirit fell upon all those who heard the word. And those of the circumcision who believed were astonished, as many as came with Peter, because the gift of the Holy Spirit had been poured out on the Gentiles also. For they heard them speak with tongues and magnify God. Then Peter answered, 'Can anyone forbid water, that these should not be baptized who have received the Holy Spirit just as we have?' And he commanded them to be baptized in the name of the Lord. Then they asked him to stay a few days" (Acts 10:44-48).

The receiving of the Holy Spirit was followed by an experience with an outward physical evidence which allowed people to tell if someone had received the baptism of the Holy Spirit. The sign of tongues reveals and confirms that the baptism of the Holy Spirit took place (see Acts 2:4, 10:44-46, and 19:6). When a person receives the baptism of the Holy Spirit, it leads to speaking a spiritual language. The Holy Spirit enables us to pray to God in our spirit, in a language we don't understand, but sometimes it can be interpreted by someone who has the gift of interpretation from the Holy Spirit. Once we are baptized in the Holy Spirit, we pray in tongues and it edifies us. When we cry out, an overflow happens, not inwardly, but outwardly in the form of spontaneous spiritual speech that overflows from the mouth.

"For you did not receive the spirit of bondage again to fear, but you received the Spirit of adoption by whom we cry out, 'Abba, Father.' The Spirit Himself bears witness with our spirit that we are children of God" (Romans 8:15-16). And also, in the letter to the Corinthians, we read, "Now He who establishes us with you in Christ and has anointed us is God, who also has sealed us and given us the Spirit in our hearts as a guarantee" (2 Corinthians 1:21-22).

The Holy Spirit has been promised by God to those who ask. The gift of the Holy Spirit must be asked for. Have confidence that God the Father will not give you the wrong thing if you ask Him for the gift of baptism with the Holy Spirit. "If you then, being evil, know how to give good gifts to your children, how much more will your Father who is in heaven give good things to those who ask Him" (Matthew 7:11).

The baptism of the Holy Spirit is receiving the person whom Jesus has promised and sent to take His place on earth.

## Beyond Salvation

The Holy Spirit is not just important for salvation but key to living a victorious life. After the baptism in the Holy Spirit, He will begin to live and dwell within us. The Holy Spirit is present in every one of God's children's lives, directing them down the path He has planned for them. The Holy Spirit's task is to help us develop Christlike characteristics through the sanctification process. He makes us more like Jesus Christ by working through our conscience to help us be more aware of sin in our lives. He convicts us of committed sin and leads us to repentance. God wants us to get rid of the things that displease Him and He uses the Holy Spirit to convict us in our conscience.

The Holy Spirit warns us in order for us to avoid falling into sin. He sends a warning against a potential sinful temptation. We can use the power of the Holy Spirit to fight against the flesh with its passions and desires. He teaches us how to submit to God's will in our lives and remain obedient to His commands. The Holy Spirit is calling us to yield ourselves so that we would allow Him to overcome issues and problems in our lives.

He wants to empower and give us strength to continue living and walking in the Spirit. He desires for us to be led by Him and to obey Him. He can guide us in our decisions, and if we obey His promptings, He will direct us through difficult situations in life. We have to do our part by asking the Holy Spirit to show us the truth and teach us how to live the life Jesus called us to live. He teaches and guides believers into all the truth, including knowledge of what is to come, and He reveals God's thoughts to us. Jesus made this clear, saying, "However, when He, the Spirit of truth, has come, He will guide you into all truth; for He will not speak on His own authority, but whatever He hears He will speak; and He will tell you things to come" (John 16:13).

The Holy Spirit enables us to understand and interpret God's Word. He reveals the truth and meaning of the Word. He also helps with our weaknesses and intercedes for us. The Holy Spirit helps us not only in our personal life but also in fulfilling the Great Commission.

Aside from being a teacher and a helper, the Holy Spirit is also a comforter and a counselor. As the Comforter, He provides comfort and calms our worries and gives us hope in the tough situations that we face regularly. As the Counselor, the Holy Spirit enables us to correctly assess what we should do in a given situation.

How do we know if we are being led by the Spirit? Our actions bear the fruit of the Spirit. This fruit continually testifies that we have gone through the entirety of the born again experience. It means the gap has been bridged between us, who used to be lost in sin, and God, who stands with welcoming arms to embrace us. Let's note some features of this new life.

> *He has delivered us from the power of darkness and conveyed us into the kingdom of the Son of His love, in whom we have redemption through His blood, the forgiveness of sins... And you, who once were alienated and enemies in your mind by wicked works, yet now He has reconciled.* (Colossians 1:13-14, 21)

Life begins after getting born again because your spiritual being resurrects to a new life. When the born again process happens, it's our spirit that gets reborn and then God can dwell inside of it. No one can fully explain what you will experience before you take this step. You have to experience it for yourself. After getting born again, we become children of God. "As many as received Him, to them He gave the right to become children of God, to those who believe in His name" (John 1:11-12).

The Spirit of God dwells in the temples of born again, sanctified individuals. Once we are a child of God, we have the Spirit of the living God dwelling in us. We become a new creation and we submit ourselves to God by living a holy and obedient life. We turn away from our old sinful lifestyle and turn toward God. The requirement for relationship with God is to be spiritually alive. Jesus said, "God is Spirit, and those who worship Him must worship in spirit and truth" (John 4:24).

After being born again, we resurrect to a new spiritual life and become a new creation, adopted into God's family. There we start a relationship with our heavenly Father. Once we have become God's children, we have access to the throne room and can approach Him boldly with confidence in prayer and fellowship with Him. Jesus' sacrifice and our acceptance of His gift of salvation brings us back to God the Father and restores relationship with Him.

The evidence of becoming a born-again creation in Christ is a transformed life. After being born again, we become saints; Christ becomes our righteousness and we are clothed in Him. As we start living a life with Jesus, we commence a journey of gradually conforming to the image of Jesus and becoming like Him through the process of sanctification. We'll never be truly happy and at peace until we are born again, because God intended for us to experience true joy and peace in His presence. Once we experience His presence, we'll never be the same. His presence is a gesture of His favor toward us.

Eternal life is expressed through a loving relationship, which starts here on earth and continues on through eternity. Everything is built around a relationship with God. There is nothing better in life than connecting with a Creator who created us for that very purpose. Accepting His love through Jesus' sacrifice, opens us to a life continually filled with His presence, knowing that His love is with us continually!

We will have the ability to overcome and resist sin, because our spiritual being will be resurrected to life in Christ Jesus. You will have the power of the Holy Spirit to assist you against sinful temptations and not to fall into sin. God will give us the power to resist sin and to overcome it so that resisting and rejecting sin will be much easier.

## Responsibility

There's a responsibility to uphold once you become a born-again child of God. As Christians, we have come into a *covenant* with God, which is an agreement with Him. A covenant is a mutual promise between two parties where both parties pledge to uphold and keep the terms and conditions for the covenant to remain valid. God is certainly keeping His part. The question is, will we keep ours?

> *To him the doorkeeper opens, and the sheep hear his voice; and he calls his own sheep by name and leads them out. And when he brings out his own sheep, he goes before them; and the sheep follow him, for they know his voice... I am the good shepherd; and I know My sheep, and am known by My own.... My sheep hear My voice, and I know them, and they follow Me.* (John 10:3-4,14, 27)

One of the indicators that we are born again is that we can have a real relationship with Jesus through fellowship, not a pretend, made-up, or make-believe relationship. Instead, this relationship is evidenced by us hearing from God and following accordingly.

Hearing from our Shepherd is a great gift. Many fail to enjoy and experience God's voice and presence because they don't see it as a gift. Others fail to establish this deep connection with God because they never truly repented and got right with God to begin with.

As believers, we have a duty and a responsibility to continually encounter God. This goes beyond our initial salvation experience and should permeate every aspect of our lives.

How can you explain a relationship with God to someone who has never experienced it before? It can be difficult, impossible actually, to fully explain a personal intimate relationship. Instead, you just have to experience it for yourself.

You can interview thousands of people who have a relationship with God and record their personal experiences with Him. But just one personal encounter with God and experiencing God in your personal life will by far outweigh all the accumulated knowledge of how thousands experience a relationship with Him. The reason some are struggling to form a personal relationship with God is that they think they know Him already due to their past religious upbringing in their knowledge about who God is. They feel that what they know about God is enough to understand who God is. Many people are convinced that they know God just because they have been taught a lot about Him, read the Bible, or attend church, but that's simply not the case. There is a theoretical knowledge of God and then there's a personal knowledge of God that can only be achieved through a personal encounter and relationship with Him.

Just like in any relationship, spending time with the other person is essential for truly getting to know them. Explanations from others, no matter how detailed, fall short of the rich understanding gained through personal interaction and day-to-day experiences. The only way for us to truly know them is by actually meeting them and spending time with them personally. We have a God-given responsibility to seek Him and learn from Him intimately throughout our lives.

Relationships are personal, so it's a personal experience that can only be acquired by an individual themselves. No one can take away or give us a relationship with God. We need to seek it out individually and experience it for ourselves. Reading the Bible without knowing its author and connecting to its author can make one mistakenly believe that they know who God is. Even praying and reading the Bible can be done without an actual relationship with Him.

People often rely on their own knowledge and wisdom to figure out who God is. They feel they know God because they believe He exists or can recite facts about Him. Anyone can claim with their mouth that they know Jesus, but claiming and *actually* knowing are two very different things. Knowing *about* God can at times get in the way of discovering God through a personal encounter. We can't figure out God on our own; we can only know Him as He reveals Himself to us when we seek Him.

If, for example, we read the Bible but don't actually have a relationship with Jesus, we will have a distorted understanding of who God is. God wants us to completely surrender to Him and not rely on our own understanding or try to figure out God on our own, but allow Him to reveal Himself to us. If our relationship with God is not yet established, we need to humble ourselves and admit that we know *of* God but do not sincerely know God.

We all want to be in right standing with God. Many believers feel like they're on good terms with God just because they've been born again and now casually attend church, read the Bible, and even pray from time to time. If I ask everyone individually if they have a relationship with God, I might get a response like, "Yes, I'm good with God."

However, if we dig deeper, the realization might come that not everything is as good as it looks on the surface. It's rare to hear someone say, "I feel like something is lacking in my relationship with Jesus. I don't have breakthroughs in my life; I don't feel complete peace," or "I don't trust the Lord fully," or "I struggle with my sinful addictions and I fall into sinful temptations easily. I need to do something about this. Please pray for me." These responses are somewhat rare. If the person was honest with themselves and would have admitted it, then they would have already done something about it. Many, through their actions and lack of desire to spend time with Him, demonstrate a lukewarm approach to Jesus.

God doesn't want us to be nominal or superficial believers

that only confess Him with our lips. He wants action that backs it. We can't please God by seeking Him superficially. People convince themselves that they have a good relationship with Jesus because they want it to be so. Some might say God is everything in their lives, but in reality, their lives testify against such things. Their motives, desires, and thoughts that eventually materialize into words and deeds reveal that this is not the case. As the saying goes, our actions speak louder than words. If we say, "I know God and have a relationship with Him," but act contrary to our words by avoiding fellowship with Him, then it shows that we accept Him with our words only while denying Him with our actions. Those who avoid fellowship with God make their own lives difficult.

People can convince themselves that everything is good in their relationship with God when that's not the case. They deceive themselves by trying to convince themselves that their relationship with God is flourishing when, in reality, it's fractured. They might not even be fully aware or realize how distant they truly are from God. In their spiritual blindness, they continue to believe they have a relationship with God, love God, obey God, and are friends of God, all the while it is just self-deception because their life is not grounded on the Word of God.

Their false conviction comes from their own understanding and interpretation of life, who God is, and the criteria to get into a relationship with Him. Pretending to have a relationship with Jesus will not help us any. We all need to come to God and genuinely pour out our hearts before Him by addressing everything that prevents us from connecting with Him. Let's ask ourselves these questions: What prevents us from reading the Bible daily? What keeps us from praying? What stops us from letting go of the past hurt? Why are we holding back from forgiving ourselves for the things that God has already forgiven us? Unforgiveness, unresolved sinful past, trauma, rejection, neglect, or abuse from others, unbelief, pride, double-mindedness, or indecisiveness are some of the things that prevent us from the progression of an already established relationship. One of the biggest pieces of evidence that a person loves God, knows God, fears God, and obeys God is if they read God's Word, meditate on it, and act upon it.

How do we gauge the quality of our relationship with God? We often tend to give ourselves a better grade than we deserve in life, and this also applies to our relationship with Jesus. We can downplay the fact that our relationship with God is in poor condition and pretend that it is adequate. God is the one who evaluates our relationship with Him. If we felt that something was off with our walk with God, we would try to do something about it to resolve our stance with Him. Those who don't have a relationship and feel comfortable where they are at wouldn't want to be helped. They will not put in the effort to change anything to get closer to God.

Talking with someone reveals their interest and how important Jesus is in their life. Living in relationship with Jesus will allow us to discern when someone talks about God in such a way that it reveals they don't have a real life with God and are not interested in their spiritual well-being but just want to give the impression that they do. They try to come across as if God is important to them and that they live in relationship with Him. You can't explain the importance of the things of God to them since they don't live with spiritual values. They simply won't understand you.

Life with Jesus is relational and experiential. There's a difference between believing and knowing. Our believing should lead to a *knowing*. "This is eternal life, that they may know You, the only true God, and Jesus Christ whom You have sent" (John 17:3).

> *Thus says the Lord: "Let not the wise man glory in his wisdom, let not the mighty man glory in his might, nor let the rich man glory in his riches; but let him who glories glory in this, that he understands and knows Me,*

*that I am the Lord, exercising lovingkindness, judgment, and righteousness in the earth. For in these I delight," says the Lord.* (Jeremiah 9:24)

If you're honest with yourself, you know whether or not you have a relationship with Him and what state it is in, and so does God. If you're honest, nobody can persuade you that you have a relationship with God if you don't have it. And if you have a relationship with God, no one can convince you otherwise. The process of believing, repenting, and experiencing baptisms in water and the Spirit are all steps of the salvation process that bridge the gap between us and God. From that place of adoption, we are endowed with the responsibility to remain close to Jesus. This is not merely done through study or accruing knowledge, but through experiential encounters with our heavenly Father. The same God that *saved* us desires to now *sustain* us.

## CHAPTER THREE

# The Sin Issue

*Therefore do not let sin reign in your mortal body, that you should obey it in its lusts.* (Romans 6:12)

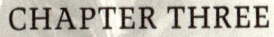

IN THE LAST chapter, we discussed overcoming a life of sin through a born again process. But how is sin dealt with once we are saved? How do we navigate temptation and disobedience once we are brought into God's family? The truth is, as children of God, we now have the ability to overcome temptation. By the grace of God, we have the ability to subject our flesh to obedience to God.

Those who have been born again cannot live in habitual, premeditated, or perpetual sin. We cannot willfully continue to live in sin after being born again. We must not fall into the same sin over and over again. To continue living in sin is a misuse of God's grace. If one lives in habitual, premeditated, presumptuous sin and knows better, then that person tramples on the blood of Jesus. Those who have committed sin but don't have repentance and remorse for what they have done have fallen away due to their silenced conscience and the voice of the Holy Spirit.

*For if we sin willfully after we have received the knowledge of the truth, there no longer remains a sacrifice for sins, but a certain fearful expectation of judgment, and fiery indignation which will devour the adversaries.* (Hebrews 10:26-27)

A born-again believer cannot practice sin. John wrote, "He who sins is of the devil, for the devil has sinned from the beginning. For this purpose the Son of God was manifested, that He might destroy the works of the devil. Whoever has been born of God does not sin, for His seed remains in him; and he cannot sin, because he has been born of God" (1 John 3:8-10). He later added, "We know that whoever is born of God does not sin; but he who has been born of God keeps himself, and the wicked one does not touch him" (1 John 5:18).

It's one thing to fall into sin and get back up through repentance, confession, and asking for forgiveness. But there is a distinction between that and continuing the practice of sinning. Sin becomes a choice when we commit it repeatedly. Jesus' sacrifice doesn't give us permission to sin but *freedom* from sin. Once you're born again, you will start living a holy life with God, free from sin.

Once you're born again, it's important to make the effort to live a holy and obedient life and not give into the temptation of perpetual sin over and over again. It's up to us to put in the effort and ask God to help us resist temptations and desires that lead to sin. Ask Jesus for forgiveness right away when you commit sin. If you mess up, fess up. Have an accountability partner who will help you avoid falling into sinful temptations. These mentors can pray for you and meet with you to talk about the temptations to make sure you are walking victoriously with Jesus.

After being born again, it's crucial to make every effort to walk with God and obey His commandments. We have to keep walking in holiness and righteousness every day by obeying God and surrendering to His will. These things will lead to maturity and growth. We are not without help, though. The same grace that saved us is the grace that will sustain us.

While born-again believers have the *capacity* to sin and will be tempted to sin, this does not mean they are subject to sin. Yes, we can still fall into sin, but we aren't slaves to it any longer. God's grace gives born-again believers the power to overcome sin. If you're born again, then ask God to help you continue living in holiness and righteousness. Make a daily choice not to give into sin and its temptations.

No matter how good our intentions, we can still be overcome by temptation to sin. That's why a strong relationship with Jesus, a commitment to holy living, and regular meditation on Scripture are essential for resisting these temptations and staying on the path of righteousness. Staying vigilant is essential to resist sin and the temptations of the devil.

By cooperating with the Holy Spirit, we become empowered to overcome temptations and sinful desires, and to resist falling into sin and continue living a holy life. However, if we do sin, we must confess it and forsake it to receive forgiveness and cleansing through the blood of Jesus Christ. Ultimately, it's up to us to put in the effort to live a sanctified life in communion with God.

After being born again, we're a new creation in Christ, but we can still choose to live by the flesh rather than the Spirit. If we gravitate toward fleshly desires, we will operate in the flesh. Prior to salvation, we had only one nature—the sinful one. Once we came to Christ, we became a new creation in Him. But presently, we still abide in the old flesh that has the remains of Adamic nature within us. This is why we still have a tendency to sin.

These two natures are always at odds with each other and pull a believer in different directions. It's a constant ongoing daily battle whether or not we are going to live in the flesh or in the spirit. We constantly have a tug of war between what the flesh wants and what the spirit wants. Our free will allows us to decide which will win. Make no mistake, our decision has consequences.

One day, believers will be completely freed from the body

of death when we are glorified with Christ in heaven, but until that day, we rely on the power of the Spirit who dwells in us and gives us victory in the ongoing battle over sin. The crucifixion of the flesh is an ongoing acknowledgement of death to the old sinful nature. It's denying one's physical self-pleasure, self-will, and self-desires.

> *For those who live according to the flesh set their minds on the things of the flesh, but those who live according to the Spirit, the things of the Spirit. For to be carnally minded is death, but to be spiritually minded is life and peace. Because the carnal mind is enmity against God; for it is not subject to the law of God, nor indeed can be. So then, those who are in the flesh cannot please God. But you are not in the flesh but in the Spirit, if indeed the Spirit of God dwells in you. Now if anyone does not have the Spirit of Christ, he is not His.* (Romans 8:5-9)

Being free from the power of sin does not make it impossible to sin; it means we're no longer under the *law* of sin. Our loyalty has changed and our predispositions have shifted. Christ has broken the sin cycle in our lives. Temptation itself will remain, just as Jesus was tempted; in fact, we can overcome temptation just as Jesus did.

> *For the law of the Spirit of life in Christ Jesus has made me free from the law of sin and death.* (Romans 8:2)

The devil knows our weak points and what to tempt us with. He sends us thoughts to provoke us so that we will act upon them. But we can make the decision to resist those thoughts and not give in. We can cultivate discipline over our incoming thoughts, training our minds to recognize and resist thoughts that contradict the truths of God's Word. By this action, we can continue living a holy life in relationship with Jesus, while resisting the devil.

As we strive to grow closer to God, an internal battle can erupt, with our flesh fighting to pull us away. The flesh will continue to tempt us to enjoy the pleasures of this world.

> *For he who sows to his flesh will of the flesh reap corruption, but he who sows to the Spirit will of the Spirit reap everlasting life. And let us not grow weary while doing good, for in due season we shall reap if we do not lose heart.* (Galatians 6:8-9)

### Distance

Before Christ, we were distant from God because of sin. After knowing Christ, distance can once again be created. Paul wrote to the Corinthians, "Awake to righteousness, and do not sin; for some do not have the knowledge of God. I speak this to your shame" (1 Corinthians 15:34). Notice, Paul called believers to "awake to righteousness." This means that even as Christians we must continually choose the path of righteousness and holiness. John spoke of this choice, saying, "Beloved, do not imitate what is evil, but what is good. He who does good is of God, but he who does evil has not seen God" (3 John 1:11), and again, "If you know that He is righteous, you know that everyone who practices righteousness is born of Him" (1 John 2:29).

> *Therefore we also, since we are surrounded by so great a cloud of witnesses, let us lay aside every weight, and the sin which so easily ensnares us, and let us run with endurance the race that is set before us, looking unto Jesus, the author and finisher of our faith, who for the joy that was set before Him endured the cross, despising the shame, and has sat down at the right hand of the throne of God. For consider Him who endured such hostility from sinners against Himself, lest you become weary and discouraged in your souls.* (Hebrews 12:1-3)

Sin violates a loving relationship we were created to have with God and other people. That's why sinning is cheating on God. Living in the new life, we journey with Him, receiving His assistance to strive for holiness and avoid sin. This pursuit of holiness is fueled by the knowledge of how much He hates sin and how deeply it hurts Him when sin separates us from Him. Our love for Him motivates us to align our lives with His character. The passage we just read on running the race with endurance is key to the Christian life. The verse says to lay aside *every* weight and sin—not just some of them. God wants us to have a zero tolerance policy for anything that slows us down.

Let's analyze how we live our lives: do we walk in holiness or do we live in sin? The more time we spend with God, the less attractive sin becomes to us. Sin is a willful choice and a violation of God's moral law. We each make a choice between living a sinful life or a holy life. There are only two options, and everyone chooses one of them. James wrote, "Therefore submit to God. Resist the devil and he will flee from you. Draw near to God and He will draw near to you. Cleanse your hands, you sinners; and purify your hearts, you double-minded" (James 4:7-8). In submitting to God, we create distance with the devil and intimacy with God. In sinning, we create distance with God and become more comfortable with the enemy.

Consider the words of Peter: "Therefore gird up the loins of your mind, be sober, and rest your hope fully upon the grace that is to be brought to you at the revelation of Jesus Christ; as obedient children, not conforming yourselves to the former lusts, as in your ignorance; but as He who called you is holy, you also be holy in all your conduct, because it is written, 'Be holy, for I am holy'" (1 Peter 1:13-16). His advice for holy conduct starts with the *mind*. Sin starts in the mind, which is the place we are to defeat it before it can manifest as action.

> But each one is tempted when he is drawn away by his own desires and enticed. Then, when desire has conceived,

*it gives birth to sin; and sin, when it is full-grown, brings forth death.* (James 1:14-15)

Sin, when full grown, brings forth death. This is no light matter. Have you been deceived into thinking that sin is harmless and fun? Sin starts with a thought, and if we entertain that thought and don't prevent ourselves from dwelling on it, then it will put roots down in our heart. God sees our decision to entertain the sinful thoughts and God sees the state of our hearts even if it hasn't yet turned into action. We might think it hasn't become action yet, so it's fine; that it doesn't count as sin. But in God's eyes, even an entertained thought counts as sin. If we keep dwelling on a sinful thought, it can produce fruit and become the action of sin itself.

Paul wrote, "Nevertheless the solid foundation of God stands, having this seal: 'The Lord knows those who are His,' and, 'Let everyone who names the name of Christ depart from iniquity'" (2 Timothy 2:19). This "departure" from iniquity happens in the space of your mind. If we do not depart from sin in our minds, we cannot depart from sin with our actions.

So, what is sin, and how do we define it? There are many definitions and explanations of what sin is. Let's look at just some of them.

- Sin is missing the mark of what God wants us to do.
- Sin is going against the way God intended us to be.
- Sin is doing something contrary to the Word of God.
- Sin is anything that displeases God.
- Sin is whatever is contrary to God's will.
- Sin is neglecting to do what is right according to the divine law of God.
- Sin is disobeying God and doing what we know we shouldn't do.
- Sin is our enemy with a temporary fleshly benefit.
- Sin is gratifying a natural desire in unnatural, unlawful ways.

- Sin is a statement and declaration of "I don't want You, God" and "I want to do it my way."
- Sin is hostility toward God.
- Sin is a rebellion against God.
- Sin is ego-driven and self-based actions to benefit oneself.
- Sin is the refusal to obey God's laws and commandments.
- Sin is going against what God intended for people.
- Sin is rejecting living by God's standard through wrongful actions, words, or thoughts.

In general terms, "sin" is any thought, word, or action considered immoral, selfish, shameful, or harmful toward God or other people.

Sin is an evil act that violates God's nature and goes against what God intended for people. Sin is a violation of a loving relationship that we were originally meant to have with our Creator. The presence of sin in a person's life makes it impossible for God to have the kind of mutual, unparalleled love relationship that He offers us as our Creator and Savior. God hates and condemns sin because it harms those He loves. God's boundaries for our lives are not a control mechanism to make us miserable. They are outflowings of His love.

If you love someone, you wouldn't intentionally hurt or upset them. Similarly, sin violates a loving relationship with God. When we sin, it hurts God whom we love and creates distance in the relationship. Sinning means being unfaithful and cheating on God in a relationship, because He created us and paid the price on the cross to redeem us to Himself. Despite His immense love for us, we sometimes disregard it and fail to cherish the relationship. Compromising with sin creates distance between us and God.

We cannot forget that continuing to live in sin carries inevitable consequences. Although no one can force us to live holy, God's all-encompassing love warns us of the danger of sin. Out of our own free will, God wants us to make a decision to repent from sin and refuse to stay in it. There's a decision to make to come clean before Jesus, who already knows what sins we have done.

Sin hurts us spiritually, emotionally, and physically. Sin is missing the mark through wrongful actions, words, or thoughts. It's going against what we were created for, which is to know God and to glorify God. It grieves God that we choose sin over Him. We displease God with our sin, and it brings Him disappointment and pain to see His beloved creation stray into something that causes them harm. Just because we fall into sin after becoming children of God, it doesn't mean that God withholds or retracts His love from us. Even when we stumble, God's love for us remains constant. However, because He is holy, He patiently waits for us to repent and continue walking in righteousness and fellowship with Him. He is waiting for us to change our minds about sin and repent so we can come back to His love, which will never give up on those who give it a chance to reveal itself.

A cherished relationship with God deepens our desire for closeness and motivates us to avoid sin. Knowing our transgressions grieve Him compels us to strive for a life that honors this connection. Relationship motivates us to avoid sinning, not out of fear of punishment, but out of love for God. We strive to live in a way that avoids causing Him pain. Jesus said, "Therefore you shall be perfect, just as your Father in heaven is perfect" (Matthew 5:48). This does not mean that we will always be perfect and sinless on earth, but it does mean that we will continue to aim toward God's perfection as we grow in maturity.

## Unavoidable Consequences

Paul wrote, "For if we would judge ourselves, we would not be judged. But when we are judged, we are chastened by the Lord, that we may not be condemned with the world" (1 Corinthians 11:31-32). What does this mean? It means that instead of living recklessly and being judged by God for it, we can judge ourselves and hold ourselves accountable, and as a result, we won't have to be judged and chastened by God. Why? Because we have already been keeping ourselves in check. If we fail to do this, we will certainly see consequences in our lives. This is not because God is cruel and mean. It is because when we, for example, drive over a road barrier and off a cliff, we are destined to feel the consequences of ignoring the barrier. The same thing is true in the spiritual life. If we ignore God's barriers, we are asking to pay a high price.

Sin's grip corrupts and destroys lives, but God, in His mercy, offers a way out. He cares for us and desires to separate us from sin's destructive power. Jesus came to reveal the harmful effect of sin and to show the solution for that sin in order to free people from their old lifestyles and addictions. Many attempt to overcome sin through sheer willpower, but ultimately fail. This is why we need God's help.

> *Do you not know that to whom you present yourselves slaves to obey, you are that one's slaves whom you obey, whether of sin leading to death, or of obedience leading to righteousness?* (Romans 6:16)

Notice the phrases "sin leading to death" and "obedience leading to righteousness." In both cases, we see consequences. In one case they are positive and in the other they are negative. Decisions that we make in this life have either good consequences or bad ramifications. When we make up our mind to commit sin, we are consenting to the consequences of sin whether we like it or not.

Breaking God's law and turning away from Him carries consequences, the first and most significant of which is a separation from God in fellowship. If one continues to perpetually live in sin to the end, then there's an eternal separation from God in hell. The choice is up to us, but we are not free from the consequences of our decisions. The consequences of our choices are not always apparent straight away, but they will eventually be revealed. We have the ability to choose whether or not to accept God's grace in the time that He gives to come to full repentance. God awaits our decision to come to Him for comfort, to be cleansed of our sins, and to embrace His loving presence. What we do with our life is up to us. No one can make that decision for us.

*For the Son of Man did not come to destroy men's lives but to save them.* (Luke 9:56)

With this passage in mind, it only makes sense that Jesus would be hurt when we dive into the very thing that destroys us. With our sinful actions, we cause Jesus pain while He shows us love. God is love, and that's why He wants us to reconcile us with Himself in order to have a personal, loving relationship. We allow our sin to stand in the way of our relationship from being restored with God.

We must live in a way that brings honor to God by walking in the holiness and righteousness that Jesus Christ bestowed upon us when we were born again. Give it all you've got in order to flee from sin. It's not having a mindset which says, 'That's okay. Jesus died for my past, present, and future sins, so as long as I remember to ask for forgiveness, I can sin all I want." If we want to find excuses to sin, we will find them. Don't underestimate the depravity of sin. Don't approach the effects and consequences of sin in your life lightly. The Scriptures say, "Of how much worse punishment, do you suppose, will he be thought worthy who has trampled the Son of God underfoot, counted the blood of the covenant by which he was sanctified a common thing, and insulted the Spirit of grace?" (Hebrews 10:29).

We do not deserve salvation or forgiveness for our sins, yet God extends mercy and grace toward us. God is reminding the sinner to repent of the sin, abandon sin, and turn toward Him. God is holy and righteous and He cannot be in the presence of sin. God loves our souls, but He hates the sinful actions that we perform, love, and entertain.

## Removing Compromise

How can a believer who knows God and knows that God knows everything continue to have a hidden sin in their life? They know that God opposes their sin but they continue to love and entertain it. Isn't it better to hate sin, get rid of it, and come clean by asking God to break the addiction to sin? God wants to deliver us from sin if we only allow Him to do so.

There are those who overlook their sin and downplay how abhorrent it is in God's eyes because it's very pleasing to their flesh. They're indifferent and apathetic to the side effects of sin being present in their lives and how it affects their relationship with God. They convince themselves that the sin they have committed is simply a shortcoming, a compromise, a mistake, a misstep, an affection, a bad deed, behavior, an interest, a hobby, or simply inherent human traits. They fall into one of two traps: either feeling their sin is less serious compared to others, or finding comfort in self-righteousness by comparing themselves to others.

Why would some people put effort into searching for something that will take away their sinful pleasures that they love? If someone loves their sin, they don't want it exposed and they don't want to give it up. They prioritize sin over God, and their love for sin surpasses the love for Him. Many are indifferent to what God thinks of their spiritual condition for that very reason. This begs the question: why would they yearn for reconciliation and a fellowship with God?

> *He who covers his sins will not prosper, But whoever confesses and forsakes them will have mercy.* (Proverbs 28:13)

God wants to carve away those areas of hidden sin and compromise in our lives. Committed sin gets in the way of our relationship with Jesus; it corrupts us and cuts us off from connecting with God, making us His enemies. Sin separates and distances us from the love of God, and we feel guilty as a result of that separation. God is waiting for us to come back to Him in humility and repent by asking for forgiveness. If we confess our sins, God will forgive us. Living in sin sets us up to live for ourselves rather than living for the God who saved us (see 2 Corinthians 5:15).

We can't get rid of sin on our own. We need to confess our sins, repenting of them and asking for forgiveness so that we can continue being in fellowship with God and enjoying His presence. If we know God, then we know how much it grieves Him to see us sin. Why would we hurt someone that we care about and with whom we have a relationship?

The goal of the enemy is to keep us feeling guilty for our sins. The enemy sends thoughts like, "You have already angered God by sinning; you have tried to quit sinning so many times and it never worked. Just give up on trying to reconcile with God." If we believe the lie, we continue in sin with no effort made toward God. Satan wants to make us feel like we have failed God too many times and don't deserve another chance to make things right with Him. He wants us to feel unworthy of God's love and feel too ashamed to approach Him to ask for forgiveness.

The enemy tries to break us through *guilt*, but Jesus offers restoration through repentance. Sin weighs people down, causing them to carry the burden of sin throughout their lives, but it doesn't have to be that way. Without walking closely with God and knowing His love for us, we might start to believe that God wants to punish us without showing a way out through repentance.

> *Who is he who condemns? It is Christ who died, and furthermore is also risen, who is even at the right hand of God, who also makes intercession for us.* (Romans 8:34)

Jesus is making intercession for us. He is rooting for our victory. Even when He corrects us, it's only out of love. Proverbs says, "My son, do not despise the chastening of the Lord, nor detest His correction; for whom the Lord loves He corrects, just as a father the son in whom he delights" (Proverbs 3:11-12).

Nothing can stop us from connecting with God except our decision to choose alternatives. Do we want sin more than we want closeness with Jesus in our lives? If we love Jesus, then any sin will be abhorrent and disgusting in our eyes. And even if we happen to fall into temptation to sin, we will run from it as though we fell into a sewer pit. Our love for Jesus will make us run to Him in order to repent and reconcile with God whenever we stray. If we linger in our sinful state and are reluctant to leave it, this means that sin has got a hold of us and overpowered us. If we truly commit to breaking free from sin, God's help is immediately available. He can help us overcome addiction as we pray and ask for His help.

### Restoration

The Bible is full of people like you and me who need continual repentance and help. After David had sinned, he knew exactly where to go for help. He prayed, "I acknowledged my sin to You, and my iniquity I have not hidden. I said, 'I will confess my transgressions to the Lord'" (Psalm 32:5). A similar concept is presented in 2 Chronicles: "If My people who are called by My name will humble themselves, and pray and seek My face, and turn from their wicked ways, then I will hear from heaven, and will forgive their sin" (2 Chronicles 7:14).

John also prescribed the same thing in the New Testament. "If we confess our sins, He is faithful and just to forgive us our sins and to cleanse us from all unrighteousness" (1 John 1:9). God is good, ready to forgive, and abundant in mercy to everyone that calls upon Him (see Psalm 86:5). As we call upon Him, He removes sin and restores relationships. We cannot love Jesus, and at the same time, love what Jesus hates. Loving Jesus means loving what He loves.

God warns us about our sin through our conscience. The

Holy Spirit convicts people of their sin; that's why they feel bad when they do things against God's law. Instead of looking for the truth, people would often rather change what they believe from the truth to lies and deception so that they don't have to deal with the voice of their conscience. If we harden our hearts to the voice of God through our conscience, then after a while, we will not want to give up our sin anymore.

If we don't abide in Christ, we are not living a holy life. Abiding in the Lord means that we continually receive, believe, and trust that Jesus is everything we need. Vigilance is key when facing the temptation of sin.

> *But those things which proceed out of the mouth come from the heart, and they defile a man. For out of the heart proceed evil thoughts, murders, adulteries, fornications, thefts, false witness, blasphemies. These are the things which defile a man, but to eat with unwashed hands does not defile a man.* (Matthew 15:18-20)

Our conscience is like our nervous system. When we touch something hot, our nervous system reminds us to pull away in order to protect our body from further permanent damage. Our conscience serves as a gauge and a moral compass designed by God. People don't accidentally sin; they do it deliberately by meditating first on what their action is going to be. When we sin, God, through our conscience, reminds us to repent of our sin.

If we're honest with ourselves, then we know when our actions lead to deterioration of our relationship with God. The purpose of the conscience is not to guilt-trip us into further sin, but to prompt us to stop and reconcile with God before sin takes hold. On the topic, John wrote, "For if our heart condemns us, God is greater than our heart, and knows all things. Beloved, if our heart does not condemn us, we have confidence toward God" (1 John 3:20-21).

The conscience is a lever God pulls to draw us back in. He uses our conscience to remind us who we are in His eyes and how awful sin is in His eyes. As a result, we use the call of our conscience as a prompt to seek a way out by humbling ourselves and reconciling with God through repentance. Repentance is a change of heart and mind toward sin. Reconciliation in a relationship involves feeling freedom from sin. He wants to re-establish that connection with us and let us know how much He loves us through forgiveness.

Isaiah wrote, "But your iniquities have separated you from your God; and your sins have hidden His face from you, so that He will not hear" (Isaiah 59:2). Some might respond with, "But I don't sin!" Here John replies, "If we say that we have no sin, we deceive ourselves, and the truth is not in us. If we confess our sins, He is faithful and just to forgive us our sins and to cleanse us from all unrighteousness. If we say that we have not sinned, we make Him a liar, and His word is not in us" (1 John 1:8-10).

If you confess your sin and repent of it, He will accept you and reconcile with you. Understanding that sin distances us from God will motivate us to put in every effort to not sin because our relationship with Jesus is so important to us. He paid the ultimate price by becoming sin for us so that we might become the righteousness of God through Him (see 2 Corinthians 5:21).

Born-again followers of Christ have Jesus as their High Priest. Jesus offered Himself once to the Father as a perfect sacrifice for our sins and now He is the High Priest who is our advocate and who intercedes on our behalf.

> *Seeing then that we have a great High Priest who has passed through the heavens, Jesus the Son of God, let us hold fast our confession. For we do not have a High Priest who cannot sympathize with our weaknesses, but was in all points tempted as we are, yet without sin. Let us therefore come boldly to the throne of grace, that we may obtain mercy and find grace to help in time of need.* (Hebrews 4:14-16)

The author of Hebrews later writes again of Christ's priesthood, saying, "Therefore, brethren, having boldness to enter the Holiest by the blood of Jesus, by a new and living way which He consecrated for us, through the veil, that is, His flesh, and having a High Priest over the house of God, let us draw near with a true heart in full assurance of faith, having our hearts sprinkled from an evil conscience and our bodies washed with pure water" (Hebrews 10:19-22).

Our relationships with God cannot continue without repentance. Repentance is telling God, "I messed up. I need You. Please forgive me." By repentance, we access the priesthood of Jesus. In this, He restores our place in Him. Make no mistake, repentance requires humility on our part. Repentance means we consciously want to give up our sinful past. A desire to get rid of the sinfulness we recognize within ourselves is the first step. With a yearning for a holy life, God's help becomes readily available. From there, we should not allow the enemy to remind us of the sins that have been forgiven and make us feel like our sins are unresolved. Paul wrote, "But now in Christ Jesus you who once were far off have been brought near by the blood of Christ" (Ephesians 2:13). The gap has been closed, restoration has occurred, and we can continue ahead as though the sin never occurred. This is the beauty of forgiveness and should motivate us to push deeper into godly living.

It is in our own best interest to be in right standing before God. God is always open to receive us and has done everything required on His part. When we enjoy, cherish, and value the time that we spend with God, we will do everything in our ability to remain holy and righteous to keep disruptions at bay. A relationship with Jesus leads to a hunger for righteousness and holiness. When we are not satisfied with God, we will start to become attracted to and seek out sin. Are you tired of letting God down? Are you tired of sinning? Are you sick of having a guilty conscience and constant reminders from within to get right with God?

Overcoming sin becomes much easier when we commit to

drawing closer to God through obedience. Experiencing His love through a relationship will give us an internal motive to resist sinful temptations. "Abstain from fleshly lusts which war against the soul" (1 Peter 2:11).

Our sin prevents us from walking victoriously in relationship with Jesus. God does not ignore us; rather, He waits patiently for our repentance because He is holy and cannot be in the presence of sin. Repentance is the only answer to reconcile back to Jesus Christ. Without a strong relationship with God, our hearts will gravitate toward worldly values.

Witnessing sin and wickedness can evoke sorrow and grief for those lost in its grip. Do we feel empathy and compassion, or do we become hardened by indifference, or worse, tempted to join their actions? If we live and operate in the flesh by loving the world, then this means we don't have the love of God. John said, "If we say that we have fellowship with Him, and walk in darkness, we lie and do not practice the truth" (1 John 1:6). We should make no provision for the flesh, to fulfill its lusts, but make provision for righteousness to show up (see Romans 13:14).

*Walk in the Spirit, and you shall not fulfill the lust of the flesh. For the flesh lusts against the Spirit, and the Spirit against the flesh; and these are contrary to one another.* (Galatians 5:16-17)

In other epistles, Paul spelled out similar truths: "Therefore, brethren, we are debtors—not to the flesh, to live according to the flesh. For if you live according to the flesh you will die; but if by the Spirit you put to death the deeds of the body, you will live" (Romans 8:12-13), and, "Therefore put to death your members which are on the earth: fornication, uncleanness, passion, evil desire, and covetousness, which is idolatry" (Colossians 3:5).

God is waiting for us to stop playing games with Him and begin taking Him and our relationship with Him seriously. Any unconfessed sin needs to be dealt with. The fact that our conscience disturbs us regarding sin is a good thing, because if it stopped disturbing us, this would mean that we have silenced the leading of God in our lives.

The apostle Paul had the opportunity to address the sin in the church of Rome, where Christians felt that grace gave them a free pass to sin and disregarded living a righteous life. As a result, he responded saying:

> *"What shall we say then? Shall we continue in sin that grace may abound? Certainly not! How shall we who died to sin live any longer in it? Or do you not know that as many of us as were baptized into Christ Jesus were baptized into His death? Therefore we were buried with Him through baptism into death, that just as Christ was raised from the dead by the glory of the Father, even so we also should walk in newness of life. For if we have been united together in the likeness of His death, certainly we also shall be in the likeness of His resurrection, knowing this, that our old man was crucified with Him, that the body of sin might be done away with, that we should no longer be slaves of sin. For he who has died has been freed from sin. Now if we died with Christ, we believe that we shall also live with Him, knowing that Christ, having been raised from the dead, dies no more. Death no longer has dominion over Him. For the death that He died, He died to sin once for all; but the life that He lives, He lives to God. Likewise you also, reckon yourselves to be dead indeed to sin, but alive to God in Christ Jesus our Lord. Therefore do not let sin reign in your mortal body, that you should obey it in its lusts. And do not present your members as instruments of unrighteousness to sin, but present yourselves to God as being alive from the dead, and your members as instruments of righteousness to God. For sin shall not have dominion over you, for you are not under law but under grace"* (Romans 6:1-14).

CHAPTER FOUR

# Indicator of Relationship

*You will know them by their fruits.* (Matthew 7:16)

HOW DO YOU know if there's a relationship with God? What is the way that we can determine whether or not we truly have a real and close relationship with Him? The truth is, some who claim to know Jesus do not actually know Him. Knowing Jesus brings about a transformation in life, which is evidenced by living righteously.

What confirmation do *you* have that you're close to God and that you're holding on to Him? How do you know that you are on good terms with Him and that He is content with you? What gives you confidence that God is pleased with you and your life? The only way to *truly* know that we're right with God is to personally receive confirmation directly from Him. Having God's approval is part of having a relationship with Him. Those who are not in fellowship with God wrongly assume their stance with God is good based on a variety of incorrect criteria, such as knowledge of the Bible, good deeds, being involved in ministry, outward appearance, religious mindset, and so forth. But what we actually need is an internal confirmation that our lives are pleasing to God, directly from Him.

Whether we want it or not, our lives will reveal if we have a relationship with God. Our lifestyle and actions reveal if we are in sync with Jesus. If we're dishonest about the condition of our relationship with God, then we deceive ourselves. If we don't walk with God, then we only have an imitation of what is real and genuine. The sign of walking with God is revealed when His Word abides in us, meaning we meditate on it, allowing it to shape our thoughts and guide our choices as we implement it in our lives. Abiding in God's Word consistently results in bearing fruit (see John 15:5). This is another way to assess our relationship with God, which involves bearing the fruits of the Spirit. If we lack these fruits (mentioned in Galatians 5:22-23), it may indicate that our relationship with Him is not where it needs to be and needs attention. As Matthew 7:16 says, "You shall know them by their fruits." Are we actively demonstrating the fruits of the Spirit in our lives? If not, we can examine our lives in light of God's Word and with the help of the Holy Spirit to identify the reasons why the fruits of the Spirit are missing. Circumstances or people cannot prevent us from bearing these fruits, because they cannot disconnect us from the love of God. So, it's up to us to review our lives and ask God, "What hinders or prevents me from living a life with You in such a way that I bear the fruits of the Spirit?"

Everyone who is born again is on a lifelong journey that requires ongoing commitment to living a holy life and allowing Him to continually sanctify us through His Word. As Jesus prayed, "Sanctify them by Your truth. Your word is truth" (John 17:17).

Want honest feedback on your connection with God? Ask yourself: How well do my choices reflect the newness of life I have received in Christ, and do they align with the values of God's Word?"

## On Display

When discussing fruit in a Christian's life, the subject of influence will inevitably come up. Our life with Jesus can't be hidden from others. We have influence for good or for bad. Our relationship with Jesus is on display and people closest to us will see and experience the fruit that we bear.

If we love God with all of our heart, with all of our soul, with all of our strength, and with all of our mind, then it will be visible to others. Our acts of obedience or disobedience toward God reveals if we are following Him. The level of obedience determines the closeness of our relationship with Him. In our walk with Christ, He is dealing with our heart issues and changing our character one step at a time in order to transform us into an image of His Son, Jesus Christ. These changes will be seen by those around us.

In our day-to-day lives, we talk the most about the topics that are important to us and that we meditate on throughout the day. That's how people in our circle know what topics interest us. How often do you meditate on God and on heavenly things? Does your speech reflect the Scriptures? If we get into the habit of setting God aside and meditating on worldly fleshly things, then whatever we focus on, that finds a place in our heart and becomes an idol. God knows whether or not we are completely devoted to Him. How do we talk about our experience with God? Is it with interest and enthusiasm? Or is it a topic we avoid altogether?

Spouses are often the people we spend the most time with in our lives. If someone were to ask your spouse if Jesus is your best friend, what would their answer be? If I were to ask your children, "Can you list ten topics that your parents discuss most frequently in the house?" would they say that God is one of the ten topics? Would God be the number one topic on the list?

If I asked your relatives and closest friends, "What are the topics you talk about the most when you are with them?" would God be on the list of those topics, and if yes, what priority would God have on that list?

Can other people outside of our close circle confirm that we have fellowship with Jesus and that He is our best friend? If a person has something off in their relationship with God, it will be revealed in some way sooner or later.

> *A good man out of the good treasure of his heart brings forth good; and an evil man out of the evil treasure of his heart brings forth evil. For out of the abundance of the heart his mouth speaks.* (Luke 6:45)

### Receiving Criticism to Better the Relationship with God

With visibility comes accountability. Because our lives are on display, we are accountable to God for our actions. We must stay receptive to correction from the Lord. Moreover, we should remain open to correction from other believers after verifying that their corrections align with the Word of God. If we don't allow God to change us in a relationship, then of course we wouldn't receive correction from other people and become defensive when they point out what prevents us from connecting with God. We will only be able to discern and accept corrections in light of our love for God because we're interested in getting closer to Him instead of becoming defensive about something that God wants to change in us.

A person willing to pay any cost to deepen their relationship with God welcomes honest feedback on obstacles hindering that connection. They seek to identify any barriers between them and God. In fact, even if their relationship with God is already healthy, they would still seek any advice that can help them grow even closer to Him.

Knowing there's always room for improvement, we shouldn't become upset, defensive, or try to justify our current condition if change is necessary. The Bible teaches discernment: is the correction true and aligned with God's word? If so, we should embrace it. Getting defensive suggests comfort with the status quo and an unwillingness to grow closer to God.

Individuals who walk closely with God, sometimes through conversation, are able to discern if others have a genuine relationship with Jesus. This provides an opportunity to pray for them or lovingly address any deception the person may have about their personal standing with God. By avoiding addressing the issue, we reveal that we're not truly interested in their spiritual well-being.

*Nevertheless I have this against you, that you have left your first love.* (Revelation 2:4)

Why do we feel guilty as Christians? Often because we know in our conscience that our relationship with Jesus is lacking. We might feel unworthy of His attention, but the reality is that He just wants us to commit to being with Him and share our hearts and tell Him everything that bothers us. He wants us to feel His love. Don't make any excuse to hold back from Him. We might feel guilty for repeatedly turning down His invitation to be in His presence, but He is still waiting for us to open our hearts to Him and repent so that we can re-establish fellowship with Him. Your first love is waiting for you.

Are you tired of relying on your own strength and abilities to hold everything together in your life? If you are not willing to give it all to Jesus and fully surrender your problems to Him, you will continue to carry them on your own. Don't approach God as if you can hide something from Him; He already knows everything about you. We can't hide anything from Him. Be honest and vulnerable.

Do you see your current situation as one where you need God's help? Do you want God's help and assistance? Are you willing to pay absolutely any price to be helped by God and to get closer with Him? God said through Jeremiah, "And you will seek Me and find Me, when you search for Me with all your heart" (Jeremiah 29:13), and again through Isaiah, "Seek the LORD while He may be found, call upon Him while He is near" (Isaiah 55:6).

If we pray, "Jesus, You are most valuable to me; I long for You. You are my best friend, my heart is fully Yours, and I look forward to spending time with You," but it is only lip service, then they are just beautiful, meaningless, empty words. When Jesus said, "If anyone thirsts, let him come to Me and drink" (John 7:37), He was referring to true thirst from the heart, not just pretty prayers.

God wants to help us, and all He needs is our willing heart to accept and receive His assistance. Don't just wish for improvement, do something about it. Prove it with your actions that change is what you really desire. Be real with God. He is waiting for us to humbly ask Him for help. He responds to our acknowledged need.

### A Prayer for Distractions

If you've let sin or distractions get in the way of your relationship with Jesus and pushed Him away, if you're ready to turn your life around and want God's intervention to achieve closeness with Him, then you can pray this prayer. Feel free to make it your own. This should be a heart cry and not merely words on a page.

> *Dear heavenly Father, I'm sorry I've ignored You in my life. Please forgive me for ignoring You. I want to reconcile with You. I ask You, Jesus, to perform any work in my life that is needed so that I can be closer to You. I don't want to pretend that I love You. I don't want to fake my love for You. I know You are the source of love and are perfectly good in every way. Please assist me in experiencing and feeling Your love. These things in my life are holding me back from knowing You. I don't want to try to keep my*

*sins and problems hidden from You any longer because I know I can't. You already know them.*

*You're all-knowing. I am having a hard time reaching out to You because I ran after sin and sinful temptations. Other people think I have a real relationship with You, but I don't. I made it look like I have a relationship with You. I pretended to know You by outwardly playing the role of a decent Christian. I deceived others and myself, and I don't want to do it anymore. I'm tired of pretending and tired of having my consciousness condemn me. I repent. Please forgive my sins. I have this addiction that I still love and cling to, but I want to be set free from it. Please help me overcome this addiction.*

*I realize that nothing is more important than fellowship with You. I'm willing to pay any price to be in fellowship with You. I have a difficult time forgiving others who have wronged me. I have unforgiveness toward this person and don't have enough strength to forgive them. Please give me strength to forgive them.*

*I keep remembering traumatic events from my past. I continue to feel guilty about those negative experiences. I'm brokenhearted as a result of betrayals by others who have broken my trust, and I'm having difficulty trusting You as a result of previous experiences with people breaking my trust. But I would like to give You a chance to demonstrate that You're trustworthy and reliable like no one else. I'm making the decision to be open and vulnerable with You. Please remove everything that stands in the way of my relationship with You. I want to grow in a relationship with You. Amen.*

## A Prayer to Revive Relationship

There's no shame in admitting that you have been wrong and made mistakes. It's a sign of honesty and humility to acknowledge your mistakes and come clean about your needs. If your relationship is stale or non-existent, you can pray this prayer to God:

> *Dear heavenly Father, please forgive me for distancing myself away from You, by sinning and disobeying You with my decisions. Forgive me for growing cold toward You. I need You more than anything in my life. I have lost my first love and passion for You, but I want to rekindle my love for You. I'm not where I want to be. I'm not hungry enough to read Your Word every day. I don't have the desire to spend time in prayer anymore. I want to pursue You, to run after You and renew my adoration for Your presence. I want to stay hungry for You, Lord. I want to have more of You. I recognize that my life is meaningless and futile without You. I'm not attracted to You or yearn for You like I used to. I want to pay the full price to follow You and obey You. I want to be closer to You through fellowship. I don't want anything else in my life to distract me from You. Please help me get rid of everything that prevents me from meditating on You. Amen.*

Allow God to cleanse every part of your life, holding nothing back. He will take away your pain, sorrow, anger, addictions, shame, and guilt. People find it hard to admit that for so many years, they only pretended to be Christian without actually living in a relationship with God. Yet when this is the case, we must humbly admit we need God's help to have a breakthrough from things that are holding us back. It takes a lot of humility to admit that we played religion for so many years.

## A Prayer to End the Pretending

We are not called to be actors as Christians—merely playing a role. God sees through our pretending. If you desire to stop the games and pursue an authentic connection with Jesus, pray this prayer:

> *I want to come clean. I open my whole heart to You. I repent of playing Christianity. I followed religion for so many years instead of following You. I'm tired of living a double life, I'm tired of hiding my true self from others, I'm tired of living in guilt-ridden condemnation of my conscience. I don't want to feel defeated and oppressed. I'm tired of trying to run my life. I'm tired of trying to control situations around me. I'm tired of being an actor and pretending everything is well in my life. I want my private life to match my public life. I'm sorry I ignored You for so long. Please forgive me.*
>
> *I want to get to know You and be in a relationship with You. I don't know You; I'll search for You no matter what until I get closer to You. I want to know You. Show me how to rekindle my relationship with You. I haven't paid enough attention to the importance of these things, Lord. I made all sorts of excuses for why I couldn't spend time with You. I've spent time with my idols instead of with You.*
>
> *I want to be drawn to You instead of my idols. I recognize You, Jesus, as the most wonderful, the greatest, and ultimate source of love that ever existed. I don't feel Your love, but I want to experience it. Please reveal Your love to me. I want to feel Your love for me so much that I will stop doubting my value and my worth. I understand how vital it is for me to experience Your love through fellowship. I ignored Your call for a relationship in the past. I made excuses to silence my conscience regarding the lack of connection with You. I was too proud to admit my true need for You.*
>
> *I used to be very passionate about our closeness, but*

*I'm not anymore. I want to return to my first love with You. I've let the vanity of life and worldly things divert my attention away from You. I stopped valuing and adoring You for who You are; I lost sight of how precious You are to me. You're the most valuable relationship I can have. I am so sorry that I have allowed myself to become attached to other things. Will You reveal to me what hinders me from experiencing You? Amen.*

Don't pretend everything is good and continue to pray without actually experiencing God. Put effort into finding the root cause and getting rid of it. Avoid things that hurt your walk with God. Ask yourself, "Is doing this hurting my relationship with God?" Without this sort of humility, we cannot grow. Many people consider humility to be a sign of weakness and thus dismiss it. Humility can be expressed as, "God, I acknowledge You know better than I do, and I trust You more than myself, so I will act as You want me to act." Humility is the bedrock of transformation.

Dishonesty, on the other hand, is pretending to be on good terms with God while having sin in our lives. It's trying to hide sin and downplaying the seriousness of it. It is pretending to know God and to have a personal relationship with Him when we do not. We might be able to trick ourselves, but we cannot fool God.

## Self-Centeredness

One of the biggest obstacles to forming and maintaining a relationship with God is self-centeredness. Selfishness works against the transformation within the relationship that God desires for us. Self-centeredness makes our own interests and desires the focal point of our lives. Christ-centeredness is when Christ and His desires sit at the center of our lives. Either our life revolves around us or it revolves around Christ. We were created to be centered on God. Self-centeredness is the biggest problem in our relationship with Jesus. It leads to comparing our performance with others and competing with them.

Christ-centeredness is a mindset of thinking about what God has already done for me and being grateful for that. Part of a Christ-centered life consists of denying ourselves, taking up the cross, and putting our flesh to death by crucifying it. The flesh will never willingly give up its seat on the throne of our heart. Crucifying our flesh is to daily dethrone selfish desires.

Dying to ourselves occurs when the flesh is yielded to God. The flesh yields to the spirit, or the spirit yields to the flesh. Naturally, the flesh will try to prevail over the spirit. To live fleshly is to be preoccupied with one's own selfish desires, needs, wants, interests, and preferences. If we are self-conscious and preoccupied with the flesh, it makes it more difficult to abide in Christ.

A Christ-centered life is to freely allow God to be the authority in my life, not myself. When Christ is on the throne of our hearts, we have a Christ-centered life and our life becomes selfless toward others, as well. Putting Jesus first in our lives is a daily decision we must make. Is Jesus the master of our lives or is it our flesh? Self-centeredness puts trust in ourselves, but Christ-centeredness puts trust in God. Self-centeredness is self-focused, self-elevating, and self-serving. It seeks to satisfy personal desires and loves self-pity. Self-centeredness leads to self-gratification, self-pleasure, and self-consciousness. It gravitates one toward self-affirmation and self-dependence in life.

God's plan for our lives is functional when we achieve Christ-centeredness. And we implement our own plans and goals when we live with self-centeredness. Before we can begin to fellowship with God, we must first surrender ourselves to Him. God will not compel someone to surrender; it must occur willingly and in obedience. The fruit of submitting to God is the action of yielding flesh to the spirit. Pride wants to stand in the way of a normal, healthy relationship with Jesus.

Let's ask ourselves, "Am I self-minded or Christ-minded? Am I self-sufficient or Christ-sufficient? Am I self-reliant or Christ-reliant? Do I value Jesus' opinion and preference over my own?"

Self-centered thoughts are as such: "How does this make me feel? How does this make me look? Is it fun for me? Is it entertaining for me? Is it pleasurable for me? How will this benefit me? This didn't work out for me. I haven't been able to accomplish that. I didn't accomplish what I wanted to." Notice the language is not that it is *Christ in me* who has accomplished things but the self-centered person takes the credit. Self-reliance aspires to be independent of God. Rather than relying on God to provide for us, self-reliance strives to maintain life on its own. Jesus presented a solution that might seem counter-intuitive: "For whoever desires to save his life will lose it, but whoever loses his life for My sake and the gospel's will save it" (Mark 8:35). Our goal is not self-preservation but self-denial.

### Pride

We were created for the purpose of glorifying God; however, acting on our fleshly desires not only fails to glorify Him but also distances us from Him. Pride convinces you that you can be good apart from God. Self-centeredness and pride go hand-in-hand, and there is not a more harmful sin to keep you from Jesus. Pride is the number one relationship killer. Pride is wanting to be independent of God. Pride puts your opinion above God's Word and your way in front of His. God requires humility for us to connect. Without it, we are acting proudly and will miss fellowship with Him. James famously wrote, "God resists the proud, But gives grace to the humble" (James 4:6).

Pride hinders or destroys relationships. A prideful heart is closed to God's voice. We can evaluate our reactions in situations that demand humility to gauge the impact of pride. To overcome pride, we must pray persistently and sincerely, seeking God's help. If we perceive pride as beneficial, we'll be reluctant to let go of it. However, with God's help, we can overcome pride and experience humility.

Pride is an attitude of the heart that shows up as an unhealthy excessive focus on oneself and holds a high opinion of one's importance, achievements, position, status, skills, and so on. Pride wants to be important and relevant; it wants to get credit and praise from other people instead of giving honor and glory to God, which rightfully belongs to Him. Pride resists help. It prefers to operate independently, relying on its own logic and experience. Pride is a mindset that declares, "I don't need God's assistance or guidance; I don't require advice, correction, or help from anyone." By rejecting God's wisdom, we rely on our own limited understanding.

For many, the biggest challenge to getting to know God is starting with the wrong mindset. They believe they already know God, and as a result, these false assumptions color how they pray, how they read the Bible, and how they grow (or fail to grow) in their Christian walk. Pride leads people to rely on their own understanding of God rather than seeking His revelation about Him. Pride manifests when God offers new revelation, and we reject it, insisting, "I understand You based on Your Word as I interpret it. I don't need further direct revelation."

This sort of person bases life on their personal philosophy and how they comprehend their reality. Their stance is, "I know how to live my life. I've already figured it out." They get angry and frustrated at what happens in their life and in the world when it goes against their beliefs. When a person is not in the right stance with God, their philosophy of life will be skewed. They put their opinions above God's.

Using their own philosophy, they create their own purpose for life and what they want to achieve. Their personal version of reality is distorted by the lies of the enemy. They prioritize their own interpretations of life's reality, elevating it above God's truth. They judge things based on their own understanding. They hold on to their personal interpretation of God's Word, being stubborn in accepting the truth from Jesus.

Until we meet Jesus and establish a relationship with Him, we can't see life for what it is because Jesus is the only real truth, and apart from Him, everything else is a deception and a lie. If we don't walk in the light, we don't have the right perspective on life. Those who walk in the darkness suppress the truth and don't want to accept it. They resist the truth of God instead of simply humbling themselves before God and submitting to God's ultimate truth and reconciling with Him. God will then begin unveiling His truths to them. We can't comprehend life itself without God's insight and revelation.

Flesh thrives on pride. Pride sustains and nourishes the flesh. We have a responsibility to curb the flesh in check and consistently deny its desires. Pride insists on standing one's ground, asserting one's identity, and prioritizing one's opinions. It fears losing respect in the eyes of others. When we become aware of how much people value our opinions, pride motivates us to protect our image and invest in maintaining our reputation, status, and position to secure their continued respect and admiration.

Pride craves external validation and is easily offended. It avoids responsibility, constructing excuses and blaming others for a lack of relationship with God. Pride refuses to acknowledge personal responsibility for an inadequate or absent relationship with Jesus, instead resorting to excuses and blaming external factors. Pride resists submission to God's will and obedience to Him. Those consumed by pride refuse to invest the effort required for a relationship with God and understanding His ways. Instead, they live according to their own desires, effectively making themselves their own gods.

Pride is self-focused, self-gratifying, self-justifying, self-indulgent, self-opinionated, self-righteous, self-seeking, self-willed, self-absorbed, self-centered, seeking self-approval, self-motivated, self-conceited, and self-important to name a few descriptions.

> *Likewise you younger people, submit yourselves to your elders. Yes, all of you be submissive to one another, and be clothed with humility, for "God resists the proud, But gives grace to the humble." Therefore humble yourselves*

*under the mighty hand of God, that He may exalt you in due time.* (1 Peter 5:5-6)

These same principles are littered throughout the Old Testament, as well. Solomon wrote, "Let another man praise you, and not your own mouth; A stranger, and not your own lips" (Proverbs 27:2). God echoed this in Jeremiah: "'Let not the wise man glory in his wisdom, let not the mighty man glory in his might, nor let the rich man glory in his riches; but let him who glories glory in this, that he understands and knows Me, that I am the Lord, exercising lovingkindness, judgment, and righteousness in the earth. For in these I delight,' says the Lord" (Jeremiah 9:23-24). Extrapolating on these very Scriptures, Paul wrote, "But 'he who glories, let him glory in the Lord.' For not he who commends himself is approved, but whom the Lord commends" (2 Corinthians 10:17-18).

Overcoming pride can be challenging as it offers the illusion of self-sufficiency and independence. While true freedom comes from seeking God, pride craves autonomy. We must honestly ask ourselves: "Have I become so reliant on myself that I neglect God's continual guidance? Have I become so assured as to believe I don't need God's help continually? Have I become wise enough to be self-sufficient? Have I become so knowledgeable that I do not long for revelations from God? Have I become so successful that it has made me proud? Have I become so confident in myself that I have become disobedient to God?"

The sin of pride is like an umbrella under which many other sins are linked together. For example, envy, jealousy, lying, hypocrisy, anger, rage, wrath, strife, resentment, revenge, retaliation, offense, unforgiveness, condemnation, judging, slander, boasting, bragging, stubbornness, rebellion, disobedience, covetousness, greed, stinginess, immorality, deception, flattery, craftiness, cunning, slyness, contempt, hate, blame, complaints, discontent, irritability, a quick temper, and frustration all find a place under the banner of pride.

CHAPTER FIVE

# Created to Love and Be Loved

*We love Him because He first loved us.* (1 John 4:19)

GOD CREATED US with a tendency to love, to experience love and be loved in return. All of us are hardwired for a need to love and be loved. Love is a fruit that grows from the union of two individuals in a relationship. In life, we long for acceptance and love from people, for example, those that are close to us like family, friends, and acquaintances. The most important reason why we were given the ability to love in the first place is to love God and experience knowing Him through a loving relationship.

We are inherently wired to crave acceptance and love from others, particularly from God. While we naturally seek affection and approval from family, friends, and society, our fundamental capacity for love is ultimately meant to experience a loving relationship with Him—to know Him and to experience His love. This relationship is the primary reason for our ability to love. God created us with that desire for Him that no other relationship can satisfy. All of us need the love of God. He really desires that we first and foremost seek His acceptance and His love above all other relationships. We don't need to resist His love, ignore it, or run away from it. All we need to do is respond and reciprocate love. We have the choice to connect with the ultimate source of love from God. He can fully express His ultimate love to those who truly desire to love Him in return. When we act upon this desire for God, it leads us to form a relationship with Him.

Our deep-seated desire for validation and acceptance often drives us to extraordinary lengths to seek attention and approval from others. We crave feeling cared for and loved. While we may pursue ultimate love through human relationships, this love is ultimately found only in God. Without a relationship with God, we may seek to fill that void through other people.

For a relationship to function and be healthy, it needs to be properly maintained through consistent care and nurturing. It must be founded on genuine love and characterized by mutual understanding, loyalty, faithfulness, respect, kindness, attention, affection, open communication, honesty, sincerity, and trust.

Most of us have been damaged by being unloved or having a lack of love in some way or another. A lack of love or being unloved can lead to depression, feelings of unworthiness, anxiety, fear, or anger. God knows our every thought we've ever had, word we've ever spoken, and deed we've ever done. He knows exactly what we went through and what wounded us and caused us pain. He is the only one who truly understands what we went through and what we still experience due to unresolved past hurt. He knows who wronged us and who mistreated us, and He knows how each of our negative experiences in life impacted us and shaped us into who we are today. He knows how the past weighs us down and keeps us from living a victorious life in fellowship with Him. He is the only one who can truly understand what we're going through and be able to comfort us. His heart's desire is to mend our brokenness, to set us free from sin and past hurt, and to make us whole again.

Maybe you feel like you don't deserve God's love because you don't value yourself, but nevertheless, He still loves you. God's ability and His genuine love toward us can heal the damage and brokenness that we have experienced in the past. We must first open our hearts to God's love and allow Him to heal the wounds caused by love's absence in our lives. As we do, we will discover the captivating power of His love.

God deeply desires our attention because He loves us immensely. Our lives undergo a dramatic transformation when we cultivate a personal interest in and a longing to know Him. The reason we often miss experiencing God's love is simply that we aren't actively seeking Him. God wants us to pursue Him in order to reveal His love and His revelations of who He is. He doesn't play hide-and-seek. If we reach out and seek Him with all of our being, we will find Him. Experiencing God's love will compel us to seek Him continually. God will not force us to love Him; He longs to reveal His heart to us, but are we willing to open ours in response?

Is Jesus only our Lord and Savior or is He also our closest friend?

The truth is, God longs to be our best friend, a confidante with whom He can share His heart. We'll feel complete only by having closeness with our heavenly Father.

Following Jesus out of love for Him is not the same as trying to follow Him formally out of obligation. Jesus is saying, "I don't want a relationship where you're not completely in love with Me. I don't want a part of your heart; I want your *whole* heart."

Because we have a free will, we can't buy love with money, we can't force someone to love us, we can't convince someone to love us; nor can you control how someone else feels about you. Real love must be *freely* given.

## Love Is at the Core of a Relationship

*We love Him because He first loved us.* (1 John 4:19)

What we love determines how we live. What we love gets our attention. Our hearts seek out what we love.

Love is at the core of our relationship with God. This is evidenced in multiple places in Scripture. For instance, "So he answered and said, 'You shall love the Lord your God with all your heart, with all your soul, with all your strength, and with all your mind,' and 'your neighbor as yourself'" (Luke 10:27). The Old Testament also reflects these truths: "Whom have I in heaven but You? And there is none upon earth that I desire besides You" (Psalm 73:25) and "With my soul I have desired You in the night, yes, by my spirit within me I will seek You early" (Isaiah 26:9).

If someone asks, "Why do you love your spouse?" you could begin by listing all of their positive personality traits, as well as what they are capable of, their attractive physical appearance, how they care for you and how they make you feel, how they raise the children and prepare food, do chores, work, and so on. You could also say, "I love my spouse simply because they exist. I love my spouse just because I choose to love them." This is the case with God—He wants us to love Him simply because He exists, just because He is, not because of what He has given us or can give us.

We don't seek God's presence for the sole purpose of assuring us of His existence. We already know He exists. But we are drawn to His presence because of our love for Him. Our spirit longs to be as close to Him as possible.

We can experience the love of God because He is a source of love and He doesn't change. The first way that God expressed His love for us is by creating us in His image. God knew us before we were born.

The second way God demonstrated His love for us was by sending Jesus Christ to die for our sins on the cross in order to redeem us and to spend eternity with us. How are we going to respond to that kind of love?

When we meditate on what Jesus endured to save us—enduring beatings, spitting, mockery, humiliation, pain from the crown of thorns, whipping, and slowly dying on the cross in an excruciatingly painful way, we realize that we can never fully grasp that kind of love for us. It compels us to respond to this kind of love by reciprocating His love, committing to Him, and dedicating time to enjoy His presence. Experiencing His love makes our time spent together effortless and enjoyable, not burdensome but pleasurable.

Some individuals are wary of the love that God offers them because they have been deprived of love by others in their lives. But God has already demonstrated His love for us in advance so that we can trust Him.

God desires us to feel loved, accepted, valued, and whole, and the only path to this fulfillment is through a personal relationship with Him. So, let's seek Him wholeheartedly, and we will find complete satisfaction in Him.

Our relationship with God needs to become second nature. This is what God desires for us to reach through personal experience.

Bob Kauflin said, "How do I know what I love the most? By asking myself a few simple questions. What do I enjoy the most? What do I spend the most time doing? Where does my mind drift to when I don't have anything to do? What am I passionate about? What do I spend my money on? What makes me angry when I don't get it? What do I feel depressed without? What do I fear losing the most? Our answers to those questions will lead us straight to the God or gods we love and worship."

Simply put, people prioritize and talk about what they love and are most interested in.

The Bible says that God is very interested in having a loving relationship with us. He is passionate about you. The question is, are you interested in having that mutual relationship with Him?

The Bible says, "Because he has set his love upon Me, therefore I will deliver him; I will set him on high, because he has known My name" (Psalm 91:14).

Anybody can say, "I love you," but if the words aren't followed up with action, they are meaningless. Do you actually experience their love that they express toward you? God's love has already been revealed to us by sending Jesus Christ to die for our sins in order to reconcile and establish a relationship with us. It's meaningless to say "I love You" to God if we do not desire to spend time in fellowship with Him. When we say, "God, I love You," He knows our hearts; He knows how we actually feel and if we are really, truly in love with Him or not. God observes how much we value and cherish His love toward us.

Love is at the core of any relationship. The most important thing that Jesus desires from us is love. He is longing for love from you. God intends to draw us closer to Him through love, enticing us into a loving relationship so that we are captivated by His love. He wants to be our best friend. Our love for God is very limited due to our humanity, compared to God's ultimate love for us, but God is pleased even with our limited ability to express our love for Him.

It's not God's fault that we haven't put in enough effort to reach out to Him and start experiencing His love. Jesus is waiting for us to respond to His love. Jesus longs to have us near Him and to give Him our hearts. Only falling in love with Jesus will make it possible to have a real relationship. We have an opportunity to fall in love with Jesus; whether we take that opportunity is up to us.

God is saying, "Allow Me to introduce Myself to you so that you can get to know Me and fall in love with Me." Do you want to be embraced in the arms of a loving heavenly Father? God desires that we experience Him as His children, and through experiencing His love, He becomes desirable to us.

God is reaching out to us; are we going to respond back to His love? Imagine a guy making a marriage proposal to a girl and she says, "I have five more guys in mind that I want to be with, and after that, you can propose and I will be your wife." Will that man accept her deal? That's what happens when Jesus offers His love to us and we say, "I want to know You, Jesus, and be Your friend and have a relationship with You, but just not today. There are more fun and interesting things that draw my attention. For me, prayer and fellowship time with You are not as important. What is important for me is to just believe in You in my heart. I will make things right with You and be Your friend on my deathbed."

Love inspires us to push past our reluctance to do things. If we really love and want something, we will make it happen. And if we don't want something, there will always be excuses, justifications, explanations, reasons, and rationality not to do it.

Being unloved, ignored, or neglected by others brings false condemnation from the past. One can start having thoughts of, *I'm not worthy of God's love* and *I don't deserve God's love*. This mindset can create a feeling of needing to earn God's love, but it's crucial to learn to shake off this hesitance and fully receive His unconditional love.

### The Intentions of Our Heart Matter

*For the eyes of the Lord run to and fro throughout the whole earth, to show Himself strong on behalf of those whose heart is loyal to Him.* (2 Chronicles 16:9)

With what heart condition are we approaching fellowship with Him when we are reading the Bible and praying? If we just go through the motions and do it as a religious check-list, it does not please God. Treating a dedicated time with God as another habitual routine can cause the relationship to cool off and gradually decline. If we don't maintain the passion and our hearts are not in it, it shows that we have started to lose genuine desire for Him. This is tragic. No one wants the other person in a relationship to be a chore, burden, or an obligation. Without experiencing God's love, the person will treat prayer time as a burden and a chore. God doesn't want us to pursue fellowship with Him out of either fear or guilt. The right approach in a healthy, loving relationship is, "I want to fellowship with God because I love Him."

Without our hearts being in it, prayer becomes a tedious religious ritual. God doesn't want a shallow, surface-level relationship with us but a real and genuine one. We could be reading the Word or praying, but our thoughts have already moved on to the next thing we're going to do when we are finished. Ask yourself: Do you really connect with God during your communion time? Do you really feel His presence? Pray and meditate until you're so lost in Him that you forget everything else in those moments except Him. It's the stance of our heart toward His heart that makes the relationship genuine. God is seeking our loyalty and a devoted heart invested in a relationship with Him. God is seeking those who cannot get enough of Him. This is the posture Jesus described when He said, "You shall love the Lord your God with all your heart, with all your soul, and with all your mind" (Matthew 22:37).

How can you love God with all your heart, soul, mind, and strength yet not be spending time with Him? The answer: you can't be. To pursue Him in this fashion means setting aside time for God with the right heart motivation.

Our relationship with God, or lack thereof, reveals if we love God with all our hearts or not. Love is the internal drive that connects us with God. When we perceive and experience God's love, it drives us to seek Him out even more. It is not just whether we love God but also how much we love Him and how we express our love for Him, how much we yearn for Him, and how much we want to know Him better. How fervently and earnestly we seek His presence is a sign of our level of love for Him. Seek God earnestly, not moderately. Go after Him with all you've got!

Love for God is expressed through worship. God's heart yearns for true worshippers who would worship Him in spirit and truth. Jesus said, "But the hour is coming, and now is, when the true worshipers will worship the Father in spirit and truth; for the Father is seeking such to worship Him" (John 4:23).

You're the object of God's love. God reveals His kindness and gentleness through love. Allow God to reveal His love in a tangible way to you. The assurance of God's love comes from experiencing it, and through that experience, we have a deeper friendship with Him.

Through a relationship, we have the assurance that we are completely loved, and we rest in Him. During the fellowship time, give your attention to God and allow Him to directly speak to you and reassure you of His love. To experience God's love frequently, we must abide in Jesus, walk closely with Him, and seek His presence continually. There are countless benefits to meditating on the immensity of God's love for us.

Is Jesus your groom? If so, then pursue falling in love with Him over and over again. God's love is independent of our circumstances. Do not try to earn His love, but instead, run to Him and let Him embrace you. Make a decision to desire nothing more than God Himself. Where do we find true satisfaction in life? Nothing compares to the fulfillment found in Him. Seeking love from people will never fully satisfy us, for only God's perfect love can truly satisfy our souls. Our relationships with others will not substitute for our relationship with God.

God knows the intentions of our heart and if we're seeking Him solely because of love or for something else. Is Jesus the true love of your life? If you obey the first commandment, then you will love God more than anything or anyone.

When we become distracted by life's busyness and drift away from God, He patiently observes whether we miss His presence and long to return to Him. God allows these times to reveal the depth of our desire for fellowship with Him.

This fellowship isn't just about checking a box on our to-do lists or completing a task on the agenda. It is more than a pursuit of head knowledge or intellectual understanding. We must move beyond simply "knowing" about the love of God and shift to *experiencing* the love of God.

### Experiencing God's Love

Relationships are intimate and personal for each individual. We have a unique journey with God that is unlike anyone else's. Once we establish a relationship, it becomes our personal experiential encounter with God.

If someone loves you, the only way that you can experience their love is through a relationship with them. Once we experience God's love, it leads us to receive His love, acceptance, healing, contentment, joy, and peace. If we spend time in prayer or meditation but lack a true relationship with God, or if sin in our lives prevents us from truly connecting with Him, then we won't notice any significant changes in our lives. Prayer may become merely a religious ritual performed out of obligation. However, if we have a personal experience with God and feel transformed by spending time with Him, that will naturally motivate us to continue seeking Him. The experience of spending time alone with God will always remain personal because we are all unique.

If we don't find pleasure in spending time with God and encountering His presence during prayer and Bible reading, we're less likely to feel motivated, interested, or eager for the next encounter. Prayer is not a one-way conversation with God. It involves encountering Him through fellowship and receiving answers to our prayers. Don't settle for praying for a predetermined number of minutes you've allocated each day. If you haven't fully experienced satisfaction and breakthrough in your connection with Him, actively seek more opportunities to be in His presence. The point of prayer is to connect with Jesus every day, not just to pray for a certain amount of minutes. Eventually, that connection leads to inner longing to meditate on Him throughout the day.

Why would we continue seeking to spend time with God if

fellowship with Him isn't enjoyable, satisfying, or fulfilling? If we fellowship with God just because we see it as a requirement and "a good thing to do," then we don't have a genuine relationship with Him the way He wants it to be. He desires that we seek Him out of love. If we don't experience pleasure and joy in God's presence, we will always seek it elsewhere.

The purpose of spending a certain amount of time in fellowship with Jesus is not to get used to doing it over and over again or develop a routine but to deepen our intimacy with Him. As we grow closer to Jesus, our love for Him grows and we want to spend more time meditating on Him and making His presence our dwelling place throughout the day.

God wants the best for our well-being, and that involves us knowing Him and acknowledging Him in our lives. He doesn't want us to be guilt-tripped to spend time with Him but to lovingly long for Him, reading His Word and praying to Him out of our own love for God.

God knows our hearts and doesn't want us to feel guilty for missing time with Him. If that does happen, our love for Him will still draw us back to seek Him again. At times, we can neglect His love by ignoring His presence in our lives. True love doesn't look for reasons or excuses to avoid being with the person they love.

Ask yourself, "Do I know *about* Jesus, or do I know Jesus *personally*?"

Everyone needs an experiential encounter with Jesus on their own. One true encounter with God changes us forever. That initial experience marks the beginning of our relationship with Him. Even if we distance ourselves from God, we will always remember that love connection we had with Him. It's challenging to imitate a relationship with Jesus if we haven't actually formed one in the first place.

God's love fills the God-shaped void and heals the absence or lack of love. Some try to make up for the absence God's love in their lives by filling the God-shaped void with temporary substitutes, seeking at least temporary satisfaction and artificial happiness. However, these fleeting pleasures ultimately leave a sense of emptiness. Real satisfaction is only possible when His love fills the God-shaped void. Only God's love can truly satisfy the longing of the human heart.

What motivates you to continually approach God? If it's anything but love, then we're not driven by the right motivation. If we don't have love motivating us, then maybe we haven't experienced Him and don't realize how valuable He is. If we haven't experienced God's goodness during our alone time with Him, we'll be less likely to seek Him out when opportunities arise. Why would I make an effort to push myself to do something I don't enjoy? Don't stop seeking God until you have felt His love; at that point, His love will captivate you.

Don't ignore how much Jesus loves you. Instead, allow yourself to experience how powerful and overwhelming His love is. In your prayer room, be captivated by His love and His nature and find deep satisfaction in worshiping Him.

Do you realize how much He loves you? Do you feel the need for Jesus every day? If a believer doesn't read their Bible or pray regularly, it suggests a potential disconnect from their relationship with God, indicating they may not feel a strong longing for His presence. That means their love for God has diminished and something else grabbed a hold of their heart. If we love Him, we will feel a need to be in contact with Jesus every day. Our soul is searching for God's love, but our flesh resists our soul's desire.

Do everything possible to abide in Jesus and remain in His love. If we love anything more than our relationship with God, it will consume us. But if our relationship with God is above all else, then we will be truly satisfied.

### Love Wants to Know

*You will seek the LORD your God, and you will find Him if you seek Him with all your heart and with all your soul.* (Deuteronomy 4:29)

Merely wanting a relationship with Jesus, or having a desire to improve an established relationship, won't make it so. We must cultivate a mindset that says, "I'm not going to stop seeking God until I reconcile with Him and become closer to Him." If we truly understand His importance to us, we'll crave for more of Him in our lives. This longing will drive us to seek Him relentlessly, regardless of the challenges.

Do we have a longing to know God even more than we already do? Don't set a goal to just know God casually, but desire to advance and grow in your love and knowledge of Him through fellowshipping with Him. Typically, a sudden, overwhelming desire to read the Bible and pray doesn't happen overnight. We must put in much effort to keep and maintain our relationship with Jesus daily. Nurturing a relationship with Jesus requires consistent discipline, persistence and perseverance.

Don't start building a relationship with Jesus and give up before experiencing His love. Persevere until you encounter Him. Eventually, you'll draw closer to God, experiencing a deepening intimacy and a greater revelation of His character. This growing connection will immerse you in His love and presence, making life without Him unimaginable. You'll cherish your time with Jesus so much that you'll eagerly anticipate your next opportunity to be alone with Him.

Think of it: at one point, your spouse was a total stranger to you, and then you made a decision to get to know them, which led to falling in love with them. In the same way, we can make a decision to get to know Jesus, and it will lead us to fall in love with Him. We can make a decision to seek God persistently until we find Him, leading to an inseparable bond. In a good relationship, neither side sees it as a burden to maintain their relationship. Their mutual love flows naturally and spontaneously.

We give ourselves and our time to God because we love Him. Our love for God provides us with the inner motivation to do what pleases Him. God desires communion with us and is looking for passion in our hearts for Him.

Even when people are in love, relationships require ongoing effort to keep that loving relationship going.

Love makes it possible to get into the habit of praying to God on a daily basis. The purpose of life is attained when we spend personal time with God, whom we love, and this becomes our favorite thing to do. This is what God intended for us in the first place, and that's how we achieve obeying the first commandment.

We can't be *kind of* in love with someone. It's impossible to be partially or moderately in love. Why do we then try to pretend that a half-hearted response to God's love is sufficient enough? Is there such a thing as loving someone too much?

How do you respond to God's love? Is it with a full effort or a half-hearted effort? It's not about being an extreme Christian versus a moderate Christian; it's about being extremely in love with Jesus. Have you ever seen a bride who was not extremely in love before the wedding? People are either in love or they're not. Some say we have to take everything in moderation, even God and our relationship with Him. There's no such thing as loving God too much, seeking Jesus too much, or spending way too much time alone with God in fellowship. People can create their own standards for loving God and investing in their relationship with Him, calling them adequate without seeking God's perspective.

Love grows over time! When we see newlyweds, we might think, "Oh, they love each other so much; they have the greatest love!" Even though newlyweds are extremely in love, their love continues to grow. But in comparison, an older couple who's in love, love each other more than the newlyweds. And do you want to know why? Because their love grew over time! When we establish a relationship with Jesus, our love for Him starts to grow. Jesus has been ready to give us all of His love, but are we willing to make a decision to receive it fully?

Each person must reciprocate love in a relationship in order to feel loved. Understanding and experiencing God's love are two very different things. How can God be number one in our lives if we don't have a relationship with Him?

Without love for Jesus, praying or reading the Bible can become just another religious experience. In the absence of love, we might feel good about dedicating a certain amount of time to God without sensing His presence or connecting with Him in fellowship. Only by loving the author of the Bible can we read it as a love letter.

Let's analyze ourselves. Are we hungry enough for God? If not, why not? What suppresses our love, our desire, and our passion for God?

A loving relationship is one where we open our hearts and pour ourselves out to God in an unrestricted way, without reservations, and are willing to spend time in stillness just to be in His presence.

Once we understand that sin and distractions hinder our relationship with Jesus, we'll be motivated to eliminate them from our lives and focus solely on deepening our connection with Him. To truly connect with Him in fellowship, we must use our free will to completely surrender to His will.

In fellowship, God reveals the state of His heart toward us. Have you ever had a relationship with someone that was burdensome? If it was burdensome, that relationship is draining and wouldn't be pleasant or long lasting. Do you think a loving God would draw you into a relationship that isn't enjoyable, pleasing, or satisfying? Of course not! Nothing can satisfy our souls like God's love can. When we spend time with God, He enjoys our presence, and He wants us to enjoy His presence and look forward to spending time with Him. We don't come to God because it only pleases Him, but because we also enjoy and love being in His presence. Give God a chance to win you over with love.

If we don't remain connected with Jesus constantly, we might start to doubt His love. Our own insecurities, misunderstandings, and problems will start to pop up, grow, and overshadow Him. It's essential to constantly remind ourselves of His love for us, His open heart toward us, and His desire to fellowship with us.

God loves us with a perfect form of love. We can't fully comprehend or grasp how much and with what kind of love God actually loves us with. But if someone says to us, "God loves you," we associate God's love with the love that we encounter through our relationships with others. We can make wrong assumptions about God's love if we have not personally experienced His love. Our ability to give and express love is influenced by our own experiences and understanding of love. It can be challenging to give more love than we have experienced ourselves, as our own experiences shape our capacity to love others. We continue to grow in our capacity to love by being in fellowship with God, which leads to discovering and experiencing more of His loving nature, which in turn expands our own love toward God and others. When Jesus was here on earth, He used different real-life examples and illustrations, in parable form, to explain our relationship with Him and with the Father. This was done so that listeners could understand the love of God by relating it to the love that they themselves had already experienced here on earth. He used numerous parables, like the child asking his father for bread and fish, as well as the parables about one lost sheep and the prodigal son.

The truth is, maintenance is required in our walk with God. In Scripture, we see a relationship that was not maintained due to lack of love:

> *Afterward the other virgins came also, saying, "Lord, Lord, open to us!" But he answered and said, "Assuredly, I say to you, I do not know you."* (Matthew 25:11–12)

Those who invest less effort in maintaining their relationship with Jesus may experience a decline in their love for Him as they spend less time with Him, eventually becoming lukewarm. Jesus points to this in Revelation: "So then, because you are lukewarm, and neither cold nor hot, I will vomit you out of My mouth" (Revelation 3:16).

There are those who were in a relationship with God at some point in their lives, but they have grown cold toward Him, lost their first love, and are no longer in fellowship with Jesus. They were born-again believers who backslid, got lukewarm, and went back into the world. They knew Jesus at some point in their lives, but they became complacent and their love for sin ended the relationship. They have not maintained their relationship with God.

### Loving God by Keeping His Word

Love for God can be demonstrated by obedience. This is apparent from many instances in the Bible. "As the Father has loved me, so have I loved you. Now remain in My love. If you keep My commandments, you will abide in My love; just as I have kept My Father's commandments and abide in His love" (John 15:9-10). "Jesus answered and said to him, 'If anyone loves Me, he will keep My word; and My Father will love him... He who does not love Me does not keep My words'" (John 14:23-24). And, "For this is the love of God, that we keep His commandments. And His commandments are not burdensome" (1 John 5:3).

Obedience is evidence. Love for God is proved through action and it's by following His commandments. If we love Him, we will obey His commandments. The more we get to know Him on a personal level, the more we will fall in love with Him and want to please Him. Believing in Jesus means living for Jesus, and loving Jesus means obeying His commandments. God's commandments are to guide our lives and to ensure our safety and well-being.

Is loving and obeying God our highest priority? We can't have love for God as our highest priority if obeying God is not our highest priority.

God is going to ask you and me, "Did you believe that My Word is the truth? What did you do with My Word? Did you follow through on what I said? Did you obey My Word and put it into practice? Did you take My warnings and consequences seriously of what I said would happen to those who do not live by My Word and obey it?"

If you're a genuine Bible-believing follower of Jesus, you will obey God and His Word. You will love to meditate on God's Word. If we believe in God, we will do everything He says in His Word to please Him through obedience.

There are some people who want to accept Jesus as their personal Savior, to wash away their sins, but who still want to continue living their lives as they see fit. They want the convenience of being saved, but they do not allow the lordship of Jesus Christ to reign over their lives. They resist surrendering to Jesus as their Lord. They refuse to obey and follow Him as the Lord of their lives. Sanctification is an ongoing process of walking with Jesus and fully obeying Him.

Some want Jesus to be their Savior but not their *Lord*, yet He has to be not only our Savior but also our Lord. We must be willing to take on the responsibility and commit to serving Him. It's possible to confess or believe that Jesus is our Lord, but not treat Him as such. There's a danger of appearing godly on the outside while inwardly rejecting God's commands and refusing to submit to His will. Will we follow our desires or obey God?

Jesus asked, "But why do you call Me 'Lord, Lord,' and not do the things which I say?" (Luke 6:46). It's a valid question that still stands. Furthermore, the question is begged, how can we obey God's commandments if we don't read His Word in the first place?

If we don't follow God's Word and put it into practice, then we're stating that we really don't believe God's warnings regarding disobeying His commandments.

Just reading the Bible doesn't necessarily make one obedient to Jesus Christ. Forsaking all to follow Jesus means placing God's commandments above everything else. Jesus said, "You are My friends if you do whatever I command you" (John 15:14).

The Bible's statutes set boundaries for our lives. God's regulations and laws are meant to protect us from sin and the enemy throughout our journey in life and it's all meant for our own good.

## Relationship Reveals Us

Throughout our lives, we have created false identities based on who we believe we are or how others perceive us. Experience and interaction in life have formed in our minds a certain perception of who we are and our identity, and we have convinced ourselves that this is the truth. Our self-perception becomes distorted without fellowship with Jesus. True self-understanding and identity are revealed only in Him.

No one knows us better than God does. How God sees us reflects our true identity, regardless of how others value us or even how we perceive ourselves.

Without a relationship with Jesus, we cannot fully understand ourselves. Our true identity is revealed only through our connection with Him. It can only be discovered in a loving relationship with Christ. The more we discover His character, the more we start to understand and discover, little by little, who we truly are. By knowing His perception of us through our relationship with Him, we can understand and gain true confidence in who we are, knowing that our worth and value come from Him alone. For our confidence to be genuine, it must be rooted in Jesus Christ and nothing else. Others' opinions of us will not shake our understanding of ourselves if we continually abide in Him.

It is one thing to be born again, but it takes effort, striving, persistence, and perseverance every day to walk in fellowship with God and obey His commandments. Following God requires daily sacrifice. Many start strong but eventually become lukewarm, backslide, and fall away from faith, succumbing to temptation, compromise, and a sinful lifestyle. While following Jesus is not easy, our love for Him enables us to overcome every challenge and persevere. When we know what we're paying the price for, then it will be easier to continue paying the cost of following Jesus.

We must actively pursue a deepening relationship with God. Neglecting this pursuit indicates a reluctance to fully commit to following Jesus. A lack of enjoyment in Bible reading and prayer suggests a disconnect in our relationship with Him. This disinterest in spending time with God signals an underlying problem. Consequently, in such cases, the best course of action is to seek God's guidance to identify and address the issue. It's in our best interest to reconcile with God.

The question is begged, what price are we willing to pay for a loving relationship? How much are we willing to shift our value system? Paul wrote, "Yet indeed I also count all things loss for the excellence of the knowledge of Christ Jesus my Lord, for whom I have suffered the loss of all things, and count them as rubbish, that I may gain Christ" (Philippians 3:8).

There are those who might acknowledge the importance and the need to establish a relationship with God but hesitate to take the steps and pay the price to get there.

A lot of things in life are difficult, inconvenient, and uncomfortable for us, but we do them anyway. Why? Because the reward and benefit outweigh the price of difficulty and inconvenience. What are some of the most difficult things you've done in your life that you'd say were well worth the effort? Our relationship with God is way more important than those things.

Maintaining a relationship is not easy. It weeds out those who are not willing to pay the price to follow Jesus. God is watching those who will respond to Him faithfully amidst life's challenges and are willing to persevere until the end. If you want something badly enough and know it's worth it, you'll pay whatever it takes to get it. If you want something badly enough and know it's worth it, you'll pay whatever it takes to get it. Where there's a desire, there's a way to achieve it. If we want to find an excuse not to do something, we will find it. If we haven't established a relationship with Jesus, it means we haven't sought Him enough.

If we don't experience enjoyment from fellowship with God, we won't value it. If we don't value it, we won't put forth the effort to pay the price of pursuing God. If we truly want to start and pursue a relationship with Jesus, we'll find a way to make it possible. Conversely, if for some reason we don't want to start or maintain a relationship with Jesus, we'll find an excuse. The only way a real relationship can succeed through all the challenges along the way is through love.

God watches those who show how much they love Him by paying the price for fellowship and friendship. The price is not burdensome if we're in love. How much effort do we invest in our family, business, or job? Shouldn't seeking God and fellowship with Him be worth even greater effort? The effort we put in each day to maintain fellowship with God reveals how valuable His friendship is to us. Those who place too small a value on Jesus will consider the cost of fellowship with Him to be very high. There are many important things in life, but as we manage them, we must not lose sight of what is most important!

Have we counted the cost of following Jesus? Relationships necessitate complete dedication and commitment. God doesn't want a half-hearted commitment. You must be fully committed to obeying and following Jesus because you desire to, not merely because it's the right thing to do. The commitment states, "I'm Yours, Jesus, and I will follow You at any cost." I'm willing to submit my flesh in order to be obedient to You and maintain a relationship with You. We can't compromise by holding onto Jesus and simultaneously living a compromised lifestyle. It's imperative that we realize that the cost of relationship with Jesus includes not just our time but our wholehearted, humble obedience.

The cost of a relationship with Jesus also involves denying yourself, picking up the cross, and following Him (see Luke 9:23).

Denying yourself means self-sacrifice and putting your preferences and wants aside. It requires having self-discipline and living in service to God and others. It means going against our fleshly desires and doing what God tells us to do. We are to surrender our lives to Jesus and live a life of sacrifice in obedience to Him, not just reading the Word of God but doing the Word and applying it in our lives.

Picking up and carrying your cross entails putting all your faith in God and completely trusting Him in every situation, no matter what is going on in your life. Picking up the cross involves dying for our ambitions, plans, and goals. This is the process of humbling ourselves.

Keep in mind, our natural inclination is to worship and serve ourselves—even if those aren't always the words we use to describe our way of life. Consequently, by our thoughts, words, and deeds, we say, "I will fulfill my dreams, I will achieve my desires, I will meet my needs, and I will not tolerate anything or anyone that stands in the way." As one's faith grows, a radical renunciation of self and an embrace of identifying with Christ and His suffering will be required. Jesus calls those who follow Him to become like Him in His suffering and self-denial. Ask God, "What do You want me to do? What should I do to carry out Your will? What is my calling? What kind of ministry should I do?"

When we get born again, we die to our old self. We also continue dying to self as part of the process of sanctification. As such, dying to self is both a one-time event and a lifelong process. Dying to self means that the things of the old life are put to death, most especially the temptation of our old sinful lifestyle that we once engaged in. "And those who are Christ's have crucified the flesh with its passions and desires" (Galatians 5:24).

The cost of a relationship with Jesus could be a loss of connection with family members, a loss of friendships, doing things that are uncomfortable for us, and so on. Jesus requires our commitment in following Him all the way. We need to understand the cost of commitment and what we're committing to before we make that decision. There's no negotiation or compromise with God. There are no discounts or sales on following Jesus Christ.

We either agree to pay the full price without bargaining or we don't commit at all.

We can't bargain with God about what we're willing to give up in order to be in relationship with Him. Jesus will point things out, things that stand in the way or distract us from Him. It's our responsibility to humbly accept His correction and obey Him, or we can choose to reject His advice and continue living as we please. There is no neutrality with God. We're either in a relationship with God or we're enemies of God.

If we tell God we are willing to pay any price for a relationship with Him, then He will honor our commitment. It's tempting to desire maximum results with minimal effort, but that approach doesn't apply to our relationship with God. What we put into a relationship is what we get out of it. God wants to be in a relationship with everyone, but not everyone wants God back. God is as close to us as we desire Him to be. We find God in proportion to the effort we put into seeking Him.

The more you pursue Jesus, the more you will find Him. We unintentionally hurt ourselves in life by neglecting to seek God. Pursuing Him is in our best interest and for our own good. God knows our flaws, issues, and imperfections. He wants to change us, but it's only possible if we surrender to His will and let Him do His work in us.

Let's not forget, "The hand of our God is upon all those for good who seek Him, but His power and His wrath are against all those who forsake Him" (Ezra 8:22). Being desperate for God reveals both our hunger for Him and His priority in our lives. How desperate are you for God? Do you truly desire a deeper connection with Him? Few are willing to sacrifice everything to fully experience and enjoy God's presence.

How can we prove that we love God? Are we willing to pay the price that will cause inconvenience or discomfort to our flesh? Why would we be willing to pay the price and deliberately put our flesh in an uncomfortable position? Many would rather spend their time and energy on things other than encounters with Jesus.

The price is not the issue; it's a matter of desiring to pursue Him. God has a relationship with those who prioritize Him over everything else. One thought that keeps coming back to mind is, "I want to live in Your presence, God. I desire You and nothing else."

In this statement to God, we reveal that His first love toward us is being reciprocated back to Him, the One who deserves it.

## CHAPTER SIX

# The Hindrances

*Adulterers and adulteresses! Do you not know that friendship with the world is enmity with God? Whoever therefore wants to be a friend of the world makes himself an enemy of God.*
(James 4:4)

SELFISHNESS, PRIDE, UNRESOLVED hurt, and bad experiences from the past are the four biggest things that make it challenging to start or keep a relationship. Some of the other things that can prevent us from having a relationship with God the way He intended for it to be are idols, apathy, negligence, laziness, vanity, busyness and the cares of life, riches, luxury, abundance, possessions or the comfort of life, and man-made traditions. All of these can play a role in a lack of desire to pursue and continue to grow in a relationship with Christ.

So the question becomes, what hinders and moves us away from our relationship with Jesus? I hope to unpack many of those points in detail in this section. First, let's look at Matthew 24:12 in a few different translations: "And because lawlessness will abound, the love of many will grow cold" (NKJV); "Because of the increase of wickedness, the love of most will grow cold" (NIV); and "Sin will be rampant everywhere, and the love of many will grow cold" (NLT).

We can analyze our lives and then ask God to reveal what hinders our relationship with Him and what prevents relationships from growing in a healthy way. Anything that hinders or prevents us from spending time alone with Jesus must be addressed and dealt with. Things that interfere with our relationship with Jesus are not worthy of our attention and need to be removed from our lives or brought under control.

## The World and Sinful Temptations

Paul made it clear: "Have no fellowship with the unfruitful works of darkness, but rather expose them" (Ephesians 5:11). If we love the world, its values, and aspire to conform to its culture, our relationship with Jesus will deteriorate. It is our responsibility to actively pursue holiness and righteousness, separating ourselves from sin to prevent worldly influences and values from infiltrating our lives. Jesus commands us not to love, cling to, or pursue anything that the world has to offer.

The world states, "Live in the moment to your heart's desire; live your life the way you want to; do whatever makes you feel happy. Enjoy life in the moment without thinking about the consequences." The world says to love yourself; God says to deny yourself. The world says self-affirmation is good; God says self-denial is good. The world only leads to fulfilling the desires of the flesh, and love of the world separates us from the love of God. Don't get caught up in the temporary artificial happiness and pleasures that the world has to offer, since becoming friends with the world positions us to be enemies of God. If we spend time flirting with sin, we shouldn't be surprised that our flesh overtakes our spirit. Worldly pleasures and worldly happiness will only last temporarily, but true, lasting joy and happiness is only found in a relationship with Jesus.

If we love Jesus, we will not love the world. It's not about loving Jesus more than the world; *it's loving one or the other.* The Word of God is often neglected by those who harbor uncleanliness, impurities, and sin as a result of embracing worldly values. To clearly hear God's message through His Word, we must address sin through repentance. Some obstacles require God's intervention, while others demand our active effort to live holy and righteous as God intended. Putting God at the forefront of our lives is pursuing His righteousness.

## Blessings

If we're not careful, we can become so focused on God's blessings that they distract us from our relationship with Jesus. These blessings can even diminish our desire to spend time with God, leading to a growing distance from Him.

God desires to bless us abundantly, but He doesn't want His blessings to hinder our relationship or lead to our downfall. Without a deep connection with Jesus, blessings can create excessive comfort, tempting us to prioritize our desires over our relationship with Him.

For instance, when Israel left Egypt, they were blessed with the blessings and gold of Egypt as they departed (see Exodus 12). Of course, we know that not long after, they were creating a golden calf from their gold. Be aware of the danger of turning God's blessings into a stumbling block.

## Idols

*For My people have committed two evils: They have forsaken Me, the fountain of living waters, and hewn themselves cisterns—broken cisterns that can hold no water.* (Jeremiah 2:13)

To have a relationship with someone, they must be available. They cannot be in a relationship with someone else simultaneously. The same is true with God and us. God cannot share our hearts with idols. When we do, the Bible says, "Those who regard worthless idols forsake their own mercy" (Jonah 2:8).

Idolatry is making God, His personhood, and His character different from what His Word reveals. Without a genuine relationship with God, we construct a distorted image of Him based on our own imagination. As a result, we mistakenly believe we are faithfully following Him and pleasing Him. Overcoming these misconceptions requires a humble pursuit of God to discover His true character. "I will set nothing wicked before my eyes; I hate the work of those who fall away; It shall not cling to me" (Psalm 101:3).

Idolatry can also involve worshiping or valuing something or someone more than God. Anything that competes for our time and attention with Jesus is idolatry. Anything that consumes us in this world can be considered idolatry. Imitating others and adopting their values can compromise the priority of God in our lives.

For example, overindulgence in food, obsession with physical appearance, fashion, or a luxurious lifestyle; excessive time spent on hobbies or interests; or idolizing sports, money, education, family, friendships, relationships, fame, influence, status, reputation, career, health, pets, pleasure, entertainment, music, games, movies, and so on. Life's circumstances can test our loyalty, revealing whether we will become attached to them, allowing our hearts to be captivated. Will we permit them to become idols, placed above God in our lives?

Even good things can be elevated above God if we are not cautious. This is why Jesus said, "He who loves father or mother more than Me is not worthy of Me. And he who loves son or daughter more than Me is not worthy of Me" (Matthew 10:37).

Once we prioritize anything or anyone over God, it becomes an idol. Even things that aren't inherently sinful can become idols when elevated above God. If something consumes us and distracts us from God, it has become an idol. Our actions reveal the intentions of our heart and where our affections lie. If we're in relationship with God, then valuing something more than God is cheating on Him.

A harmful mindset is believing, "I give God most of my effort, so now I can indulge in my desires, even though I know God disapproves." Our heart is fully committed to God or it isn't; there's no middle ground.

The Scriptures ask, "What does the Lord your God require of you, but to fear the Lord your God, to walk in all His ways and to love Him, to serve the Lord your God with all your heart and with all your soul?" (Deuteronomy 10:12).

We aren't to tolerate idolatry but to flee from it (see 1 Corinthians 10:14). What holds a special place in your heart? Our priorities reveal the true desires of our hearts. What do we cherish most in life? What consumes our thoughts throughout the day? Is it family and shared experiences? Is it our career or business success? Is it friendships or hobbies? Perhaps it's education, social media, fame, influence, or material possessions? Or maybe it's entertainment, sports, or simply pleasure and comfort? We see a remarkable parable in Luke's gospel that speaks to these things:

> *Then He said to him, "A certain man gave a great supper and invited many, and sent his servant at supper time to say to those who were invited, 'Come, for all things are now ready.' But they all with one accord began to make excuses. The first said to him, 'I have bought a piece of ground, and I must go and see it. I ask you to have me excused.' And another said, 'I have bought five yoke of oxen, and I am going to test them. I ask you to have me excused.' Still another said, 'I have married a wife, and therefore I cannot come.' So that servant came and reported these things to his master."* (Luke 14:16-21)

Viewing this parable as an invitation to fellowship with Jesus reveals various distractions preventing people from joining Him. "I bought" represents work and business; oxen symbolize possessions; land signifies property; and marriage illustrates relationships. Any of these, or a combination, can create distance between us and Jesus. Compromise in our relationship with God begins when something or someone else is prioritized over Him.

If work, business, sports, hobbies, or interests become more important than our connection with Jesus, then they become our idols. Similarly, if specific activities control our lives or relationships distract us from God, it's essential to seek God's guidance on how to manage them so that He remains our priority. Some of these things might seem harmless on their own, but they become idols when they captivate our hearts and distract or distance us from our love for God.

Aside from Jesus, nothing can quench our thirst for what we are chasing after. The flesh will always demand more and more. Our spiritual being will only find full satisfaction in Him. We cannot simultaneously crave both spiritual and worldly fulfillment, as one will inevitably overshadow the other. "No one can serve two masters; for either he will hate the one and love the other, or else he will be loyal to the one and despise the other. You cannot serve God and mammon" (Matthew 6:24).

If we recognize something competing for our attention with God, we can pray to Him, saying, "This has a hold on my heart, but I want to be free from it. Please remove it from my life. I dislike how it captivates my heart and distracts me from You. I acknowledge that You are infinitely more valuable to me than this addiction. Please help me! I don't want my desires to control my life. I want to love You above all else."

## The Devil

The enemy will try his best to keep us from connecting with the Creator. He wants to prevent us continuing our relationship with God by any means possible. The devil intends to keep us away from Jesus by distracting us as much as possible. He tries to achieve this through various means, including white noise, other people, our own desires, and the sinful temptations offered by the world. He offers a wide range of choices that can disconnect us from our relationship with God. Things like sin, compromise, pride, negative influences, selfishness, fear of man, interests, vanity, and life's worries, among others, can all damage and undermine our connection with God.

The devil seeks opportunities to sow doubt, preventing us from establishing a relationship with God. He opposes a connection between the Creator and His creation, driven by his hatred of God and rebellion against Him. He harbors no love for humanity, created in God's image, and desires only to harm us.

The devil will try to deceive us by sending us condemning thoughts and convincing us that we don't deserve a relationship with God, that we're unworthy of His attention, that He will never truly accept us or forgive us for our sins, and that our attempts to reach out to Him will fail.

Even after experiencing God in our lives, if we neglect to connect with Him regularly, the enemy will sow seeds of doubt in our minds. His goal is to keep us away from God's presence and love. This can lead to doubting God and His ability to preserve us, as well as doubting His power to complete the sanctification process He began.

The enemy's job description is clear: "The thief does not come except to steal, and to kill, and to destroy. I have come that they may have life, and that they may have it more abundantly" (John 10:10). Paul pointed to this also, writing, "But I fear, lest somehow, as the serpent deceived Eve by his craftiness, so your minds may be corrupted from the simplicity that is in Christ" (2 Corinthians 11:3). His ultimate goal is to sever our relationship with God. He seeks to steal existing connections or prevent them from forming altogether. His aim is to keep us disconnected from God's love, ultimately leading to eternal separation from God in hell.

To avoid the enemy's trap and be led by God's voice, we must test everything we hear in our inner being with the Word of God. The enemy will try to separate us from God by any means necessary. The methods or the time it takes are irrelevant as long as it works. One tactic is to distract us with activities that consume our time and energy, reducing our desire for daily communion with God. This can be achieved through worldly pleasures, entertainment, vanity, or worries. The enemy wants to separate us from God by tempting us to sin, reminding us of past failures to induce guilt, and shaming us, all in an effort to make us feel unworthy of approaching God for forgiveness, thus preventing us from re-establishing a connection with Him. He seeks to prevent us from experiencing and abiding in God's love, a love he himself lost due to pride and rebellion, resulting in his expulsion from heaven.

The enemy wants us to focus on our weaknesses, failures, and flaws, making us feel unworthy of God's attention. He seeks to sow doubt about God's love and care for us, discouraging us from seeking His help for our needs.

The enemy tries to persuade us with lies about God's love. His tactics aim to diminish our passion and hunger for Jesus. The enemy distorts the truth, planting thoughts like, "You should doubt God because..." or "You don't have time for daily fellowship with Jesus because..." He may also suggest, "You're not valuable to God; you don't deserve His attention or mercy. There are more important things than reading the Bible or praying.

We can discern whether our thoughts originate from God, the enemy, or ourselves. If a thought contradicts God's Word, it's not from Him. We can also ask God for confirmation on the source of any thought.

It's up to us to remain vigilant in our relationship with God and work hard to fight back against Satan's attacks with God's Word.

## Separation

The enemy tries to convince us that God is distant and doesn't fully love or care about us. He also suggests that God is angry with our wrongdoings, discouraging us from seeking reconciliation through repentance and forgiveness. The enemy wants to persuade us to believe that we need to earn God's love and favor through our efforts. He whispers doubts, like, "You've failed God too many times. He won't forgive you."

The enemy aims to separate us from God and then defeat us in isolation. He sends thoughts of discouragement and disappointment when we become complacent in our walk with God, deterring us from pursuing Him further. By regularly immersing ourselves in God's Word and meditating on its message, we equip ourselves to defeat the enemy's attacks.

The enemy exploits our sinful actions by making us feel bad without offering a solution. When we sin, he tries to shame us into avoiding God. While God is displeased with our sin, He desires reconciliation through repentance. He wants us to know there is a way back to fellowship with Him. He seeks a repentant heart fully surrendered to Him. We cannot earn Jesus' love through our efforts, for His love is freely given. Sin alone separates us from God's love and must be addressed. We must reconcile with God and live holy and righteous lives to please Him. God patiently waits for us to recognize this and return to Him.

God's love for us is perfect; all that remains is for us to embrace it. He chose to love us before we existed; His decision to create us flowed from that love. Why, then, do we doubt His love when we sin? God remains faithful even when we distance ourselves from Him. Instead of fleeing His presence, we should humbly approach Him, confess our sins, and seek forgiveness.

Satan sends thoughts suggesting we avoid confronting the issues that have created a rift between us and God. He proposes escaping the discomfort of reconciliation through distractions. "Why not relax with a TV show or game?" he tempts us by masquerading his words as our own thoughts.

Some, feeling overwhelmed by life's challenges, eagerly embrace these distractions. They immerse themselves in activities to silence the inner voice urging them to confront their spiritual condition.

God, however, did not create us to escape the reality of our separation from Him through pleasure and entertainment. He wants us to face our struggles and bring them to Him for transformation.

### Flesh Versus Spirit

The flesh and the spirit constantly oppose each other. There will never be a truce between them. There will never be days where the flesh is not demanding anything.

We either operate in the spirit or we operate in the flesh. When we wake up, our flesh says, "Listen to me and do what I want!" Our flesh tells us to do the opposite of what our spirit wants. The flesh will always dictate what it wants, and it will never be fully satisfied. The flesh will entice us to have our lives revolve around materialistic things and desires. Our feelings based on these fleshly desires will deter us from pursuing God. It's important to recognize the source of these feelings and to continue seeking God, even when we don't feel like it at times, knowing that these feelings originate from our flesh.

Once we're born again, we have the ability to subject our flesh to obedience toward God. When we give up our selfish ambitions and practice self-denial on a regular basis, we make progress in our relationship with God.

Let's avoid having a carnal mindset! "It's not a big deal if I don't feel like reading the Bible today or praying, because there's always tomorrow for these things." If we prioritize our fleshly desires over our spiritual needs, it's no surprise that our fleshly desires will dominate our lives and dictate our choices.

While engaged in constant battle with the flesh, we experience both victories and defeats. Daily self-examination is essential. Am I obeying God? Are worldly attractions pulling me away? Do I meditate on God regularly? Have any areas of my life become idols? Do I express love for God through obedience? Do I anticipate time spent with God? Am I consumed by vanity and busyness? Do I struggle with temptation? Is my prayer life disciplined? Is my ministry hindering my fellowship with God? Am I maintaining my first love for Him? Are my friends negatively impacting my relationship with God?

**Talk Reveals Interests**

Observe the topics of conversation at your next social gathering, and you'll likely find that God is rarely, if ever, the focus. Even when God or spiritual matters are mentioned, they're often quickly dismissed and the conversation moves to a new topic.

A person's enthusiasm and passion when discussing their interests reveal how valuable these things are to them and shows their priorities. If similar enthusiasm isn't evident when talking about God, His work in their life, His love, or the revelations they receive from Him, it may indicate a deeper issue in their relationship with Him. We can't expect those who don't live and walk with God to talk passionately about their relationship with Him.

If you speak with someone about God, His Word, and what He has done in your life, and they remain disengaged, show no interest, or lack similar experiences to share, this suggests a lack of personal relationship and importance they place on God. If the person doesn't have a real relationship with Jesus, they are consumed by worldly things and desires. This naturally draws them toward what the flesh craves, focusing on everyday life topics and activities. Their connection with God may not be a priority, and they might not be interested in maintaining a relationship with Him. While everyday pursuits aren't inherently sinful, when they take priority, control us, and fill our thoughts, they disrupt our continuous connection with God. Also, that means they can, over time, potentially influence us to drift away from God's presence and become complacent in our walk with God.

As we experience the life-changing love of Jesus, we yearn for others to discover the same fulfillment in communion with Him.

Those we interact with may pursue God casually, but even if they don't prioritize seeking Him, it doesn't mean we should compromise our own stance with God by adopting the same worldly interests as them. We must not become attached to the worldly values that entice those close to us.

> *Do not love the world or the things in the world. If anyone loves the world, the love of the Father is not in him. For all that is in the world—the lust of the flesh, the lust of the eyes, and the pride of life—is not of the Father but is of the world. And the world is passing away, and the lust of it; but he who does the will of God abides forever.* (1 John 2:15-17)

Many don't want to put in the effort to pursue Jesus or reignite their first love for Him, which they've lost. The quality of our relationship with Jesus is evident in our lives. People don't need to pry into our personal lives to discern whether we love Him. Our actions and our fruits reveal the state of our hearts. If someone lacks a genuine relationship with Jesus, then it's guaranteed that they have some kind of spiritual problem in life or sin that keeps them from approaching God. Our lives will reveal our state before God to others, whether we want it or not.

If a person doesn't have a victorious relationship with Jesus, they will definitely have one or more of the following: idols, ongoing sin, unresolved past hurt, excessive focus on work, family, or business, or adhering to man-made traditions rather than God's truth.

The absence of visible examples of believers actively seeking God, can affect our perseverance in our own pursuit of Him. While finding a community of those hungry for God can be a source of encouragement and inspiration, this lack shouldn't discourage us. We must prioritize our connection with God, for it is through Him, not others, that we find ultimate love and perfect fulfillment.

## Building Blocks in a Relationship

So how do we overcome these hindrances? The key to overcoming hindrances in a relationship is honesty, sincerity, humility, and childlike simplicity. Honesty is about intellect; it's accepting the truth through the mind. Sincerity is about emotion; it's accepting the truth through the heart. Honesty is being truthful and sincerity is having genuine feelings.

The word "honest" comes from the Latin word *honestus*, meaning "honorable." It deals with displaying integrity and not being deceptive or fraudulent.

The word "sincere" comes from the Latin word *sincerus*, meaning "pure" or "clean." It is usually used to indicate the quality of being genuine, without hypocrisy or pretense.

Honesty is a moral virtue involving a disposition to tell the truth. Sincerity is the disposition to be authentic and respectful.

Honesty is essential in a relationship; that's why we need to ask God to reveal what displeases Him in us. No one knows our spiritual condition or what we need to change in our spiritual life better than God, and He will remind us what He doesn't like in our lives and what needs to be changed.

Let's be really honest and sincere with God regarding our relationship with Him. If our relationship with God is not where it needs to be, we can tell Him, "God, my relationship with You feels distant. I'm tired of going through religious routines without a real connection. I don't want to pretend I love You more than anything, or act like I know You when I don't. I yearn for a deeper connection, to truly know You. I confess my hypocrisy, the gap between how I live in public and in private. I want to be Your friend, to live a life that reflects Your love. I want to enjoy spending time alone with You, and to have a heart that turns to You throughout the day."

True humility before God starts with honesty. Knowing He already knows your life, be transparent and sincere, expressing your struggles, your doubts, your true feelings. This vulnerability – laying bare your heart – is the essence of humility. It reflects a modest view of oneself, acknowledging weaknesses and admitting when you're wrong. Humility involves putting others above yourself and having a heart of servitude, willing to help others.

Childlike simplicity in a relationship refers to a state of mind or character trait where an individual approaches the relationship with the innocence, openness, and unpretentiousness often associated with children. In a relationship, a childlike simplicity trait is marked by an absence of pretense, a willingness to trust and connect, and a desire to avoid unnecessary complications. It involves embracing a straightforward and open-hearted approach.

In a relationship, marked by childlike simplicity, trust and genuine authenticity shine through, free from the complexities of an ego-driven behavior. This behavior demonstrates vulnerability without fear, expressing their emotions openly and honestly. It expresses a sincere interest in understanding others' thoughts, feelings, and experiences. It lacks ulterior motives or hidden agendas, fostering a deep sense of trust and emotional intimacy.

Maybe you're complicating your communication with God. Don't make it harder than it needs to be. Be straightforward and honest with Him by telling Him everything. God, our Creator, understands our limitations. He speaks to us in ways we can comprehend, knowing the limits of our human brains. So, communicate simply and honestly. He doesn't require complex or formal language. He knows your past, your joys and burdens. Talk to Him about everything – what troubles you today, your hopes and concerns for the future. Ask God to reveal His plans for you and your calling in life.

# CHAPTER SEVEN

# What Leads to Success?

*But without faith it is impossible to please Him, for he who comes to God must believe that He is, and that He is a rewarder of those who diligently seek Him.* (Hebrews 11:6)

SUCCESS IN YOUR dedicated times of fellowship with God require a few ingredients like desire, discipline, persistence, and perseverance. You might think, *I have no discipline.* The truth is, we're all disciplined in some areas of our lives. If it's important to us, we'll be willing to pay the price; we will put in the effort and be disciplined to achieve what we're striving for. To be successful in any area of our life, we apply some or all of these qualities. The issue is shifting those qualities to our relationship with the Lord.

We usually don't have to discipline ourselves to make time for our spouse; it happens automatically because there's love involved. When we come to spend alone time in fellowship with God, He sees the motive and intention of our hearts. He knows whether we come to check off a box or genuinely long for His presence and look forward to meeting Him. Don't think, "I need to spend time with God today or I will feel guilty," but instead learn to approach Him out of love. If we are in love with Jesus, it won't be difficult to be disciplined to spend time with Him. If fellowship is important enough for us, we will continue to put effort into maintaining it.

We are disciplined enough not to risk being late for work - the consequences are severe. Shouldn't our relationship with God require even greater commitment? We live in a society where instant gratification is promoted everywhere. People don't want to wait for delayed gratification. They frequently switch their focus on something that will reward them instantly instead of exercising discipline through waiting. And that's why many fail at being disciplined in spending alone time with Jesus. It also helps to have an accountability partner who can encourage us to continue and not lose focus in achieving consistency in our walk with God.

The best way to break a habit is to create a new one that takes its place. Maybe some of our current habits make it hard for us to fellowship with Jesus. We used to spend our time doing what we wanted and living our lives as we desired. The cost of our relationship with God requires us to break our old, unproductive habits and old ways of doing things. We can seek God to help us with this.

Discipline creates habits, habits make routines, and routines become who we are.

It's important that we establish structure in our lives to have dedicated time with the Lord. Discipline is what gives us the inner drive to reach out to God and continue our relationship with Him. Discipline prevents inconsistency in a relationship. Discipline yourself to spend time with God and be intentional in your pursuit of Him.

God is devoted to us, and He wants us to be devoted to Him just like our relationship in a good, healthy marriage. We need to put in effort through discipline to set aside time just to connect with Him. When planning to spend time with God, block off time and mark it on the calendar to prevent something else from occupying that time of the day.

Perseverance embodies the inner strength and determination to keep pushing through challenges, setbacks, and discouragement in pursuit of a goal. Persistence is the unwavering commitment to maintaining or achieving something, even in the face of resistance or obstacles.

## Wholehearted Versus Half-Hearted

Through Jeremiah, God said, "Then you will call upon Me and go and pray to Me, and I will listen to you. And you will seek Me and find Me, when you search for Me with all your heart" (Jeremiah 29:12-13). The Psalms echo similar things: "Blessed are those who keep His testimonies, who seek Him with the whole heart!" (Psalm 119:2).

Let's reflect on our lives. Why would we put effort into something that we don't find to be valuable? If we don't value Jesus, that means we haven't discovered how valuable He is.

Do you make an effort to get to know Jesus and follow Him with all of your heart? Wholehearted means *completely* and *sincerely* devoted and determined in pursuing with enthusiasm and earnest commitment. A wholehearted approach entails completely surrendering to Jesus, with no reservations.

Half-hearted means doing something without any real effort, interest, or enthusiasm. It's not fully being invested in something or someone.

God is seeking those who are fully committed to being in a relationship with Him. Give God your whole heart.

Ask yourself, "What effort do I put into following Jesus?" Do you have the intention of being fully committed to walking with Him? If we're wholeheartedly and sincerely seeking God and putting Him first in our lives by getting rid of things that He tells us to, then it's a guarantee that our relationship with Him will flourish. It might not happen as fast as we want it to or exactly as we want it to, but we will move in the right direction even if we encounter hardships along the way.

We need to analyze our life and ask ourselves, are we willing to be faithful in our relationship all the time or only from time to time? Do we feel burdened by spending personal time with Jesus? What makes us avoid fellowship with Him? Do we really put effort into our walk with God? Are we determined to seek God in our lives, regardless of our circumstances? If we're not careful then we might express carelessness, indifference, and apathy toward what matters most in life.

Relationship necessitates total surrender to Jesus. It takes effort to be vigilant and remain so that no worry, vanity, or distraction draws our attention away from our relationship with Christ.

Many expect God to be in a good relationship with them while not contributing much time to develop that relationship. We can't expect God's favor over our lives if we are not interested in maintaining a close relationship with Him.

If we haven't experienced starting a new life with Jesus and established a relationship with Him, that means we haven't given all of our effort to find Him. Maybe we're not willing to pay the full price because we are still holding on to something else. God wants us to be completely committed in our relationship with Him—to be all sold out for Jesus.

Everyone wants to reap the benefits that comes out of a relationship with Jesus, but not everyone wants to work and put effort into spending time with Him. If we want to get the most out of a relationship with God, we will need to put in maximum effort. Let's ask ourselves, do we really put all of our effort into seeking God?

Paying the full price in a relationship involves being completely faithful to Jesus. What percentage of the time would you expect your spouse to be faithful to you? Anything other than 100% would not be acceptable. Jesus wants our whole heart. He doesn't want a cheating bride. He wants our complete loyalty and nothing less.

It takes effort to live a pure life, seeking righteousness and holiness. This shows that we desire to put in effort to have fellowship with the holy God.

What we want to get out of a relationship is directly connected to how much we invest in it. If we're not fully invested in seeking God, then something will always draw us away from Him. Life gives us a lot of distractions and temptations that try to get us to stop focusing on Jesus. If we act upon our fleshly desires, then we will not want to keep pursuing a relationship with God. We might hesitate to make the sacrifices that are needed to keep that relationship going.

It's up to us to dismiss and give up everything we love that is of the world—all of our dreams, pursuits, and desires—in favor of Jesus.

Make a decision to chase after God, regardless of the cost, and maintain that relationship no matter what. Do it regardless of the distractions and regardless of what others think or say. Pursue God and do whatever it takes to achieve and maintain a relationship with Him. Get to the point where you're naturally drawn to be in His presence. A consistent prayer life and Bible reading help maintain a healthy relationship. Every day we have the opportunity to get closer to God. God is waiting for us with open arms to fellowship with Him.

Choose friendship with Jesus regardless of your past. Choose Jesus no matter how much people have hurt you. Don't compromise on the value of Jesus.

If it doesn't cost us anything, it's not a sacrifice. Sacrifice requires us to deprive ourselves of something. It is necessary to offer God a sacrifice that reveals how much He is valued by us. The sacrifice is to deny our own will, a continuous sacrifice of self-denial.

God knows how hungry you are for Him. He knows the hardships and difficulties that you have to overcome in order to continue being in fellowship with Him. What is the cost you're paying to be in fellowship with Jesus? Don't let anything come between you and your relationship with Jesus. Defend your relationship at all costs. Pay the price to remain in fellowship with Him. It's not always easy, but it's so worth it!

Have you completely surrendered your life to God and His will, or do you seek Him when you're in need and when it's convenient for you? Not everyone will pursue to seek God due to the high price. What we get out of a relationship with Christ is more than worth our effort that we put into it.

It's always enticing to want to compromise in order to live partially for God and partially for our own selfish desires and ambitions. An easy, comfortable life can makes it more challenging to pay the price of living fully for God. We have to be vigilant that the comforts of life don't get in the way of our relationship with Jesus.

If we seek approval and recognition from others by following the crowd and trying to fit in, it can ultimately lead to compromise in our relationship with Jesus. Everyone needs to have their own personal walk with God. If you don't see many people around you who have a healthy relationship with Jesus, this shouldn't discourage you from continuing to earnestly pursue Him.

When it comes to seeking God, our actions speak louder than words. If we claim to seek and desire God but fail to actively pursue fellowship with Him, our actions contradict our words, revealing our true attitude toward God. Jesus paid the ultimate price to be with you. What are you willing to pay to be with Him?

We must be willing to forsake everything else in order to obtain Him.

Take some time off and get away from the noise of life. Spend those days seeking God in prayer and reading His Word. Isolate yourself, even from technology. Fast or bring food and water so that you can completely focus on Him with no distractions. Pray,

"I will seek You no matter what. I won't stop seeking You until I get closer to You."

An intensified and fervent prayer of a righteous believer is very effective. No one can hold us back from a relationship with God. There's no justifiable reason not to have and maintain a relationship with Jesus.

### Love Means Mutual Enjoyment

As discussed, the main prerequisite to establishing a relationship with God is to get born again. Once we are born again, we are adopted into God's family and become God's children. In a healthy, loving relationship, both parties reach out to each other and look forward to fellowshipping with one another. As long as we maintain our love for God, we will have a longing and a desire to spend more time with Him in order to know Him better.

As we read the Bible, we become more aware of God's heart stance toward humanity, His personality, His nature, and His love for people. And as we begin to spend time alone with God, we will feel drawn to embrace His presence. We will continue to fall in love with Jesus as we learn more about His character. Spending time with Jesus captivates our attention, and we'll be more and more enthralled by His love, beauty, and presence. The more we pursue Jesus, the more He will reveal Himself to us.

Looking back on times when fellowship with Jesus was lacking, we might realize moments where we hadn't put enough effort into pursuing God. We might notice where we readily excused ourselves from fellowship with Him.

The realization of our condition without Jesus gives us motivation to seek Him every day. Spending time with God reveals the reality of total reliance and dependence on Him.

God understands that we all need certain amounts of time to function in life and carry out our daily routines. He knows how busy we are, but most importantly, He created us for a relationship with Him. This connection with Him is our most important purpose here on earth. He will always have time to listen to us. Therefore, no matter how busy our lives are, if we truly desire it, we will find an opportunity to spend time with God.

If we are born again, our spiritual being will yearn for communion with Christ, but we can choose to suppress inner voice. We all understand that in order to grow, love must be upheld and maintained. It's important to make an effort to long for and thirst for Jesus' presence in our lives. Genuine, loving fellowship with God is not a religious ritual.

What is the time limit that two individuals, who are in love, should set aside for their fellowship together? Is any amount of time considered enough or too much? True love is not satisfied with seeing and interacting with loved ones on occasion. A relationship with Jesus starts out of love and continues by allowing that love to grow. It entices us to Him with a desire to pursue Him more intimately.

One of the actions of love is to spend time with the person you love. Deeply valuing relationships, we readily sacrifice time to nurture them, finding the effort enriching rather than burdensome. In the same way, we express our love for Jesus by spending time with Him in a quiet place, for this strengthens our relationship. Let us examine our free time and see how much of it we devote to God on a daily basis.

He wants us to enjoy spending time in His presence as His loving children and experience His love. Relationships are about giving and receiving. This means genuine love is characterized by mutual enjoyment of one another and pleasure in spending time together. As we continue in fellowship and prayer, they will become so enjoyable that we will not be looking forward to its ending.

How eagerly we anticipate and look forward to spending time with Jesus is a sign of how much we love Him. In our eagerness, God sees our desire to grow closer to Him, examining our hearts. A prayer goal is the passionate desire to know Him even more on a deeper, more intimate level, beyond simply experiencing His presence.

In life, time is one of the most valuable things we possess. Precisely because it's so precious, how much time can you give God daily? What plans or events are so important to you that you're willing to spend time on them instead of fellowship with God? If not our time, how else can we prove or show that we love God more than anyone or anything in our lives? Let's ask ourselves again, do we love God more than anything else? Is He the most important in our lives? In the midst of your busy life, God sees the moments you willingly set aside to be with Him.

God does not want a once-in-a-while relationship. For some it's perfectly normal to have occasional encounter with God every now and then. They don't feel the urge to pursue God more frequently in their lives. "As long as God speaks to me, it's all good. There is no need to put effort into growing the relationship and improving its closeness." God wants to reveal His heart to us, but are we willing to put in the effort and time to listen?

Imagine a husband who tells his wife, "I love you," often but avoids spending time with her. Will his wife feel loved by him if he doesn't spend time with her? The same is true with God. How do we express our love for God? Saying "I love you" to God is just an empty phrase without really having our hearts attracted to talk to Him. If our deeds don't confirm our words, then our words are not really genuine.

Fellowship is not appealing to those who don't value the person they have fellowship with. They will perceive that fellowship as burdensome and a waste of their time.

God invites us to spend alone time with Him, simply to be in His presence and share our hearts. It's important to dedicate a specific time each day for prayer. Once you start to enjoy His presence, you will not count minutes but will be fully immersed in the conversation with the Creator.

Picture yourself talking with someone and knowing they're

not really interested in your conversation with them. Maybe they're in a hurry and can't wait until the conversation is over so that they can move on to do other things. How would that make you feel? The same thing is happening when we read Bible verses, say a short prayer, and run to do other things without having our heart in it. We can feel obligated to give God at least some of our time as a tribute, so we can feel we're in His good graces and avoid His anger. We can also treat meeting with God as a chore. Our actions prove where our heart is and confirms how much we value Him in our life.

Instead of thinking, "Okay, God, here's the time I dedicate to having another fellowship with You. I'm hoping You keep track of all the minutes I put in and reward me accordingly," our mindset should be, "Thank You for giving me another opportunity and privilege to talk to You again."

James wrote, "Draw near to God, and he will draw near to you" (James 4:8). Let's be intentional with our time spent with God. If our prayer life does not result in life changes, then perhaps our time spent with God is superficial and we don't want to apply what He is telling us to change in our lives.

*Call to Me, and I will answer you, and show you great and mighty things, which you do not know.* (Jeremiah 33:3)

How can God express His intimate love for us if we don't spend time with Him? A lack of hunger for God inevitably leads to prioritizing our own plans and desires in how we manage our time.

We need God more than He needs us, but He makes it look as if He needs us more than we need Him. Embrace the mindset that you are here to enjoy God's presence rather than merely allocating time to Him. God misses spending time with us and is patiently waiting for us to make time for Him in our day. He doesn't want to force us to spend personal time with Him. He desires that we make a decision that comes out of love for Him. If we don't miss being in God's presence, we'll make excuses for not spending time in our prayer closet. This reveals a diminished dependence on Him in our daily lives.

The things we truly love don't require excuses; we make time for them because they hold such importance in our lives. God is patiently waiting for the day and time when we will decide to reconnect with Him. He values the joy of friendship and the time we spend together.

A heartfelt moment spent with Jesus is more valuable than hours without true connection. Imagine your cousin, who's not very close to you, visited you from another country, and you felt the responsibility to show her around the city and spend time with her. You take your cousin to all the tourist hotspots. The conversation flows politely, but you struggle to find common ground beyond the weather and generic observations about the city. And then later on, your best friend comes over to your house and you only have thirty minutes to talk to them, but you pour out your soul and share your heart with them. After this conversation, you felt so much better spending time with your best friend than with your cousin, despite the fact that you spent far less time with your best friend.

When you are best friends with someone, you don't want to meet up with them once in a while; you want to meet up with them as much as possible because of the closeness of your friendship.

Having tasted the love of God through friendship, we crave a deeper closeness with Him, seeking it out as often as we can. Spending time with Jesus is a cornerstone of expressing our love for Him. How else can we translate this love into actions that reflect our devotion in everyday life? God loves us, and He is jealous when we prioritize someone or something over Him.

## The Ultimate Investment

We can't fast-track relationships to grow deep. There's a natural pace at which relationships grow and cultivate.

A relationship is built over time and requires an investment of time. Devoting time to any relationship is crucial for its success. As a relationship grows over time, so will the frequency and amount of time we spend with God.

We will never find a better way to get to know someone than by spending quality time with them. What is the evidence that God is our best friend? How can we prove to others that God is number one in our lives and that we love Him more than anything else? If He holds the highest place in our hearts, we wouldn't trade time spent in fellowship with Him for anything else. A true best friend is someone we confide in and share openly with. Is our relationship with God reflecting this kind of open communication? If we consider Him our best friend, yet rarely talk to Him, there's a disconnect between our beliefs and actions.

Developing, growing, and maintaining a relationship with Jesus requires an investment of time, nurtured by love, communication, mutual commitment, intimacy, and trust. Regular personal time with God is essential, for it strengthens the connection we share with Him and fosters our spiritual growth. We can't fast forward the development of that process. Relationships don't flourish by rushing them. They grow naturally over time. As we spend private prayer time alone with God, simply enjoying His presence, He will reveal more of Himself to us. God desires for us to have deep intimacy with Him and to be transparent with Him in everything.

The consistent practice of daily prayer fosters a sense of satisfaction as we experience God's presence. This leads to motivating us to run and talk to Him throughout the day whenever we get a chance. As our desire for Him deepens, so too does our yearning for connection, prompting us to meet with Him more often in prayer. Knowing God listens, even when we don't feel His presence, strengthens our faith and leads to a more persistent prayer life. As we put effort into spending more time in His presence, we'll be able to sense His presence more frequently in our lives.

It's important for us to ask ourselves, What keeps us from reading the Bible and praying on a daily or regular basis? God knows if we approach Him out of love or obligation.

Life sets the pace, but we have the power to choose a different rhythm, to slow down and get serious with God. We can't keep chasing after fleeting pleasures and indulging the flesh. If we are not actively seeking to satisfy our spirit, we will naturally gravitate toward satisfying our flesh.

How we spend our free time reveals what truly matters to us. In light of that, Jesus sacrificed His life to be with us. What are we willing to sacrifice for a deeper relationship with Him?

Many dedicate a portion of their time to fellowship with God. Some make a dedicated effort, giving a significant amount of their time to this pursuit. Still, a select few prioritize constant connection, seeking fellowship with Him whenever possible. We can choose to put forth effort and progress to the point where spending time with God becomes our favorite pastime. If we truly want to pursue God, no one will stop us.

Some believers may feel they don't experience a strong connection with God after praying. This could be because cultivating a sense of God's presence takes ongoing effort. God hears our prayers, but the issue is that we impatiently leave His presence too early to hear Him. The ability to hear and recognize His voice comes from spending more time with Him. The priority should not be seeking God to speak to us, but rather to seek Him just to be in His presence. When we seek His presence, He will speak to us. For some a prayer becomes a means to an end, a way to quickly get what they desire. This approach often leads to a desire for fast results while neglecting the importance of cultivating a consistent prayer life. Relationships are not mechanical; they're organic and every encounter is different. We find contentment simply by experiencing His presence.

Growing in fellowship with God requires true surrender and

dedicated time. We can choose, every day, to make room for God amidst our daily obligations.

Effective time management is crucial. Prioritizing the most important things ensures we fulfill our commitment to a continuous walk with God. Although our busy lives limit the time we can spend in quiet meditation with God, let's not be discouraged. Every opportunity to connect with Him, even briefly, is a precious gift.

Busy schedules and competing priorities can tempt us to compromise fellowship time with God for something that seems more valuable. We're constantly faced with the challenge of replacing our consistent prayer time with something else.

The saying goes, 'If there's a will, there's a way.' When we truly desire a connection with God, with God's grace and our own effort, we'll find ways to make it a daily pursuit. God's love is ever-present, waiting patiently for our hearts to turn towards Him. That's why disciplining ourselves to pursue God daily is crucial, isn't it? Jesus is waiting for us to come back to Him and let go of the things of the world, the worries of life, and our own vanity.

Sometimes our wants might appear as needs, and this can lead to mistakenly prioritizing more time toward our wants, which reduces our time set aside to spend with God. There's nothing more fulfilling than offering our hearts in worship to God and seeking His presence.

We dedicate time to what is important to us. Do we make a decision and commit to setting everything else aside for the time specifically dedicated to fellowship? Each day, we have a choice to make in favor of fellowship or not.

Make an intentional plan to pray and follow through with it. Don't think, "If I have spare time later on and feel like praying, I'll pray." We can deliberately avoid time alone with God by making all sorts of excuses. In our eyes, those excuses can be justifiable, but not in God's. Don't say, "I will have fellowship with Jesus at the next available opportunity." Create opportunity! Sometimes we can focus on our mood or our desire to determine if we should spend time with God. Don't rely on your flesh, knowing that your flesh resists your spiritual needs.

We're responsible for our inconsistent experience of God. God always wants to have a connection with us. Remember, God's love is constant, even if we feel distant. If we feel that we have lost connection with God, then we need to run to Him, repent of our sins, ask Him what prevents us from connecting with Him, and allow Him to fix whatever His hand is pointing to in our life that needs to be changed. It's always something in our hearts that prevents us from allowing Him to be close to us.

If we dedicate only a few minutes to a relationship, how much will a relationship like this grow? People spend very few minutes of their time in fellowship with God and expect the relationship to be amazing.

In life, everything and everyone is competing for our time and attention. Everything in our lives is measured in terms of time. Throughout the day, a constant tug-of-war for our time and attention unfolds. Events, errands, and people compete for our time, each demanding a decision: to engage, and if so, for how long. God is jealous for us because of His great love for us.

If Jesus was here visibly before you and asked, "What portion of your time can you set aside to fellowship with Me?" what would you say to Him? He still stands at the door of hearts and knocks to see who will invite Him to fellowship with Him.

God whispers to us constantly, by giving us little reminders of Himself every day. He is waiting for us to quiet the noise and truly listen. Life's distractions can easily drown out His whispers. Let's not forget that our time with God is the most important part of our day.

Could it be that we're so preoccupied by life that we forget He is actually the source of life? Can we say that we don't have time for Jesus, who gave us physical and spiritual life and wants us to spend eternity with Him?

While living here on earth, how can we prove that we want to spend eternity with Jesus? Some people desire to spend eternity with Jesus but are unwilling to spend limited amounts of time with Him each day here on earth. This inconsistency raises the question: Can we truly desire an eternal connection with Jesus without cultivating a daily one?

Throughout our days, we often invest time in financial pursuits for physical well-being. However, our spiritual life holds far greater importance. Nurturing it through a relationship with God is key to its sustenance.

If we want more of Jesus in our lives, what needs to change to make time for Him a priority?

Some see time spent alone with God as futile, but those who've encountered Him are drawn to His presence. They know nothing compares to the satisfaction of being with Him.

### Maximize Moments

Aside from your dedicated alone time with God, seek for *moments* to connect with Him even for a short time. Take the initiative to pursue God and get to know Him on a deeper level in those slivers of time.

Cultural norms keep us occupied 24/7, but chase those quick times of intimacy with God to keep your heart on fire throughout the day. Take a moment to reflect on your daily routine. Analyze the activities and events that occupy your time. How much time do you dedicate to each one? Ask yourself a crucial question: "How can I rearrange my schedule to create more space for God?" If spending time with Jesus is a top priority in your life, then consider what adjustments you can make to accommodate that desire.

When the busyness of life, our worries, or earthly concerns take priority over spending time with Jesus, it can be a sign that our intimacy with Him needs attention. Life is a gift from God, but we can get carried away so much with the gift that we forget the Gift Giver. Our relationship with God is not only important but also vital to our lives. Make time for the very purpose we were created for.

Our heart's intention matters; it determines the quality of our relationship with God. There's a big difference between doing something and *loving* to do something. It's not just about going through the motions. Are we reading the Bible just to study it, or because we find enjoyment in it and are drawn to find deeper revelations of who God is? Does God's love captivate us? It's about enjoying and treasuring time with God that makes it quality time.

Prayer is not a one-way street. During prayer, we also have an opportunity to hear from God if we're being receptive and expectant! He wants to speak to us more than we want to speak to Him. Having experienced God's presence draws us to a relentless pursuit to encounter Him again and again and we won't settle for anything less.

It's crucial to remain diligent and apply God's Word to ourselves daily, not just occasionally when life slows down or when we feel inclined. When we have a sincere desire to learn God's instructions through His Word, we can ask for help, and He will reveal its meaning to us. When we embrace and actively apply the Word in our lives and remain teachable in His hands, He will continuously shape us, molding us into His perfect masterpiece to be revealed in the end.

Neglecting the importance of spending time with God every day can cause us to drift from Him and become complacent in our walk with Him over time. God is waiting for us to put distractions aside and simply seek Him.

Take the example of a fisherman who is passionate about fishing. He works during the week, and then on Saturday, he has a desire to sleep in, but he also loves fishing. He knows that fish bite when they are hungry, which is very early in the morning. So he has to wake up around 4 a.m. to make it to the river around 5 a.m. to catch some fish. And even though he got less sleep on the weekend than on the weekdays, he doesn't see it as a burden because he considers it to be time well spent. Why? Because he enjoys fishing and considers it his favorite pastime!

Restructure your priorities and treat this like a mission-critical task, because it is!

God desires loyalty and a devoted heart. He seeks those who yearn for His presence, longing for a close connection. These individuals actively pursue knowing Him, making time for daily encounters and sacrifices to nurture that relationship.

Why emphasize these things so clearly? Because, at the end of the day, shallow relationships are unsatisfactory and burdensome. Without experiencing the deep satisfaction of encountering God in prayer, we might settle for a quick, five-minute routine that lacks true connection. God doesn't want formality in prayer. He wants a prayer that is sincere and personal.

When we neglect or limit our fellowship time with God, it leads to the deterioration of our relationship with Him.

A genuine relationship with God requires holiness, for a pure heart is essential to encountering Him. This desire for closeness motivates us to continue living a holy life with His assistance. Holiness isn't just about following rules, it's about aligning ourselves with God's character and aligning our desires with His will.

Ignoring Jesus' call for a relationship not only grieves Him, but it also deprives us of the blessings that come from encountering Him. At times, we can disregard His will through our actions by neglecting His voice and failing to obey Him by not acting upon what He says.

For deeper commitment and discipline in fellowshipping with God, consider an accountability partner to support your time with Jesus.

A lack of fellowship with God is dangerous business. Without regular fellowship with God, doubt creeps in. It weakens our faith in His Word and ultimately in Him. Paul wrote, "But without faith it is impossible to please Him, for he who comes to God must believe that He is, and that He is a rewarder of those who diligently seek Him" (Hebrews 11:6).

Without a continual relationship, how can we be confident of our standing and approval from God? A growing distance from God can sow seeds of doubt about our salvation. Without regular communication with the author of our salvation, these doubts can take root and erode our confidence. Distancing ourselves from God and His love can lead us down paths of isolation, negativity, or self-destructive behaviors. Doubting His love can fuel fear, worry, uncertainty, depression, loneliness, and anxiety. However, when we embrace God's love, we find the strength to overcome these challenges. It becomes the foundation for a life filled with peace, joy, and a sense of belonging.

Our personal desire to please God and maintain our relationship with Him prevents others from undermining our faith or diminishing our love for Him.

We all cherish justice, opposing its absence not only in our own lives but also in the lives of others. Isn't it profound injustice that the Creator, who loves us immeasurably, is often denied the loving relationship He desires with His creation? We cannot afford indifference, apathy, or ignorance towards Jesus. A relationship with God is truly essential.

We have a responsibility to be good stewards of our time. A day without spending time alone with God is a day where we miss out on the very purpose for which it was created.

## CHAPTER EIGHT

# The Secret Place

*But you, when you pray, go into your room, and when you have shut your door, pray to your Father who is in the secret place; and your Father who sees in secret will reward you openly. (Matthew 6:6)*

THE SECRET PLACE isn't confined to a specific location within the house such as a separate office or room, and it's not solely about intentionally connecting with God in solitude at a designated time of the day. Instead, it expands to the notion that once we have developed the habit of identifying an opportunity within our daily routine, we can use that opportunity and dedicate that time to commune intimately with God. The psalmist wrote, "He who dwells in the secret place of the Most High shall abide under the shadow of the Almighty" (Psalm 91:1).

Let's increase in our pursuit of the Lord Jesus through alone time in the secret room and grow in our knowledge of Him. The secret place is a place where a date between two loving hearts occurs. This place is a key to God's heart.

The best gift we can give to Jesus is our undivided attention. He longs to be with us and wants our attention, which shows our affection for Him and that our hearts are drawn to His presence. This is a hallmark of the secret place.

Doing chores while listening to worship music, listening to sermons while working or running errands, or listening to an audio Bible while commuting are all valuable activities, but they shouldn't replace one-on-one time with God in full attention. This is what truly counts as quality devotion time. Separating from other things allows us to really concentrate solely on Him. This is why God desires our full attention to truly connect with Him without distractions.

Would you be fine if you came to someone's house as a guest and, while having a conversation with you, the host started to get distracted by cleaning the house while continuing to speak to you?

Make an effort to be in a quiet environment during the day in order to meditate on God and His Word and allow God to speak in a still, small voice inside your heart. Remain still in His presence and experience Him.

Every opportunity to spend time alone with Him away from distractions should be treasured. Don't let your thoughts scatter, for a distracted mind hinders your connection with Him. To truly pay attention, discipline your mind to resist distractions and gently shift your focus back to Jesus whenever they arise.

In your quiet time with God, you might not always feel His presence immediately, and your mind may wander. This is normal! Just remember to keep seeking Him, and focus will come. Don't get discouraged if you don't feel the presence of God every time you pray. Just realize that God knows you're there to dedicate time to Him and are waiting for Him in your alone time. Our reverence for God is demonstrated through our patience in awaiting His presence during prayer time. Keep focusing your attention on Jesus, knowing that you will succeed in overcoming any distractions that try to get in the way.

The Bible shows us the fruit of our time in the secret place: we begin to connect with God and meditate on Him throughout the day. The psalms declare, "But his delight is in the law of the Lord, And in His law he meditates day and night" (Psalm 1:2) and "I have set the Lord always before me; Because He is at my right hand I shall not be moved. Therefore my heart is glad, and my glory rejoices; My flesh also will rest in hope" (Psalm 16:8-9). Job also says, "Receive, please, instruction from His mouth, And lay up His words in your heart" (Job 22:22).

An internal dialogue runs throughout our day. We are constantly bombarded by various thoughts. We hold the power to choose what thoughts we linger on, and to let go of those we don't want to dwell on any further.

Why is it so important to remain vigilant? Because if we don't, we will be controlled by our own thoughts or by thoughts from the enemy, and those thoughts will determine our words and actions. Therefore, if we desire our words and actions to be approved by God, it is crucial to steer our thoughts in the right direction. Holiness is not only reflected in words and actions but also in our thoughts.

Throughout the day, our thoughts can be a silent form of conversation with God, especially if He holds the greatest place in our hearts. This act of meditation is echoed in Malachi 3:16, which highlights its importance: "So a book of remembrance was written before Him for those who fear the Lord and who meditate on His name."

What do we think about most throughout the day? When we love someone, we don't force ourselves to think about them and the things connected to them in some way. We don't force ourselves to meditate on them and find it burdensome. Do we sense the need to think about God throughout the day? Do we feel a lack of peace if we don't connect with Him in our thoughts on a regular basis? If we don't meditate on God, then the question is, what people, things, topics, or interests steer our thoughts away from God? How can we meditate on heavenly things if we're busy finding out things about other people's lives and sharing them with others?

We're all busy with things in life during the day, but it doesn't mean that you stop thinking about your spouse. It doesn't mean you don't ponder on your last conversation or things you did together in the past. It doesn't mean that you don't prepare for what you want to say to your spouse when you meet up again. The same holds true for God, if He is the love of our lives.

We can examine what occupies our minds throughout the day, what grabs our attention the most, and what captivates our hearts. Analyze your life and see what topics dominate it. Those topics compete with our ability to hear from God and can easily overpower the still, small voice of the Holy Spirit. It's crucial to be vigilant so that our thoughts about life don't overwhelm us to the point where we can't hear God's voice when He speaks. God sees what we think about throughout the day. He is a jealous God and sees how important He is to us. He sees if we are not fully dedicated to Him. Whatever we love and hold in high regard that contradicts God's ways will get in the way and interfere with our relationship with God. When we let these things take hold, they can easily intrude on our moments of quiet reflection with God or our attempts to meditate on His Word throughout the day. Keep things out of your mind and heart that could distract you from focusing on Him.

Being vigilant in a relationship means being aware of God's presence throughout the day, following His lead, and walking under His guidance. Remain attentive so that nothing overtakes and overpowers your thoughts while meditating and focusing on God throughout the day. God didn't intend for us to be in fellowship with Him once in a while or from time to time.

If we have a healthy, committed relationship with Him, why do we then think it's okay to skip fellowship time with Him? We shouldn't limit our time with God to a certain time of the day only. The goal of spending time alone with God is to eventually live in His presence. This is when our prayer time becomes our prayer life. He intended for us to be in continuous connection with Him throughout the day. The ultimate goal is to achieve a life of living in a continuous sense of God's presence, where it becomes habitual and natural for us to dwell on Him. No, it's not easy to maintain a constant connection to God throughout the day and avoid getting distracted with everything that comes our way. It's not easy, but it's very rewarding.

Is it normal to long for Him and pursue Him only from time to time, or should it be all the time? Spending our time in the day meditating on Jesus and being aware of God's presence may appear extreme and excessive to some, but our love for God steers us in this direction and this is how God intended for us to live. His plan is for us to remain in the state of experiencing His love, to communicate with the Holy Spirit, and to share our hearts with Him. Those who don't have their first love for God will find this to be too extreme to desire, to have such love and passion for God. We can dedicate a large portion of our free time to God in fellowship, but if we live for ourselves the rest of the time, it's not going to help us.

We can't put our relationship on hold when we're not in our prayer closet. God hears our thoughts and speaks to us through them. The goal of spending quality time alone in a prayer closet with God is to develop the habit of meditating and communicating with Him in our thoughts throughout the day and to be constantly aware of Him in our hearts and minds. We can have continuous inner conversations with Jesus in our spirits, where we can ask Him questions, consult with Him, seek His guidance, share our heart with Him, thank Him, and worship Him.

Jesus doesn't want to be our friend from time to time; He wants to be our closest friend *all* the time. Some treat their dedicated fellowship time with God as a stand-alone event. They pray and read the Bible, then go about their lives without meditating on God throughout the day. This disrupts the continuous connection He desires with His children. His heart is open to communicate with us throughout the day. We make mistakes and won't get it right all the time, but it's important to continue growing stronger in our walk with God. God desires that we live in union with Him rather than encountering Him occasionally and living our lives as we see fit the rest of the time. Relationships lead to partnership and cooperation in all aspects of our daily lives with God.

Abiding in Jesus means nurturing a constant awareness of His presence in your thoughts throughout the day. Practicing to focus our thoughts on God in our prayer closet prepares us to dwell on God even when there are distractions and noise around us. Practicing mindfulness helps us refocus on Him throughout the day, even when distractions compete for our attention. We're still capable of distractions, but we need to bring our focus back to Him whenever distractions occur. Cut off distractions that take your focus away from meditating on Jesus. If we don't focus on Jesus, the enemy's temptations can easily influence our thoughts without our awareness.

As you move through your day, actively cultivate an awareness of His presence. Strive to run after God persistently instead of occasionally. He is only a thought away. By filling up with God, you prevent filling your mind with fleshly, worldly things, and you're practicing seeking God so that it becomes second nature to you.

Pray, "Jesus, talk to me. I want to hear Your voice. Lead me where You want me to be. Jesus, I need You so much; I want to spend more time with You. I'm already looking forward to our next meeting. I love being with You and just meditating on You. Thank You for Your love that never fails."

Ask Him questions, tell Him about details of your life, and act upon the words He sends in your thoughts. Throughout the day, ask Jesus for guidance. "What do You want me to say now? What do You want me to do now? What should I do in this situation?" The frequency with which we think about God reflects our level of love for Him.

As our days unfold, the constant busyness can easily distract us from noticing when God's voice is speaking to us. When this happens, we miss hearing from God. Therefore, we can cultivate discipline and focus our thoughts on meditating on God, His Word, and heavenly things. God speaks to us in many ways, but we might not always recognize His voice. Developing a consistent awareness of God throughout the day takes time and practice. It's a journey of learning to refocus our thoughts on Him, sense His presence, and recognize His voice.

Even when we make it a priority to occupy our minds with God, there will always be temptation to be preoccupied with life and, in the process, take our eyes off Jesus. Become accustomed to thinking about God often during the day. It takes effort to avoid distractions, stay connected to Jesus, and cultivate a sense of awareness of Him in our daily lives. He knows what your heart longs for most in life, your passion, and even the thoughts that fill your meditations. He desires to be the most treasured object of your contemplation, the focus of your meditations. With this in mind, can you recognize His presence when He is speaking to you?

Don't be distracted by everyday matters, the cares of the world, or the busyness of life. Focus your efforts on cultivating a connection with Jesus. Don't let external circumstances pull your attention away from your inner focus on Him. A daily connection with Jesus prevents us from becoming complacent in our spiritual journey. Therefore, it's in our best interest to make a daily effort to maintain this connection with God.

### Meditating on Him

We must steer our thoughts to meditate on Jesus. The psalmist prayed, "Let the words of my mouth and the meditation of my heart Be acceptable in Your sight" (Psalm 19:14). To pull this off, Paul gives us insight: "[We should cast] down arguments and every high thing that exalts itself against the knowledge of God, bringing every thought into captivity to the obedience of Christ" (2 Corinthians 10:5).

We will meditate on what is in our hearts because we cherish it, and that's the reason why we allowed it to be placed in our hearts in the first place. As we focus more on Jesus, other things tend to fade away. This takes effort, but it's so worth it. "Keep your heart with all diligence, for out of it spring the issues of life" (Proverbs 4:23).

Monitor what thoughts you allow to enter into your heart and take up residence there. If left unchecked, those thoughts that take up residence will dictate our feelings, emotions, words, and actions. Mindfulness helps us redirect our thoughts towards what we choose to meditate on.

Where our treasure is, there our heart and thoughts also be. A close relationship with Jesus fosters a longing for Him and a focus on heavenly treasures. Without focusing on heavenly things, our thoughts naturally drift towards the fleshly, worldly, and sinful. All that is worldly and fleshly is perishing and passes away, but spiritual values remain forever. Notice Paul's intentional words, "Set your mind on things above, not on things on the earth" (Colossians 3:2).

> *For those who live according to the flesh set their minds on the things of the flesh, but those who live according to the Spirit, the things of the Spirit. For to be carnally minded is death, but to be spiritually minded is life and peace.* (Romans 8:5-6)

God wants to reveal His heart to us, but are we willing to listen? Our focus should remain on Jesus, and we should be conscious of His presence. When you direct your thoughts toward Him, He gives you sensitivity to God's things and understanding of the circumstances and people in your life.

Focus your thoughts on connecting with God. With consistent practice, this will become habitual during prayer. When focusing on Jesus, if distracting thoughts arise, acknowledge them and return your attention to Him. While daily tasks occupy our minds, keeping our connection with God throughout the day is vital. By remaining mindful during chores and errands, you can weave this connection into the fabric of your day. The more we fix our gaze on Jesus, the less we are swayed by the fleeting attractions of the world.

Meditation on God cultivates awareness of temptation, allowing us to resist it with His Word and avoid sin. In addition to meditating on God throughout the day, it's important to implement prayer in tongues which has numerous benefits listed in the Bible. Praying in tongues allows the Holy Spirit within us to express our deepest needs and desires directly to God.

How often do you want to experience His love, joy, and peace? We make that decision by choosing whether or not to abide in Him, to remain in His presence, and to be alert and ready to hear His voice.

David wrote, "Oh, how I love Your law! It is my meditation all the day. You, through Your commandments, make me wiser than my enemies; For they are ever with me. I have more understanding than all my teachers, For Your testimonies are my meditation" (Psalm 119:97-99). Similar thoughts were repeated by Jesus when He said, "Man shall not live by bread alone, but by every word that proceeds from the mouth of God" (Matthew 4:4).

## External Noise

Have you ever tried to listen to two people talking to you at the same time? Most likely you didn't hear what either of them was saying clearly. By quieting the external noise, we prepare our hearts to be receptive to God's voice. The problem is not in God's speaking but in our listening. Job says, "For God may speak in one way, or in another, yet man does not perceive it" (Job 33:14).

Minimizing distractions such as background noise allows us to more readily focus our thoughts on God throughout the day. Because of the constant activity of our minds, it is challenging to keep our minds still and to give God the attention He deserves. Growing in our faith requires practice in quieting distractions and keeping our hearts centered on Christ when our minds wander.

Remember throughout the day that Jesus is always close. Have this mentality that Jesus wants to be in fellowship with me. Focus on Jesus rather than your sinful past or temptations because Jesus is already at work in you and all you need to do is keep walking in His righteousness.

God talks to us through the day in our spirit, and we can unintentionally ignore His message. Jesus will not raise His voice to speak over the white noise we surround ourselves with. We need to eliminate white noise and concentrate on Jesus to hear what He is saying to us. Do we yearn to hear God's gentle whisper? Then intentional stillness becomes the key to staying receptive to Him. As we cultivate this internal stillness, He will speak to us in a personal, unique way that resonates with our heart.

We might start wondering, "Does God really speak to us outside of dedicated fellowship time?" The truth is, God is speaking to us throughout the day, but we may miss it if we're not open to hearing His voice.

The more distractions and white noise we have, the harder it is to hear God and be attentive to His still, small voice. White noise drowns out God's voice in our lives. We must pay attention and be perceptive to His quiet voice.

Everything is competing for our attention, making it difficult to find stillness and focus on what truly matters. External distractions, like audible white noise from TVs, radios, music, traffic, or conversations, can be disruptive. In addition, internal noise can be just as disruptive. When our minds are preoccupied with thoughts, it can be challenging to hear God's voice.

What do we fill our minds with, externally and internally? Externally, it can be radio, TV, conversations, etc. Internally, we are bombarded with thoughts, which we allow to fill our minds.

Headphones can eliminate audible white noise, but even with them, we still need to make an effort to bring our thoughts back to focus on Christ when they wander and tempt us to think about other things. Quietness is the absence of external noise. Stillness is the absence of internal noise.

The constant noise of life around us threatens to drown out the still, small voice of God. It can feel like God is silent when too many noises have grabbed our attention. Eliminate the noise around you and create a space to hear Him. Quiet your mind. Get into the habit of interacting with the Holy Spirit even in the busyness of day.

We are responsible for shutting God out of our lives by deciding to focus on something else that we find more important than Him. We need quietness in our minds in order to focus on His voice. It's up to us to take the initiative to quiet the distractions and cultivate stillness within ourselves in order to hear God's voice.

**Face Before Hands**

A key element of abiding in Jesus is the seeking of His face. The Scriptures are replete with passages on this: "When You said, 'Seek My face,' My heart said to You, 'Your face, Lord, I will seek'" (Psalm 27:8) and "Seek the LORD and His strength; Seek His face evermore!" (1 Chronicles 16:11).

If we're not careful in prayer, the focus can be on ourselves and our own words as opposed to God. It's all about Him; it's always been about Him. We just fail to recognize it at times. Allow Him to receive all the glory. We are called to seek His face, not just His hands. In other words, we seek God for who He is, not just what He can do.

Can any relationship be considered healthy and normal if one party always asks for their needs and desires to be met but doesn't contribute with regular socializing in return? Of course not!

Have you ever had a friend that only contacts you when he or she has a need? They call and you know exactly what they're going to ask of you. How do you feel when people seek something from you rather than just have a casual conversation with you?

It wouldn't be our preference to be in a relationship with someone who seeks us out mostly to get something from us. These shallow, surface relationships are based on selfishness, personal gain, and personal agendas and don't take into consideration the needs or preferences of the other person. They just focus on their own needs and self-serving goals that must be met. Their approach says, "What will I get out of this relationship? How will this benefit me?" And then they get disappointed because they don't receive what they hoped for.

Using others for personal gain shows selfishness and can potentially destroy that relationship. The same applies in the relationship with God. If God hasn't answered their prayers straight away, or in a way that they want, people get disappointed with Him. If God doesn't answer us, it could mean He wants us to grow in faith, trust, and patience. He is testing us to see if we will turn to alternative solutions to resolve the problem or wait for His guidance.

If this approach is unwanted between people, why would we think it would be okay with God? Why would we think it would be okay to seek Him mostly for what He can do for us? If we prioritize seeking His hands to bless us instead of seeking His face just to talk to Him, then this reveals that we don't understand His godly nature. This shows that we don't value Him more than what He can give us.

This type of need-based prayer focuses mostly on fulfilling our own desires. The wrong motive for being in a relationship is seeking God for what He can do for us instead of seeking Him just for Himself. Love in a relationship is revealed when we focus on God as an object of our adoration rather than focusing on God for provisions. Make it a priority to seek Him for Himself, for who He is, and make it secondary to ask Him to answer your needs and solve your problems. God is more valuable than His gifts and blessings. That's why it's important to cultivate a relationship with Him, centered on who He is, rather than just what we can receive.

Those who lack a devoted and healthy relationship with God will have need-based prayers focused on getting something. They seek blessings from Him, unaware that God's blessings come through simply spending time with Him. When we have a loving connection with the Creator, God fulfills our needs.

Instead of presenting our plans to God for approval, we need to discover His will for our lives. By spending time with Him, we can align ourselves with His plan and walk in it with confidence. His plan, after all, will always succeed because He is in it.

Healthy relationships nurture a deep connection through quality time, mutual respect, and care, expressed through enjoying each other's presence and the giving and receiving of love. At times, we might find it challenging to be fully encompassed by Jesus, especially if we got used to asking Him to fulfill our needs.

In prayer, make seeking His presence your primary focus, instead of receiving His blessings, for it is through seeking Him that blessings come. God desires to be acknowledged for who He is. He doesn't want a relationship based on answered prayers alone. He longs for us to worship Him, to truly know Him, and to focus our hearts on Him. Knowing that God already understands our challenges and worries, we can trust in His perfect timing. Since He is in control, His answers may involve a period of waiting. Seeking Him isn't just about immediate solutions; He may sometimes work behind the scenes to address our needs even before we ask.

Selfish prayers, fueled by our own needs and wants, reflect the desires of a human heart. They focus on external things like possessions, success, or controlling specific outcomes, without considering God's will or our own spiritual growth. These prayers are essentially self-centered attempts to manipulate God for personal gain.

A needs-based prayer focuses on presenting one's genuine needs, concerns, and desires before God. It involves acknowledging and seeking help for personal or collective needs. It includes asking God for physical healing, support, provisions, and blessing. The difference between selfish and needs-based prayer is that selfish prayer tends to prioritize personal gratification or gain, often disregarding the welfare of others. In contrast, needs-based prayer recognizes one's own needs but may also encompass the well-being of others, acknowledging that they too have legitimate needs.

While physical blessings and breakthroughs are important for our lives, it's the spiritual breakthroughs that truly impact us and our walk with God. So, instead of focusing mainly on physical needs, let's seek the needs that are most important for our spiritual life. In prayer, we can yearn for a deeper love for Him and for others, a stronger understanding of His will, and a growing trust in His guidance, asking for the humility to submit to His will and the desire to be refined by Him. By prioritizing these desires in prayer, we cultivate the qualities that strengthen our relationship with Him and lead to a more fulfilling walk with Him.

### Demand or Request

When we demand in prayer, it's as if we're saying that we know what is better for us and God is not giving us what we want or is delaying our request. We're trying to help God by trying to urge Him to speed up answering our prayers. We are telling Him what we want Him to do. "This is what I think needs to be done, so please bless my ideas and my plans and my projects."

In contrast, a *request* in prayer involves seeking His heart's desire and asking Him, "What do You want me to do? How should I go about this situation?"

Instead of focusing solely on our own desires in prayer, we can seek God's will by asking Him to reveal His plan for our lives. During prayer, try listening attentively for His voice, or being open to His guidance. Say, "Jesus, I want what You want. Please reveal Your will to me."

Often in prayer we can set up the wrong expectations by desiring God to do something in our lives as opposed to just enjoying Him. We might even try to rush through praise and worship in order to move to the part where we ask Him for needs. At times, it's tempting to have personal ambitions that go beyond just simply enjoying Him for who He is and appreciating His presence. God does not want us to seek Him only when we are in trouble or when there is a problem that we cannot solve on our own. Seek Jesus and His direction in all areas of your life, not just when issues arise.

Frequently, the emphasis is on the gift rather than the gift-giver. God wants to spend time with us as our best friend. Without a personal encounter, our perception of Jesus' love for us would be measured through materialistic blessings. There are those who gauge His love by the amount of blessings that they receive from Him, and in their mind, this determines how much He loves them.

Prayer time is not about us but about Him. Focus on Him in prayer rather than yourself. Focus your thoughts on Him alone to minimize distractions during prayer. When you communicate with God, imagine that the whole world ceases to exist. It's just you and God.

Seek God's heart in fellowship with Him, rather than focusing solely on asking Him to meet your needs. God's favor and provisions naturally follow those whose heart is after His heart. A consistent prayer life deepens trust in God and the assurance that He will direct us and meet our needs according to His will. He will direct and guide our next steps in life as long as we are obedient to Him and His Word and put His Word into practice in our lives. When we enjoy His presence without asking Him for anything, God will not neglect our needs or overlook our wishes, even if we don't ask Him directly to intervene and resolve them.

## The Voice of God

As you lean in and abide in Jesus, you will begin to hear His voice. Conversation with God is just that—conversation. This means a dialogue between two parties. God communicates with us whenever and however He decides to. As a sovereign God, He communicates with each of His children in unique ways, tailoring His messages to best reach their hearts.

For instance, if you have a random thought that keeps coming back, and it aligns with God's Word, it is probably God trying to speak to you. When God starts to speak through various channels, we need to respond promptly. If we hear God's voice but fail to respond through obedience, it becomes disobedience.

During our quiet time with the Lord, we can sit still in His presence and say, "Jesus, I love You. I'm here for You. Jesus, thank You for Your sacrifice. I'm so grateful for all You do in my life. God, You're so wonderful, You're holy, You're amazing." Then continue sitting in His presence, and you might get a word, a sentence or two, a number, a picture, a vision, an impression, or a memory of a person that you have met.

He speaks through ideas or thoughts, and we gradually begin to recognize God-sent thoughts and ideas and distinguish them from our own thoughts. The more time we spend with God, the better we start to recognize His voice. The Holy Spirit teaches and guides us in all things in life. The Holy Spirit speaks by sending spontaneous thoughts that align with Scripture, and sometimes you can even feel His presence while He speaks. Some of the ways that the Holy Spirit speaks to us is through Scriptures; through lyrics of a song; in a still, small, inner voice; through our consciousness; through impressions in the mind; in visions and dreams; by words, symbols, colors, and objects; through numbers and signs; and through nature and other people.

God communicates with us in specific ways, offering guidance, urging us to pray, or even warning of potential challenges. After receiving revelation from God, we have the opportunity to ask for more clarity on what He is revealing to us. Keep a separate journal to record these revelations, writing down anything you sense from God, including signs, interpretations of Bible verses, revelations, impressions, or pictures. In addition, God can speak to us through other people and situations. This practice will help you refine your ability to recognize and discern His voice and follow His guidance.

In our time with Jesus, sometimes we'll sense God's presence, and sometimes it won't be that obvious and we won't tangibly feel it. Sometimes we'll hear the still, small voice of God and sometimes we won't. Remember, in prayer we pursue God Himself in order to know Him more not just His presence or messages. As we pray, we know He sees and hears us even if we don't feel His presence. Don't be discouraged by this absence, for faith guides us, not fleeting feelings. Seeking time with God in order to know Him more intimately should be our highest priority.

Prayers might be answered immediately or later on. God might send the answer through other people, through His Word, through dreams, and so forth. God hears our prayers even if we don't receive immediate confirmation.

I encourage you to pray, "God, please make me more receptive to Your heart as a Father." In this, we will get personal revelations for our lives and also receive words for others. Experiencing God's presence in the secret place and hearing His voice in that setting is all part of our abiding in Him. The rich benefits of seeking God far outweigh the cost of seeking Him, to the point that they cannot even be compared.

CHAPTER NINE

# The Types of Prayer

*Therefore I exhort first of all that supplications, prayers, intercessions, and giving of thanks be made for all men, for kings and all who are in authority, that we may lead a quiet and peaceable life in all godliness and reverence.*
(1 Timothy 2:1-2)

IN THE SAME way that there is not just one type of communication from person to person, there is not just one type of prayer from people to God. Prayer can include worship, praise, thanksgiving, confession, intercession, petition, supplication, and requests. A prayer can include some, all, or just one of these components.

The goal with this chapter is to both unpack the various forms of prayer as well as provide some sample prayers to help you as you engage with heaven. The Bible says, "The effective, fervent prayer of a righteous man avails much" (James 5:16). Put simply, this means our fervent prayer works! John agreed, writing, "And if we know that He hears us, whatever we ask, we know that we have the petitions that we have asked of Him" (1 John 5:15).

## Worship

Worship is verbalizing praise to God for who He is, His works, and stating that God is worthy of praise. Worship and praise need to be prioritized in our prayers, because God deserves all the glory and praise. Prioritize some prayer time specifically for glorifying, worshiping, praising, thanking, and adoring Him. When we realize that everything good in us is from Him, it will be easier to give God the glory He is due.

## Adoration

Adoration is praising God just for being who He is. We do this by seeing Him as an object of our exaltation and praise without necessarily even taking into consideration all of His worthiness and attributes. It's good to have dedicated prayers just for that: to adore God and express our appreciation for Him.

## Thanksgiving

Thanksgiving is expressing thankfulness and gratitude towards God and giving thanks to Him for what we're grateful for and what He has done in our life, the lives of others, and all other things He has done or is currently doing.

## Confession

Confession involves both a repentant heart towards God and a desire to forsake the sin committed. Confession is a self-evaluation of our lives in which we recognize our sin, admit that we have sinned, and show that we are willing to truly repent and turn away from any involvement in sin by asking God for forgiveness and receiving reconciliation with Him. True repentance is marked by a change in behavior, reflecting a genuine turning away from sin.

## Intercessory/Petition Prayer

Intercessory prayer, also called petition prayer, involves praying for the needs and requests of others on their behalf. This includes offering intense prayers, fervent supplications, and earnest pleas to God for their well-being. We can intercede for a wide range of people, including all humanity, believers facing various challenges, those who have strayed from their faith, individuals yet to find salvation, church leaders and ministers, the sick, our enemies, nations of the world, those in authority, and the nation of Israel.

## Supplication

Supplication is a type of prayer that is used to ask God for help and guidance on what to do. This kind of prayer often expresses a deep sense of dependence on God to seek His mercy, support, or favor. It can encompass various aspects of life, including personal hardships, difficulties, or matters concerning the well-being of the community or the world.

As we navigate these modes of prayer, let's prioritize honoring, worshiping, praising, thanking, and adoring God. This is a beneficial way to start our prayer time, reflecting a heart that yearns to say, 'While I live I will praise the Lord; I will sing praises to my God while I have my being' (Psalm 146:2).

Consider making these words your own: "Yours, O Lord, is the greatness, the power and the glory, the victory and the majesty; for all that is in heaven and in earth is Yours; Yours is the kingdom, O Lord, and You are exalted as head over all" (1 Chronicles 29:11). The New Testament also declares, "For of Him and through Him and to Him are all things, to whom be glory forever. Amen" (Romans 11:36).

Worship is the main and most important part of a relationship in which we acknowledge, adore, and exalt God for who He is. It's expressing thankfulness, appreciation, and gratitude for His goodness and greatness. It allows us to acknowledge His qualities for which He deserves praise, glory, and honor. Worshiping is proclaiming His faithfulness, mercy, and love. The Bible says, "Whoever offers praise glorifies Me" (Psalm 50:23).

During prayer, it's important to practice giving God glory, honor, worship, and praise with a joyful and grateful heart. For many, this is the starting point and closing point of their time in prayer.

### Simplicity in Prayer

Don't make prayer complicated, and don't overthink when you talk with God. When we overcomplicate things, we limit God, and this prevents us from getting closer to Him during our fellowship time. God hears heartfelt prayers. We simply need to humble ourselves before Him, pour out our hearts, and tell Him everything. Speak to God from your heart in what you're going through in life. Be yourself with Him.

Praying doesn't need to happen in beautiful, sublime, and exalting memorized words and expressions but naturally in simple words from our hearts. God desires childlike simplicity, sincerity, humility, honesty, affection, and adoration. It's a constant challenge not to complicate the simplicity of our fellowship with Jesus. A daily walk with the Lord requires humility and obedience. We need to get back to childlike simplicity and sincerity in our relationship with God.

God is waiting for us to give up on our ambitions and completely surrender to Him during our prayer. God is looking for a willing and humble heart. To become childlike is to humble oneself and be honest. Don't complicate things in your relationship with Jesus. Approach Him with childlike simplicity. There is no right or wrong way to pray as long as we live righteously and approach God with sincerity in prayer.

We need to simply communicate with God, coming before Him and genuinely pouring out our hearts, expressing our wishes and desires. Come to Him without any reservations. Tell Him everything that's significant to you. Describe your spiritual walk with Him, life situation, what you're going through, what you're ashamed of, what concerns you, what bothers you, what frustrates you, life's challenges, things you don't understand, and what you need advice and guidance in. Ask Him to give you confidence and assurance by allowing you to see who you are in Him. Share your encounters with other people; what makes you sad, upset, or angry; what brings you joy and happiness; and what you're thankful for.

Ask Him to fill you with joy and peace, especially during difficult times. God is aware of your joy, worries, problems, concerns, and trials, but He still wants you to express and discuss them with Him. Thank Him for creating you, saving you, continuing to work in your life, protecting you, and blessing you. Speak to God about everything that prevents you from living a holy life, about your struggles with sin, and then confess your sins by repenting of doing them. Thank Jesus for dying on the cross for your sins and express how grateful you are for the gift of salvation. Tell Him how much you love Him, how much you value Him, and how much you admire Him. Express gratitude for how amazing and wonderful He is.

There's no wrong way of expressing yourself before God. Just be honest and humble in your approach. Talk to Him simply, without any religious framework or form. Don't try too hard to impress God with beautiful words during your alone time with Him; just focus on Him and be yourself when speaking to Him. Feel free to address any concerns you have about your journey with Him. Don't try to suppress things that are important to you, thinking that it's not important for Jesus to hear. Delight in being with Him. Develop your ability to dwell in the presence of the Most High. Spend some quiet time with the Lord, waiting for Him to say something, and just staying in His presence, resting in Him. When we rest in His presence, God speaks to us. In His presence, we cultivate the practice of giving up and surrendering until we have surrendered everything about us.

It's okay to cry before God even if you're an adult, because in

His eyes, you're always a child. If you genuinely feel like crying before God, don't withhold your emotions. There is nothing to be ashamed of. It's between you and God. Tears express our deepest emotions, whether they are tears of despair, tears of hopelessness, tears of brokenness, or tears of tenderness and joy at feeling His love and presence. Knowing that our loving heavenly Father will never make fun of us, push us away, or condemn us for expressing our heart to Him will make it much easier to open up to Him like we wouldn't open up to anyone else. Let's recall a time we wept tears of gratitude before God, overwhelmed by His greatness.

**Responses**

When you find yourself in a difficult situation in life, take time to worship God, even before asking Him for anything. In moments of mistreatment, neglect, or rejection, turn to God by remembering who He is to you and who you are to Him. We can get closer to Him and open up our hearts by telling Him our whole situation in prayer, asking Him to bring us peace and comfort and to resolve our problems.

When we lose peace or there's some kind of burden or turmoil, we just need to run to God, sit silently by dwelling in His presence, and find comfort by focusing on Him. Meditate on Him and His beauty, majesty, power, and glory. This gesture reveals that we trust Jesus not just with our words but also with our actions. We turn to Him for assistance, confident in His ability to answer our prayers and provide guidance, rather than solely relying on our own limited capabilities. In His presence, we discover peace, even when the situation appears unresolved.

Losing our peace can happen for several reasons. One reason is failing to abide in Christ and focusing too much on ourselves. Another reason is when the enemy sends negative thoughts that tempt us to lose the peace we have in Christ.

Pray using God's promises. There are more than seven thousand promises in the Bible that God has left for us. Find these promises, read them, and discuss them with God during your prayer time.

### Prayer Models

As a disclaimer, you don't have to follow these words in your prayers word for word; they are just examples and suggestions for what can be said during times of prayer. There's no standard for how to talk to God. Just start.

With that in mind, consider the truth of some of these phrases and how these elements might be worked into your prayer life.

### Acknowledge God and thank Him for who He is and His character:

I thank You for who You are.
You're perfectly good in all Your ways.
You're the ultimate love.
There's no one like You.
You're holy.
You're righteous.
You're just.
You're self-sufficient.
You're sovereign.
You're wise.
You're all mighty.
You're all powerful.
You're magnificent.
You're majestic.
You're the greatest.
You are El Shaddai (Lord God Almighty).
You are Elohim (God).
You are Adonai (Lord, Master).
You are Yahweh (Lord, Jehovah).

You are Jehovah Rapha (The Lord That Heals).
You are Jehovah Jireh (The Lord Will Provide).
You are Jehovah Shalom (The Lord Is Peace).
You're the Self-Existent One.
You're the All-Sufficient One.
You're the Everlasting, Eternal God.
You're a wonderful Creator of all.
Lord, You're glorious.
I bless Your holy name.
I exalt You above all in my life.
You are the King of kings and Lord of lords.
You are Alpha and Omega.
All praise is for You, my King.
The whole world is full of Your glory.
You are the source of love.
I acknowledge Your might and power.
You're perfect in all of Your ways.
I honor You with fear and reverence.
All the glory and honor belongs to You.
You deserve all the glory and praise.
Jesus, I worship You.
You are my Shepherd.
I want to know more of who You are.
You're faithful.
You're trustworthy.
You're reliable.
Your wisdom holds everything in place.
You pronounce perfect justice over evil.
Your knowledge is beyond my understanding.
Your mercy is higher than heavens.
Your love is beyond comprehension.
You're gracious.
You're patient and long-suffering to my wrongdoings.
You're kind and merciful to me.

## Talk about God's love for you and express your love toward God:

You're the love of my life.
Jesus, I'm so in love with You.
You are love itself. You're the definition of love.
What have I done in my life to deserve Your love?
I can't get enough of Your love; You're so dear to me.
Thank You for loving me.
I want to love You more.
My heart belongs to You.
Thank You for Your loving heart.
I want to be embraced by Your love.
I adore You so much.
I'm valuable in Your eyes.
Your love has captivated my heart.
I don't deserve Your love, but You still show it to me.
I don't want anything else in life more than You.
I want to give myself completely to Your love, without any reservations.
I'm grateful for Your love.
I want to feel loved and accepted by You.
I worship You. Oh, how I need You; how much I adore You.
Jesus, You're everything to me.
I'm grateful that You're in my life.
No one can take You away from me.
There's no one like You.
I want to experience Your love.
I want to grow in love with You.
I'm Your child.
I want to live to glorify You.
Let Your name be glorified in my life.
I'm here for You, and only You.
Thank You for loving me.
You're everything I've ever needed.

I don't want to doubt or question Your love for me.

### Thank Jesus for salvation and for continuing to sanctify you:

I have no idea how valuable I am in Your eyes or how difficult it was for You to obtain my salvation on the cross.
I'm cleansed by Your blood, Jesus.
Thank You for gifting me the clothes of righteousness.
You're my righteousness.
Thank You for the gift of salvation.
You loved me before I knew You.
I'm grateful to You for salvation.
There's power in Your blood, Jesus.
Jesus, Your name is above all names.
You have authority over everything.
Sanctify me through Your word.
I surrender my entire life to You, God. Please use me for Your glory. Do whatever You can in my life to cleanse me so that I can walk with You.
Please reveal to me what You want me to change in my life.
I give You permission to work in my life and change anything that isn't right or that keeps me from walking with You.
I'm grateful for salvation and what You did on the cross to save me, Jesus.
Reveal to me what displeases You in my life.
Refine me, purify me, and cleanse my heart.

### Thank Him for what He has already done, what He is doing now, and what He will do in the future:

Thank You for revealing Yourself to me.
Thank You for Your salvation on the cross.
Thank You for redeeming me.
Thank You for adopting me into Your family.

Thank You for taking me in as Your child.
Thank You for Your patience.
Thank You for Your goodness.
Thank You for being faithful to me.
I can never thank You enough for what You have done for me.
There's no one who can help me like You can.
You deserve the highest honor, praise, and worship.
You're all I need.
Thank You for helping me when I wasn't even aware that You were there.
You are my life, and You sustain me.
I live only because of You.
I'm so grateful to You for life.
I cherish having You in my life.
Thank You for revealing Yourself to me.
I'm grateful for my life's journey with You.
I'm so grateful for even the little things in life.
I'm eternally grateful for what You've done in my life.
I depend on You. I need You. You're my shield. You're my fortress. You're my rock.
Jesus, thank You for all the work You have done in my life.
Thank You for everything You do, because I don't deserve anything good, but You provide for me and sustain me out of Your loving kindness.
You gave me Your life; how can I doubt You?

## Express gratitude for the opportunity to be in fellowship with God:

Thank You for Your presence.
I am thankful for the chance to come before You and spend time in Your presence.
Thank You for giving me the opportunity to reconnect with You in prayer.
Thank You for allowing me to share fellowship with You.

There's nowhere else I'd rather be than in Your presence.
Nothing and no one else will substitute for You in my life.
Nothing else will satisfy me like You do.
I love being in fellowship with You.
I want to abide in You.
I long to be with You, to be united with You.
I want to be closer to You.
Jesus, reveal Your heart to me.
Thank You for letting me experience Your presence.
I want to forget myself while being captivated by Your beauty.
I want to enjoy more of You.
Make my heart receptive to Your voice.
I want to be more sensitive to Your voice.
I adore You and seek Your approval in all that I do.
I want to pay any price to be close to You.
I won't give up seeking You at every available opportunity.
I will not stop until I have a breakthrough with You.
Please reveal to me what I need to do on my part to improve the relationship.
I want to abide in You and be in Your presence throughout the day.
I treasure our time together.
I hunger for more of You; I long and thirst for You.
Thank You for giving me the time and opportunity to seek You out and spend time with You.
I want to pursue You with all of my heart.
Thank You for revealing Yourself to me.
Thank You for allowing me to approach You.
I want to have more time to spend with You.
Your presence means so much to me and I value it greatly.
I come to Your feet to be with You.

**Express your need and desire to know Him more:**

Show me how I can improve my fellowship with You.

Do whatever it takes to help me follow You.
Show me Your heart, heavenly Father.
I'd like to get to know You better.
I need more of You in my life.
I want to connect with Your Spirit.
I want to be closer to You.
I want to know what's on Your heart.
I want to pay the full price of following You.
I'd like confirmation that my life pleases You.
I want to be more open with You, Jesus. I want to be more vulnerable with You and share more of myself with You. I want to learn how to trust You in order to open up to You and share my most personal things that are important to me.
Jesus, help me see my need for Your presence every single day.
Jesus, please let me recognize how much I depend on You in my life.
I just want You. I don't ask for any of Your gifts or blessings because You alone are far greater than anything that You give. I just want You.
I want to dwell in You.
Teach me how to approach You.
I want to have close communion with You.
Jesus, please teach me to recognize Your gentle voice.
I would like to know what's on Your heart.
Jesus, how can I hear You better?
Make me more sensitive to the voice of the Holy Spirit.
Speak clearly to me so that I can recognize Your voice and not doubt You.

**Talk about your relationship with Him:**

Free me from anything that prevents me from connecting with You.

Take away everything that prevents me from growing in my relationship with You.
I don't want anything to distract me from You.
I want to know You more. What do I need to change or get rid of in my life?
Point out things in my life that do not glorify You.
What do I need to do to get closer to You, so I can hear Your voice better?
Take away everything that prevents me from approaching You.
Jesus, show me how I can spend time with You more effectively.
Jesus, free me from the need to focus on anything else more than Your presence.
I don't want to lose sight of You.

**Pray to help you better understand Him and His will:**

I want to know Your will for my life.
Please reveal Your will to me so that I may live by it.
I want to live according to Your Word.
I don't want to disappoint You with my actions.
I don't want anything in my life that You don't approve of.
I want You to be glorified through my life. You have devised a life plan for me; please guide me in accordance with Your will.
I don't fully understand Your will or Your work in my life, but I trust You.
I trust that You're in control of my situation and will resolve it at Your appointed time.
Direct my path.
I want to be obedient to Your guidance and direction.
Give me wisdom and understanding of Your Word.
I allow You to complete Your work in my life.
Show me what I need to do to bring Your name glory.
I only want to do things that You approve of.
I trust that You know what You're doing.

I'm tired of doubting You. I want to fully trust You without any reservations.
I want to do Your will, Jesus, no matter how much time, money, or effort it will involve.
Lead me. Reveal to me what I need to do.
Please reveal Your plan to me.
I want to be led by You, Holy Spirit.
Direct my steps daily.
I want to fulfill Your will here on earth.
I thank You for being in my life and guiding me.
Holy Spirit, guide me in truth. I want Your counsel in life.
I want to do Your will, regardless of how unpleasant or uncomfortable it will be for me.
Holy Spirit, I need You. I desire Your presence. Please direct my steps and advise me on what I should say or do.
Holy Spirit, reign in my life.
I ask for Your encouragement, counsel, guidance, and understanding.
I seek Your counsel in all things.
What should I do today, God?
Search my heart and reveal to me what I need to work on.

## Talk about allowing God to change you:

I trust You with my life, and I give You permission to do everything You need in my life to sanctify me, discipline me, correct my ways, and remove things that don't glorify You.
Lord, transform my life.
Humble me if I become prideful.
Help me to overcome my fleshly temptations.
Tell me what I am doing wrong in this situation.
You are aware of my circumstances.
I'm willing to go through any changes You require in my life.
I surrender my life to You.
Prune and refine me.

Deal with my heart.
Please remove and eliminate everything that You don't approve of in my life.
Free me from anything that hinders me from walking in freedom.
I submit to Your refining.
I recognize my dependence on You.
I want to remain humble before You.
Jesus, point things out in my life that You want to change or get rid of.
Break every stronghold in my life formed by the lies of the enemy.
Jesus, I believe You have the power to free me from any fear, anxiety, anger, depression, loneliness, low self-esteem, insecurities, feeling unworthy, guilt, and condemnation.
Jesus, I can't fix this issue, but You can. Please help me.
I want to grow in character and become more like You.
Please give me Your peace and joy.
I ask that You continue to shape my character so that I can be a vessel for Your glory.
Jesus, I want to grow spiritually.
I'm thankful for Your mercy and grace. I appreciate Your corrections so that I can be purified and sanctified even more in order to live a victorious and a sin-free life.
Let me see myself as You see me. Let me see others as You see them.

### Present your requests before Him and ask for your needs in prayer:

Jesus, please lead me to make correct decisions.
Give me spiritual strength to overcome obstacles in my life.
Strengthen me to overcome sinful temptations.
You know my physical and spiritual needs.
You sustain my life.
You know better what I need in my life.

I need Your help.
I give this problem over to You.
I trust You and want to continue to grow in that trust.
You're the provider for all my needs.
Jesus, please take away the fear from my life.
I cast my cares, worries, and fear at Your feet.
I know You're in control of my life. I need Your assistance.
I can't do this task unless You enable me.
My life is in Your hands.
Please give me Your peace.
I want to trust You more.
Keep me humble.

## Ask for spiritual, emotional, and physical protection in life:

Protect my heart from emotional harm that comes from interacting with others.
Protect me from people who want to manipulate and control me with flattery and craftiness.
Protect me from the actions of the enemy.
Protect me with the blood of Jesus.
I plead the blood of Jesus over me, my family, and my house.
I desperately need Your help to protect me from my adversary.
Deliver me from the evil schemes of the enemy.
Remind me to meditate on Your Word.
Warn me through my consciousness of things that don't please You.
I will continue to rely on You as my protector.
You're my shield.
You're my fortress.
You're my rock.
You're my hiding place.
You will never fail me.
You will never abandon me.

I can wholeheartedly trust You.
I will not be afraid when I'm with You.
My confidence is in You.
My identity is in You.
You will never leave me nor forsake me.
In You, I will find refuge.

### Talk about sin and sinful temptations:

Help me to overcome any sinful temptation that comes my way.
Guard my heart and my mind.
Cleanse me from sin and inequities.
I repent of my sin.
I want to live a holy and righteous life in Your eyes.
Jesus, I don't want to love anything in the world. Help me to resist temptation, sin, and sinful behavior.
Please forgive me for not following Your instructions correctly.

### Talk about hardships and difficulties that you face:

Help me with that difficult project at work.
I have this problem that I don't know how to resolve. Please help me with it.
I'm tired of having doubts, insecurities, guilt, and condemnation in my life. I want to be free from all of that.
Please help me in my effort to stay in Your Word, to meditate on You, and to live a spiritually victorious life.
Please send me friends that will help me to get closer to You.
I want to be at peace with whatever happens, knowing that You are aware of my situation.
Take my pain away.
I give You all my difficulties, problems, and worries.

I'm having trouble trusting You right now, but I choose to stand on Your promises.
Regardless of how I feel right now, I choose to worship You.
I lay all of my burdens and anxiety at Your feet.

### Talk about your relationships with others:

I need Your assistance in dealing with people who are unjust to me.
Help me to deal lovingly with people who are offending me.
People misunderstand me and I don't know how to resolve this situation.
Help me to love others like You do.
I forgive everyone who hurt me, who broke my trust, and who wronged me.
Heal my heart from all the wounds caused by others.

### Pray regarding the needs of others:

I pray that You will help them with the hardships they go through.
Soften the hearts of sinners so that they can accept the truth of who You are.
What need exists in this person's life that You want me to pray for?
Give the unbeliever a repentant heart and open their spiritual eyes to see their true condition and help them make a decision to repent and get born again.
Help those who don't have peace in their heart to receive Your peace.
Fulfill the needs of those who struggle in difficult situations.
With whom should I share this verse or revelation with?
Heal those who are hurting and suffering at the moment.
I ask that You grant them wisdom, discernment, and courage as they make their decisions.
Reveal the truth to those who are walking in darkness and sin.

I pray that more will hear the message of the gospel and will come to salvation.

Help meet the needs of the local community of believers and strengthen their faith.

I pray for the persecuted believers worldwide. Help ease the suffering that they're enduring for Your name's sake.

Encourage those who evangelize and proclaim the news of salvation to others.

### Asking for a word for others:

What message do You want to give me to this person?
What specific need do You want me to pray for this individual?
What is the reason You wanted me to meet with this person? What should I tell them?

### Holy Spirit

At the end of the day, prayer is a rich conversation with the Creator. Talk to Him about your day and what you're going through. Share your heart with Jesus. He is interested in the details of your daily life. Tell Him what is going well and what is not, what is challenging and what you are looking forward to. Learn the art of interaction with the Holy Spirit in your life. Paul wrote, "The grace of the Lord Jesus Christ, and the love of God, and the communion of the Holy Spirit be with you all. Amen" (2 Corinthians 13:14).

God has given us the Holy Spirit as a gift in order to nourish, edify, help, comfort, and renew us throughout our life here on earth. Jesus said, "But the Helper, the Holy Spirit, whom the Father will send in My name, He will teach you all things, and bring to your remembrance all things that I said to you" (John 14:26). The Holy Spirit is a person and He was sent as a Helper to assist us in our prayers. As we pray in tongues, the Holy Spirit will intercede for us, guide our spirit, and give utterance to what to pray to God the Father. It gives us a way to pray for situations we might not otherwise be aware of. The Holy Spirit, who knows everything about our circumstance, is able to intercede on our behalf regarding these situations. In the same way, He also provides a way for us to pray for the needs of others on their behalf. The Holy Spirit knows everything that we have need of.

We become more obedient to His voice and what the Holy Spirit wants to accomplish in our lives when we continue praying in tongues at His prompting. The Holy Spirit wants us to walk in His presence. By being aware of the Holy Spirit's presence in our lives, we have the chance to interact with Him at all times. We can constantly communicate with and consult the Holy Spirit in all aspects of our lives. This creates a partnership, allowing us to seek guidance before we act. Simply ask if you should proceed with something, and listen for His leading. Share the details of your day with the Holy Spirit. Ask the Holy Spirit for guidance and advice, even with small and insignificant things. He wants to assist us with anything we are having difficulty with, because He cares about our well-being. The Holy Spirit comforts us in all of our sorrows.

The Holy Spirit longs to connect with us, desiring us to share what matters most to us. He offers guidance, helping us navigate life's decisions. We can lean on Him to assist us in every aspects of our life. Empowered by the Holy Spirit, we overcome sin and glorify God by living for His purpose.

We can, however, ignore the voice of the Holy Spirit. Only those who choose to walk with Him have unhindered access to His strength and guidance. Walking in His ways is a sign of reliance on the Holy Spirit. We pay attention to what He says, heed His warnings, and follow His instructions. Following the Holy Spirit's prompting requires surrender. While not always easy, it leads to the fullness of life. The Holy Spirit supplies everything we need to live a godly life, and He produces His amazing fruit in us.

It's natural for God's children to live under the guidance of the Holy Spirit. When we turn our thoughts toward Him, He gives us sensitivity and wisdom to understand situations in our lives. Our character growth depends on how willing we are to let God continue to produce His work in us.

The more time we put into being aware of the Holy Spirit's presence and focusing on Him and His voice, the better it is for our spiritual growth. Prayer and the Holy Spirit's guidance empower us to live according to God's will.

### The Purpose of Tongues

*He who speaks in a tongue edifies himself.* (1 Corinthians 14:4)

Praying in the spirit means making prayers that are led and guided by the Holy Spirit. Praying in the Spirit allows us to pray without ceasing. Paul wrote, "Likewise the Spirit also helps in our weaknesses. For we do not know what we should pray for as we ought, but the Spirit Himself makes intercession for us with groanings which cannot be uttered" (Romans 8:26).

When you pray in tongues, your spirit speaks directly to God. To speak with God in tongues is to communicate with Him in a heavenly, supernatural language. *This* is praying in the spirit, and it is highly encouraged in the Bible. "And pray in the Spirit on all occasions with all kinds of prayers and requests. With this in mind, be alert and always keep on praying for all the Lord's people" (Ephesians 6:18). And, "For he who speaks in a tongue does not speak to men but to God, for no one understands him; however, in the spirit he speaks mysteries" (1 Corinthians 14:2).

The more we pray, the closer we will grow in our relationship with God. The more we pray in tongues, the more His power will manifest through us and change the lives of others. Jude wrote, "But you, beloved, building yourselves up on your most holy faith, praying in the Holy Spirit..." (Jude 1:20).

When we live by the Spirit, we produce spiritual fruit, which is to live out the salvation we have received by continuing to focus our mind on the things of the Spirit. We allow the Holy Spirit to empower us to overcome sin and deeds of the flesh. Paul said, "If we live in the Spirit, let us also walk in the Spirit" (Galatians 5:25).

We permit the Holy Spirit to act within us and carry out His will as He directs. In order to continue to walk in the Spirit, we must give the Holy Spirit permission to exercise control over our thoughts, feelings, will, words, and deeds. When we live by the Spirit, we produce spiritual fruit.

To walk in the Spirit, we have to relinquish desires that go against the Holy Spirit. If we engage in desires of the flesh, then we are walking in the flesh. It's essential that we walk in the identity we have in Jesus Christ because our life is now in Him.

Throughout the day, engage in continuous interaction with the Holy Spirit by sharing your thoughts and experiences, asking questions with a seeking heart, and yearning even deeper revelations of the nature of Jesus Christ.

## Walking in the Spirit

Our desires and intentions give us away and reveal if we actually live in the flesh or in the spirit at the moment. The flesh always attempts to do what it wants. It takes effort, persistence, and perseverance to live by the Spirit and walk by the Spirit. If we walk in the Spirit, we will not do the works of the flesh. While we walk in the Spirit, we aren't sinning. Strive to live spiritually instead of carnally. The carnal mind cannot please God (see Romans 8:7-9).

Walking by the spirit means looking to Jesus for our direction. It is a daily journey of asking ourselves what the Lord wants us to do. What will honor and please Him? It involves examining our lives, and if we recognize the works of the flesh within us, we need to repent and ask for help from the Holy Spirit. Walking by the Spirit is living your life continually in the presence of the Spirit of God. It's having Christ foremost in all your affections. It's pursuing God with all of your heart, as we're commanded to do in the first and greatest commandment. It's to have no other idols before you, no other gods before you, but to serve God alone with all of your heart.

To walk in the Spirit is to become aware of your thoughts, choices of words, actions, and reactions. It is being conscious of doing the right thing at the right time, not with our own strength but with the help of the Holy Spirit. Because what we consume will be revealed in our words and actions.

Walking in the spirit is our ability to become aware of ourselves so that we can detect and discern when the devil comes to tempt and to whisper lies into our ears. It's being sensitive and watchful. Stand guard at the door of your heart. It's having discernment of the content we come across: does it align with the Word of God or not?

God's Spirit not only provides guidance but also strength, because we are unable to obey God in our own strength. The Holy Spirit gives us everything we need to live a godly life. He also works in us to make His fruit manifest in our lives.

The Holy Spirit gives us the ability to live for God's purpose and glory. Walking in the Spirit requires ongoing practice of yielding to the Holy Spirit. As we surrender to the Holy Spirit's guidance, our walk in the Spirit becomes more natural. Through this ongoing practice, we strengthen our discipline, making it easier to overcome the desires of the flesh. However, we always have the choice to follow the Holy Spirit's guidance or resist it.

Paul wrote, "Now the works of the flesh are evident, which are: adultery, fornication, uncleanness, lewdness, idolatry, sorcery, hatred, contentions, jealousies, outbursts of wrath, selfish ambitions, dissensions, heresies, envy, murders, drunkenness, revelries, and the like; of which I tell you beforehand, just as I also told you in time past, that those who practice such things will not inherit the kingdom of God. But the fruit of the Spirit is love, joy, peace, longsuffering, kindness, goodness, faithfulness, gentleness, self-control. Against such there is no law. And those who are Christ's have crucified the flesh with its passions and desires" (Galatians 5:19-24). And later, "Do not be deceived, God is not mocked; for whatever a man sows, that he will also reap. For he who sows to his flesh will of the flesh reap corruption, but he who sows to the Spirit will of the Spirit reap everlasting life" (Galatians 6:7-8).

Action that comes out of walking in the Spirit includes denying yourself, crucifying your flesh, humbling yourself, putting others' needs first, forsaking the world, and walking in holiness. Open your heart to the Holy Spirit's feedback on your life and your relationship with God.

What we set our mind to dictates our lifestyle. The carnal mind is set on fleshly things and it directs our flesh how to act. If we don't put effort in walking in the Spirit, then by default we will walk in the flesh. The Bible says that sowing into the spirit will bring the fruitfulness of the character of Christ into our lives. The flesh will try to stop you from sowing into the spirit. As long as we continue to sow in the spirit, we will produce the fruit of the spirit.

Why bring out these subjects during a chapter on prayer? The truth is, often in prayer, we want God to change our things. In reality, God wants to change our minds. And from there, our actions, speech, perceptions, and more. Don't underestimate the power of all types of prayer in your daily walk.

CHAPTER TEN
-----

# Our Authority

*For I delight in the law of God according to the inward man.*
(Romans 7:22)

WHAT IS THE Bible? Put simply, it is a revelation of the heart, mind, and character of God. God's Word is the absolute standard of truth and the true foundation for our lives. His will has been revealed in His Word. God's will should define our lives, not merely be a small part of it. The truth is, God is not what people say about Him. God is what He says about Himself. In Scripture, we can see how He communicates with people. The only way we can really know God is by personally spending time with Him and reading His Word. All of God's words will come to pass.

Everything you read in the Word of God is true and has already happened, is happening, or will happen at some point. Stand on God's Word as a firm foundation, independent of your own beliefs. We need to know the author of the Bible personally through a relationship. This is how we can know the truth and won't doubt His Word or what He says in it. If we believe and know God, then we will believe in His Word. A personal, experience-based relationship with Jesus leads to such confidence in God's Word as the truth, where we don't have a shadow of doubt of its credibility.

It's essential that we continue to seek the revelation of Jesus in the Word of God. Paul spoke of this, saying, "That the God of our Lord Jesus Christ, the Father of glory, may give to you the spirit of wisdom and revelation in the knowledge of Him, the eyes of your understanding being enlightened; that you may know what is the hope of His calling, what are the riches of the glory of His inheritance in the saints, and what is the exceeding greatness of His power toward us who believe, according to the working of His mighty power which He worked in Christ when He raised Him from the dead and seated Him at His right hand in the heavenly places, far above all principality and power and might and dominion, and every name that is named, not only in this age but also in that which is to come. And He put all things under His feet, and gave Him to be head over all things to the church, which is His body, the fullness of Him who fills all in all" (Ephesians 1:17-23).

Note, Paul speaks of our need for the *spirit of revelation* and then goes on to reveal detailed aspects of Jesus' character. Revelation in the Bible provides us with insight into God and we can trust that it is fully reliable. The Scriptures speak of their reliability continually: "for prophecy never came by the will of man, but holy men of God spoke as they were moved by the Holy Spirit" (2 Peter 1:21); "For the word of God is living and powerful, and sharper than any two-edged sword, piercing even to the division of soul and spirit, and of joints and marrow, and is a discerner of the thoughts and intents of the heart" (Hebrews 4:12); "For this reason we also thank God without ceasing, because when you received the word of God which you heard from us, you welcomed it not as the word of men, but as it is in truth, the word of God, which also effectively works in you who believe" (1 Thessalonians 2:13).

The longest chapter in the Bible, Psalm 119, is full of passages on hiding the Word of God in our hearts, meditating on His precepts, and delighting in God's statutes. God is speaking to us through His Word; therefore, it is necessary to feed our soul with the Word. His Word should fill our minds, hearts, and souls. Our appreciation of God's Word comes from reading it and following it with obedience.

Ask God for the discernment to understand the revelations of His Word, the discipline to stay true to it, and the willingness to obey. If we do not have a healthy relationship with God and do not spend enough time in God's Word, reading and meditating on it, we run the risk of not taking God's Word seriously as the truth or allowing it to be the ultimate authority in our lives. If we don't fully trust or rely on God, we can fall into the trap of deceiving ourselves. This may involve distorting the truth of His Word, twisting Scriptures, or interpreting them out of context to fit our lifestyle. Instead of trying to fit the Bible into our worldview, we need to adjust our worldview to match the truth of the Word.

Discerning the truth of His Word is critical. The reason we read the Bible daily is so that we can align our lives according to biblical truth and walk in relationship with God the way He intended. The Bible is the truth, and it is an unchanging truth. If we don't follow God's Word to the letter and obey it in practice, then we're saying that we really don't believe God's Word and don't trust Him. The Bible's truth stands independently of human experiences, opinions, and feelings. Look at your life before God and evaluate it in light of God's Word. Examine your life and see what the Bible tells you to change in it. We can check any information that we come across by asking the question, "Is the information backed up by the Word of God or not?"

We need to study the Bible, contemplate on it, reflect on it, and apply it to our lives. The whole purpose of reading the Word is to continually meditate on what was read and then put it into practice. This defines living out the Word of God. This helps us to grow our faith and nourish our soul. Also, by meditating on the Word of God, we don't leave any room for fleshly desires to enter our minds. Abide means to live, remain permanently in, and align yourself with the Word of God. Abiding in the Lord means that we continually receive, believe, and trust that Jesus is everything we need.

If we don't rely on God's truth as authority, then we can make incorrect assertions of who God is. Over time, this wrong belief can make us hardened to the truth of God's Word. God is who He says He is through His Word. We must abandon the framework of our own understandings, views, and limitations about who God is and how He works in our lives. God expresses His nature through His Word. He left His Word with us so that we could reconcile with Him and know Him.

Spiritual breakthrough and growth in our relationship with Jesus don't come from reading the Bible occasionally; they come from reading it consistently and putting it into practice.

If we don't read the Word, how can we meditate on it? If we don't meditate on the Word, how can we put it into practice in our daily lives? We can't afford to get complacent with the Bible.

> *All Scripture is given by inspiration of God, and is profitable for doctrine, for reproof, for correction, for instruction in righteousness, that the man of God may be complete, thoroughly equipped for every good work.* (2 Timothy 3:16-17)

What makes the Bible so reliable? First, it's inspired by God. Second, because it is of God, it is eternal. Life circumstances will change and shift, but God's Word will not. Jesus said, "Heaven and earth will pass away, but My words will by no means pass away" (Matthew 24:35). Peter also incorporated the Old Testament passages in his writings on the subject: "...having been born again, not of corruptible seed but incorruptible, through the word of God which lives and abides forever, because 'All flesh is as grass, And all the glory of man as the flower of the grass. The grass withers, And its flower falls away, But the word of the Lord endures forever'" (1 Peter 1:23-25).

Read a certain passage or a certain verse from the Bible and meditate on it until God reveals that passage to you in a new light and you have a fresh revelation. It's not enough to interpret God's Word properly; we also need to apply it in our lives. Don't just read the Bible, but live it. Bible memorization is good, but it is not enough on its own. Of the Pharisees, Jesus spoke, "You search the Scriptures, for in them you think you have eternal life; and these are they which testify of Me" (John 5:39).

We can become accustomed to reading one or two chapters in general and believing that God is pleased with us because we read His Word. What truly matters is whether our hearts connect with God and find joy in His Word.

For example, if you read a few Bible verses and then meditate on them throughout the day and share your revelations with others, this would be far better than mechanically reading three chapters daily and not having your heart in it or applying it to your life.

Embrace the combination of prayer and reading the Bible together. You can read some verses from the Bible and then prayerfully ask about what you have just read: "God, what are You saying to me through these verses? What do You want to reveal to me today? Make known to me the revelation so that I can incorporate this into my life. Your Word sustains my spirit and gives life. I desire to be fed by Your Word. I want to be taught by the truth of Your Word. What do You want me to learn today from Your Word? I want to put Your Word into practice in my life. Please open the understanding of Your Word. I want to grow in the knowledge of You through the Word. What lesson can I get from this story or passage? How do I put what You've revealed to me into action? With whom should I share this revelation?"

This is how we become doers of the Word and not hearers only (see James 1:22 and Luke 11:28). Jesus said the wise man who builds his house on the rock does not merely *hear* the sayings of Jesus but "does them" also (see Matthew 7:24).

God gave us the Word to judge our actions. We have to compare our actions according to the Word of God to see if we live and walk according to the Word.

Some people might have made-up excuses such as, "It's not necessary for me to read the Bible daily. I meditate on God here and there throughout the day anyway."

Read the Bible until you fall in love with its author, and then you will start loving your Bible reading. It will become a love letter, not just a set of instructions. Read the Bible until you feel His peace.

## Healthy Relationships Grow

An indicator of a healthy relationship is that it constantly grows. Starting a relationship with Jesus is a beginning, but there's an ongoing price that is required to maintain and grow in that relationship. It's one thing to establish a relationship, but it's another to maintain and continuously develop it. What counts is the sustained effort that reveals how valuable a relationship is to us. We can sustain and cultivate our relationship by spending daily alone time with God in private prayer.

Our overall purpose is to love God more and grow closer in relationship with Him. As long as we foster the relationship, it will grow, get stronger, and get deeper over time. If we have a relationship with Jesus and spend time with Him every day, we will grow closer to Him, whether we notice it or not.

Let's examine our lives and ask ourselves, "Where do I stand when it comes to my relationship with Jesus? Do I love God more than I did when I got born again? Do I know God more now than when I was first born again? Do I spend more time with God now than when I was first saved?"

Relationships can always improve. How much do we desire to deepen our relationship with Jesus? How much effort are we willing to expend to get to know Him better? Even though a relationship with Jesus creates a desire to know Him more, it still doesn't come automatically and we still need to invest ourselves into this relationship.

All born-again believers are embarked on a lifelong journey of growing closer to God. While we may not know the specifics of each other's walk with Him, we can all still support and encourage each other in deepening our relationships.

Let's not look at others and compare our relationship with God to theirs. We are all at different stages of our walk with Him. Everyone's unique background, upbringing, and experiences shape their relationship with God. Remember, you will only be held accountable for your personal relationship with Jesus, not the relationships of others with Jesus. Make sure that your relationship with Jesus grows and becomes stronger every day.

God desires to cultivate a flourishing relationship with us, to the point where we regularly reflect on Him and interact with Him and it becomes natural throughout our day.

Are you content with where you're at in your relationship with Jesus? If so, then you aren't growing, because a real relationship with Jesus will always keep you hungry and longing for more of Him. There's a risk of becoming complacent in following Jesus by relaxing and taking it easy when it comes to our walk with God.

It doesn't matter how much we know God, there is always more of Him to know. If we feel content and aren't moving forward in our relationship, then this means that our love for Jesus has cooled off and we've stopped pursuing Him further.

God is far greater and vaster than we can ever imagine. He is much bigger, more amazing, and more awesome than our wildest imagination of Him or what others tell us about Him or try to describe Him. God is immense and immeasurable in all His greatness, glory, might, and power, and we will never be able to know Him completely.

We try to figure out and understand God with our limited

minds, attempting to confine Him within a box so that we can comprehend His character and nature. However, we have barely scratched the surface of knowing God with our very limited human minds. We will never fully comprehend Him, so we should stop pretending that we understand God and know enough about Him to live and function in life without the need for further exploration of who He is. We should not believe we can entirely grasp, understand, or figure out His nature. He will reveal Himself to us piece by piece when we seek Him and walk with Him.

We need to repent of this and say, "God, forgive me for trying to limit You and Your might, Your power, Your glory." Eternity will not be enough to fully discover and grasp who God is, along with all His nature, ability, characteristics, and attributes. It's important to approach God in humility during our prayer time and be ready to learn from Him, desiring to receive ongoing revelations about who He is, His thoughts and opinions, in order to know God in a relational way.

There isn't enough time for us to grasp all the information currently available through what others have written or spoken about who God is, whether it be in sermons, teachings, seminars, conferences, or books. However, even though we all have limited time to learn about God from others and seek Him individually, He still desires us to express interest in getting to know Him and to actively pursue Him. Let's make sure we invest our utmost desire and effort into discovering more about Him and take pleasure in the process of uncovering who He is. It's normal to maintain an insatiable hunger for knowledge about God and a deep longing in our hearts to know Him more and more, because a genuine relationship with God is one where you can never get enough of Him. We will never attain full knowledge of God, but this reality shouldn't deter us from seeking to understand Him.

A healthy relationship never stands still; it always grows and develops, bringing even more closeness between two parties. Being content means that we like the current state of a relationship and don't desire to exert more effort in order to get rid of things that keep us from pursuing Him further. If we are honest, we will seek the root cause and a way to remove every obstacle that prevents our relationship from growing. We can pray and ask Jesus to reveal what hinders the growth and why we lack the hunger to know Him more. We won't rest until our relationship with Him becomes healthy again. We can't just assume that we're good in our relationship with God. We have to know this by having confirmation from Him.

The degree to which we enjoy God is proportional to the degree to which we know Him. So, the question is, do we have the desire to enjoy Him greater? The more we spend time with Him, the more our intimate knowledge of God increases and the closer our friendship bond becomes.

### Trust in Relationship

The Bible says, "Trust in Him at all times, you people; Pour out your heart before Him; God is a refuge for us" (Psalm 62:8), and, "Trust in the Lord with all your heart, And lean not on your own understanding" (Proverbs 3:5).

Trust is the cornerstone of any thriving relationship, requiring mutual ongoing effort to build and maintain over time. As our relationship with Jesus continues to grow, we'll feel comfortable sharing anything and everything with Him.

Before being born again, we trusted ourselves, and now we need to break that habit and start growing in our trust in Jesus. When we repented and believed in Him and His Word, we put our trust in Jesus and believed that what He said was the truth. When we face obstacles and problems, things can appear bleak and uncertain with no clear path or direction to follow. At this point, God is looking to see if we really trust Him or if we're ready to give up and use our own strength and wisdom to resolve the situation before He comes through with a breakthrough to our problem. If we feel something is off, the best response would be to talk to God about it to resolve it and find a solution from Him. Don't put it aside as something insignificant.

If you hesitate to open up to God and share your heart and what concerns you in life, then you will never have the opportunity to have real closeness and trust with Him. Building trust with God begins with getting to know Him better. We must strive for closeness and cling to Him with all our hearts. "Blessed is the man who trusts in the Lord" (Jeremiah 17:7).

We either put our trust in God or in other things, other people, or ourselves. When we doubt God, then we tend to rely on someone or something else. If we don't have God in mind when we face hardships, difficulties, and problems, we'll turn to our own logic, strength, and intellect to try and resolve the situation. When trust is placed on anything or anyone but God, it will invariably fail to live up to our trustworthiness and then our faith will collapse. God will test how faithful we are to Him and if we are going to continue to walk in trust with Him even when we face difficulties and challenges. Everyone's faith will be tested! When we're in trouble and we run to Him and receive His peace and answer to our problem, then this kind of experience of His trustworthiness will compel us to seek Him again in future difficulties.

Throughout our lives, we have learned to build defenses in order not to get hurt by others in relationships. Those defenses are actually preventing us from trusting Jesus with a childlike trust. Not trusting God reveals that we doubt His love. And if we don't trust Him fully, we can't move on with Jesus in our relationship with Him.

Isaiah recognized, "You will keep him in perfect peace, Whose mind is stayed on You, Because he trusts in You" (Isaiah 26:3). It may feel comfortable to be in control of our lives and trust ourselves, but God wants to have a chance to earn our trust by being in a relationship with us so that we can grow in trusting Him in all things. The most difficult part is making the initial decision to trust God. Once we take that step, He will reveal His trustworthiness and reliability to us. Trust may not always make logical sense. When we choose to trust God, rather than relying on our own understanding of how things should be resolved, we are taking a leap of faith. Trust, then, becomes a response of faith.

Living by logic often contradicts walking by faith, obstructing our ability to trust God. But if we persevere in placing our trust in Him, He will never let us down or put us to shame for trusting in Him. Trusting God, even when we don't understand what is happening, allows Him to prove His trustworthiness to us. God's actions in our lives will continually reinforce our trust in Him. Trust is a mindset, not a fleeting or occasional condition.

The more we know someone, the more we will trust them. Once we experience God's trustworthiness and establish trust in Him, it becomes a continuous relationship that grows stronger over time. Trust is a lifelong process. By believing God's word written in the Bible, we are called to act upon it, testing God's truthfulness and trustworthiness through our actions. Inevitably, fear and doubt will try to take away our trust in God. When we encounter a problem, do we trust in Him and run to Him for a solution; or do we first run to someone knowing they can help us? These challenges test our reliance on God. If we don't feel that God has our back and we can fully rely on Him, then we'll feel like we need to rely on ourselves in life, or rely on someone or something else. This reveals that we don't find God worthy of our trust. God wants to have our complete trust and confidence in Him. God sees our hearts and what we put our trust and security in.

If it's not in Him, we often place our trust in our job, business, savings, investments, family, friendship, abilities, wisdom, network, strength, experience, knowledge, future plans, and so forth. At times, we hesitate to allow God to interfere with our plans. By placing our trust in God, it deepens until we can completely rely on Him in any situation or circumstance. God is speaking to us, "You have tried your own way to fix the situation. Do you want to keep trying or will you finally let Me do the work?" Once we say, "God, I trust You," He will come through. God will test our trust in Him if we really believe what He says to us, even if it goes against our logic and rationality.

We would like to be in control of situations and the future, but God wants us to trust Him and live by faith. Our faith is tested when we face uncertainty. Jesus is asking, "Do you trust Me that I'm capable of helping you?" Jesus wants us to test Him and His trustworthiness to prove that He will never abandon or betray us. Take God's word for it! Give God a chance to reveal Himself to you through a personal, experiential relationship. We will learn to trust and place our dependence on God in times of need. Trust is formed when we find security in God. He will show up. As the Scripture says, "Commit your way to the Lord, Trust also in Him, And He shall bring it to pass" (Psalm 37:5).

If we feel that we can resolve some area of our lives without God's help, then that demonstrates that we rely on ourselves and don't trust God. Don't let what the circumstances reveal distract you from your focus on His promises. God is able to resolve any issue, so continue to seek Him through Bible reading and prayer. Whatever happens around you, just keep trusting God with all your effort. Worries, discouragement, fear, and anxiety come when we stop trusting Jesus.

Experiencing God upholding our trust, through resolved problems, strengthens our faith in the Lord. Jesus will never disappoint us, deceive us, abandon us, backstab us, betray us, or fail us. Jesus will always help us and encourage us. Knowing this and actually experiencing this is what makes the difference between knowing God and knowing *about* God. Knowing God comes from a personal revelation and makes us feel safe and secure. God sometimes delays answering our prayers to see how long we are willing to wait. How long will we continue to trust Him before we become anxious and seek a solution elsewhere? The relationship allows us to put our trust in God, because we have firsthand knowledge of how loving He is to us. By being sincere and hungry for God, we open ourselves to experiencing His trustworthiness and love, confirming our decision to place our trust in Him.

> *And those who know Your name will put their trust in You; For You, Lord, have not forsaken those who seek You.* (Psalm 9:10)

The more time we spend alone in fellowship with Jesus, worshiping Him, the more our trust will grow. Relationship leads to trust of giving ourselves completely to Jesus.

When we practice trusting God with childlike simplicity, it leads our minds to be completely at rest, even if we don't have answers for what to do or what tomorrow holds. He permits hardships so that we can learn to trust Him even when we can't see a way out or how to resolve the problem. Childlike simplicity and trust mean trusting God wholeheartedly without questioning His decisions. *Tested* faith becomes *strong* faith.

As we grow in intimacy with God, we become vulnerable toward God. Relationships require intimacy, which means letting the Holy Spirit into every part of our lives, even the parts where we don't let other people in, because they are too private. Intimacy and openness in a relationship builds trust, but at the same time, they make us vulnerable, and that's exactly what God desires from us.

We shouldn't be afraid of being vulnerable with God, because being vulnerable makes relationships more intimate and builds trust. He wants us to be vulnerable with Him, which shows that we're fully trusting Him to remain faithful to us and that He won't break our trust. Being honest with God means opening up and telling Him everything that bothers us; what causes us concern, worry, or stress; or what causes us joy and happiness.

## Holiness and Righteousness

To live righteously involves aligning one's life with the moral standards defined by God. It's making an effort to live in obedience to God and in accordance with what God holds to be right. "Put on the new man which was created according to God, in true righteousness and holiness" (Ephesians 4:24).

To walk in righteousness that Christ gave us, we need to prioritize God above all else in our lives and live in a relationship with Him, acting according to His will. Abiding continually in His Word produces holiness and sanctification. John explains this concept: "Sanctify them by Your truth. Your word is truth" (John 17:17). Additionally, we need a daily posture of repentance to approach a holy God. This humility allows us to recognize our shortcomings and receive His perfect grace. Through this ongoing repentance, we can grow closer to God and experience the joy of His forgiveness. Paul wrote, "Therefore, having these promises, beloved, let us cleanse ourselves from all filthiness of the flesh and spirit, perfecting holiness in the fear of God" (2 Corinthians 7:1).

Holiness is a means by which we can approach a loving God. God is holy, and sin is lawlessness in the eyes of God. Committed sin distances us from a holy God. We're confronted with choices every day. The choice that we make will reveal if we desire to live holy and righteous or to live in sin. If we love God, why would we make a deliberate decision to entertain sin in our lives, which will distance ourselves from Him? If we're in a relationship with Jesus, we would not want to hurt Him with our actions. When we understand that falling into sin affects our relationship with Jesus and causes Him to be upset and mourn our wrongdoing, it gives us that much more motivation to live holy lives and avoid sin. Every time we disobey God, our consciousness reminds us to get right with Him by repenting and asking for forgiveness in order to obtain a clean heart.

Our righteousness comes from Jesus, so we need to continually abide in Him in order to remain righteous. A relationship with God leads to pleasing God, which implies holiness and righteousness. Holiness means keeping away from and abstaining from wickedness, evil, and sin. God is seeking clean hands and purified hearts so He can fill the clean vessels with His presence.

We live in a world full of sinful temptations and in the midst of those who love to sin. Whether we like it or not, this has an effect on us and makes it necessary for us to have an ongoing process of sanctification. Sanctification is a continuing process where God, with our cooperation, works in our lives to remove any impurity and everything that doesn't glorify Him. Over time, He brings correction and disciplines us in a way that helps to gradually cleanse us of anything that defiles us. Through the process of sanctification, He shapes us more and more to become like His Son, Jesus Christ. God will continue to sanctify us as we allow Him to do so, refining us to the extent that we are willing, ultimately drawing us closer to Himself. He is not going to force Himself on us, because He values our free will. We must give Him permission to be continually sanctified and we must also try to live holy lives and walk in integrity before God. Part of our relationship with Jesus involves confronting the sins that prevent us from walking in holiness. If we're receptive, Jesus will gently guide us to see the things that hinder our walk in holiness.

Do you know if what you're doing is right based on God's feedback in your life? Are you sure that you have favor in God's eyes? How do you know He is pleased with you and your actions? Only by knowing Him would you know this! Ask yourself, "What does God require of me based on His Word?" Obeying Jesus is the key to living a holy life.

## Fear of God

*If then I am the Father, Where is My honor? And if I am a Master, Where is My reverence? Says the Lord of hosts.* (Malachi 1:6)

Solomon, the man of great wisdom, summarized life with God, saying, "Fear God and keep His commandments, for this is man's all. For God will bring every work into judgment, Including every secret thing, whether good or evil" (Ecclesiastes 12:13-14).

Fear of God is realizing that He is just and holy. It's the understanding that God is not only a loving heavenly Father but also a righteous, just judge of all the earth. Fear of God arises from the knowledge that He holds accountable those who reject Him. Fear of God is recognizing that His perfect, holy standard will determine judgment on the world for sins not repented of and not covered by the blood of Jesus on judgment day. This acknowledgment brings us to a place of reverence for His justice. A healthy fear of the Lord is not optional, but it is the starting point of wisdom and understanding (see Proverbs 9:10).

Reverence for God's sovereignty acknowledges His absolute power and dominion over all creation. This sovereignty encompasses God's supreme authority and His right to govern creation in accordance with His will.

Respect and reverence stem from the realization that our lives are in His hands, that He has the power to do anything with it, and that He can take it away at any time. Fear is the realization that God is terrifying to those who decide to resist, disobey, and reject Him all their lives until their end. The Scriptures record this powerful statement: "In truth I perceive that God shows no partiality. But in every nation whoever fears Him and works righteousness is accepted by Him" (Acts 10:34-35). Jesus said, "And do not fear those who kill the body but cannot kill the soul. But rather fear Him who is able to destroy both soul and body in hell" (Matthew 10:28).

Fear of God brings a desire to please Him and honor His name. Fear means having reverence and utmost respect for God and having a sense of awe and submission to Him. It is not being afraid of God to the point of timidity or shrinking back from Him. It's recognizing Him for who He is: His majesty, His power, His might, His wisdom, His glory. When we revere and admire God's authority as the almighty, all-powerful, and omnipotent Creator who created everything, we experience God's fear.

Fear of God leads to honoring and obeying God with our lives completely. This also shows our understanding that God knows everything that we think, say, or do. This leads us to see God as an authority over our lives, to accept His authority, and do what is right by obeying Him and His Word. Fear of God involves absolute reverence for Him as the almighty God, having great admiration of knowing how powerful He is and what He is capable of. The fear of God makes us take Him more seriously than anything else in life, including other priorities and other people's opinions.

The reverence of God leads to despising sin so that it becomes repulsive to us. The Bible says, "The fear of the Lord is to hate evil" (Proverbs 8:13), and instructs, "Do not be wise in your own eyes; fear the Lord and depart from evil" (Proverbs 3:7).

We bring God pain and sadness when He sees how much our sin affects us. Knowing that our sin is abhorrent to God instills the fear of God in us and gives us that much more motivation to strive to live righteously with His help.

Fear of God means hating sin, wickedness, and evil and keeping away from it. Walking in God's fear entails being aware of how much God despises sin and how committed sin upsets and angers Him. Fear prompts us to avoid upsetting or angering God out of respect and reverence for Him. Fear of God makes us value God's presence in our lives over anything else.

The fear of God and holiness are intertwined, because godly fear leads to avoiding wickedness and sin. Without the fear of God, we won't treat sin with all the seriousness and gravity it deserves. "Therefore, since we are receiving a kingdom which cannot be shaken, let us have grace, by which we may serve God acceptably with reverence and godly fear. For our God is a consuming fire" (Hebrews 12:28-29).

Fear of God brings an understanding of our accountability for our actions before Him. Fearing God motivates us to live in obedience to His will. This reverence for God leads us to habitually follow His commandments and compels us to live each day in a way that avoids displeasing or angering Him.

The fear of God involves obeying God without compromise. Reverence for God can serve as a gentle reminder when distractions pull us away, prompting a renewed focus on strengthening our connection with Him.

A relationship with God leads to growing in the fear of the Lord. As we grow in our relationship with Him, we will receive greater knowledge and revelation of Him and become more in awe of how magnificent He is.

## CHAPTER ELEVEN

# Unresolved and Unhealed Past

*Brethren, I do not count myself to have apprehended; but
one thing I do, forgetting those things which are behind
and reaching forward to those things which are ahead.*
(Philippians 3:13)

YOU MAY BE reading all of these principles and thinking, "This all sounds great. I want this type of relationship with God. I want intimacy with God in my future." But you have one major hurdle: *your past*. The truth is, unresolved and unhealed past hurt and negative experiences can prevent us from a connection with God's love to begin with.

While we could throw this section on the past into the "hindrances" chapter, it is such a universal struggle that it warrants its own chapter.

Truth is, we are born into a broken world due to sin, and we are all broken in one way or another. Everyone is broken differently due to being stained by the effects of sin in this world.

The consequence of brokenness through sin results in traumatic memories from the past, emotional wounds, and scars. If sin is not dealt with, then strongholds are formed in the forms of depression, anxiety, fear, pride, jealousy, anger, lust, guilt, rejection, loneliness, stress, unforgiveness, insecurities, self-hatred, toxic relationships, hopelessness, emptiness, or some other kind of hurt.

When broken people interact with one another, they intentionally or unintentionally cause pain and suffering to others by hurting them through words or deeds. They commit injustice and express a lack of love for one another or even the absence of love. When people don't get enough love and affection, they are usually unable to provide real, genuine love in the right measure and affection toward others. People might have lied to us, been mean to us, hurt us, cheated on us, hated us, mistreated us, neglected us, rejected us, abused us, backstabbed us, betrayed us, talked badly about us, taken advantage of us, made fun of us, and looked down on us. By being treated unjustly, it causes people to carry these burdens all their lives. This negative past experience is what prevents them from really opening up to Jesus to be healed to start a connection with Him. If your parents did not love you, if your siblings ignored you, if your classmates or co-workers bullied you, if your spouse was unfaithful to you, if your relatives betrayed you, if your friends rejected you—any of these and other reasons that you could come up with are still not valid reasons not to seek and find God in a relationship. How people treat us shouldn't affect how we treat God. Don't give people the power to harden your heart against God.

God desires to restore us and heal our brokenness. This is why Jesus was sent: to restore us from our broken state so that we would experience His ultimate love and, as a result, have the ability to love others around us. The restoration process begins with repentance and getting born again.

> *The Spirit of the Lord is upon Me, Because He has anointed Me To preach the gospel to the poor; He has sent Me to heal the broken hearted, to proclaim liberty to*

*the captives And recovery of sight to the blind, To set at liberty those who are oppressed.* (Luke 4:18)

Unresolved past hurt in our lives is due to the presence of sin, be it in the form of offense, bitterness, resentment, or unforgiveness towards others. Having self-condemnation, self-criticism, or blaming ourselves for what has happened in the past and believing that these hurts define us, creates a barrier to accepting God's love and keeps us distant from Him.

People who have experienced hurt by others in the past and haven't found healing still carry that brokenness inside of them and endure suffering as a result. They have inner wounds that haven't been addressed and resolved with God's help. They feel like dealing with and unraveling the past is too painful. These individuals might harbor fears, doubts, insecurities, and suspicions leading them to distrust others for fear of being hurt again. And as a result, they try to keep a distance between themselves and others. This distance prevents healthy relationships from being formed. It's the same way they treat Jesus: by being doubtful of Him, wary of His love, and hesitant of fully trusting and relying on Him.

People who have an unresolved past continue to live in their brokenness. Many who have unresolved past hurts become fixated on the pain and perceived injustice they've experienced. This focus on their pain makes it difficult to accept help, as it can require humbling oneself before God. By rejecting help, they may inadvertently reject the healing which God offers. They feel like it's their battle that they have to deal with and resolve on their own. But actually, the answer is to humble themselves and to allow God to provide a solution. Insecure, easily offended, and burdened by unresolved past hurts, these individuals choose apathy towards the pain they carry. They ignore the weight of their past and overlook the importance of breaking free from its grip. Failing to realize how important it is to deal with their past, they don't live victoriously in relationship with Christ.

Past hurts can leave us guarded and hesitant to open ourselves up to the vulnerability of new relationships. This fear of potentially being hurt again, often rooted in unresolved emotional baggage, can act as a formidable barrier which can prevent a relationship with God from ever forming. Our negative past life experiences can limit us from connecting fully with God. Our previous experiences, out of lack of love or the absence of love, hinder us from fully accepting God's love. Those who don't want to deal with the past, who don't want to allow God to resolve it, continue to carry their past along with them, which affects their present. They allow the unresolved past to control them, and as a result, they have a lack of fellowship with God. Unhealed past hurt will eat away at a person and continue to harm them if not dealt with properly with God's help. God doesn't want us to hold on to our past hurt and dwell on it. Remember that no one can hurt us beyond God's ability to heal us. We need to be willing to be free from our past.

Don't associate people's actions with God's actions. People, out of their free will, make decisions to hurt us, but this is not a reason to reject God and push Him away. Do not let the hurt caused by others to harden your heart against God. His main goal is for us to be free from the past and end up in His presence. He wants to restore us so that we will be complete in Him.

Our family members and friends can try to help us with our problems and bring us some temporary relief, but they cannot resolve all of our problems completely because they have limited abilities.

Those who haven't received healing from God for past trauma, negative experiences, or emotional pain can get stuck reliving those moments in their thoughts. This can lead to continued hurt and self-retraumatization, making it harder to open their hearts and talk about their vulnerability and emotions with God.

Don't try to fix your past with your own effort in order to approach God already restored. Come to God as you are and He will heal you and restore your past so that you can have a successful relationship with Him and bring joy into your life.

## The Blame Game

If we're continuously upset at life's circumstances, we're indirectly upset at the Lifegiver for giving us that life. People can feel anger towards God due to the mistreatment by others. This anger stems from the deep emotional wounds caused by the actions of others or events beyond their control that inflicted pain in their lives. We may experience mistreatment, abuse, betrayal, and broken trust, which can be deeply hurtful. However, these experiences don't give us a reason or an excuse to abandon seeking God and pursuing a relationship with Him. Don't give other people the power to prevent you from establishing or continuing a relationship with your heavenly Father. While it's not God's fault that people have sinned against us, their free will allows them to make choices that impact others. They will be held accountable by God unless they repent. In contrast, those who develop a relationship with God and understand His character of perfect love will not blame Him for what has happened to them in the past. Through this relationship, they will come to know that His nature is perfectly good and perfectly just. They will experience His love, kindness, mercy, and goodness firsthand, "Every good gift and every perfect gift is from above, and comes down from the Father of lights, with whom there is no variation or shadow of turning" (James 1:17).

Sometimes, we try to blame God or become consumed by anger, bitterness, or resentment over past experiences. This often happens when we struggle to understand why things haven't gone as planned. Perhaps we hold onto beliefs about God that don't reflect His true character. This not only reveals our limited knowledge of God but also raises the question of whether we truly know Him at all. We may have misconceptions about His plan, believing He is unfair or responsible for others' wrongdoings. However, clinging to these ideas distances us from God's love.

Holding onto past hurts and offenses prevents God from performing the healing process in us. Healing can't continue until we fully surrender the situation to God by choosing to forgive those who wronged us. Blaming others for causing us injustice and hurt will hinder us to find closure and move forward. When we forgive people who have wronged us, our actions declare, 'I want to walk in the freedom that Jesus acquired for me on the cross.

If we continue to express regret for committed past sins and failures and place the blame on ourselves after we have asked for forgiveness, then this means that we don't believe that God has forgiven us or that we haven't forgiven ourselves. We shouldn't compare ourselves with others. Comparing ourselves with others, especially not in our favor, leads to a defeated mindset. This mindset says, "My life is not as good as others. My path does not feel as blessed as theirs. I was given more hardships and difficulties than so and so. I don't deserve such a difficult life. Why do so many have it so much easier than me? Why did God allow these problems to be in my life? What others have done to me can't be undone and I will never be free from my past."

Having a victim mentality and feeling self-pity leads to blaming others, grumbling at life's circumstances, or acquiring a defeated mindset. This mindset says, "I'm not interested in putting effort to pursue relationship with Him, because my life didn't work out the way I wanted it to. The time is gone now, so I can't make up for it or undo what has happened. I can't rewind my life and relive those parts again to undo what has happened, but I wish I could."

While some blame God or the people around them, others wrestle with guilt, unable to forgive themselves for past mistakes. This relentless self-blame takes a heavy toll, persisting even after seeking forgiveness from God and others they've hurt. But if God forgave you, you must forgive yourself. Jesus came to set the captives free. If He sets you free from sin and you continue to blame yourself for sins of the past and carry guilt and shame, then you're not completely free from guilt. You might not feel like you deserve to be free. You might feel that forgiving yourself is a selfish way of absolving yourself of the responsibility for what you have done. You might feel like self-condemnation is a fair price to pay for your past sins, but that's not true. This is not the way to receive freedom from God.

If we have asked God for forgiveness for our past, and He forgave us and we felt His forgiveness, we need to forgive ourselves. God wants us to forgive ourselves and move on. Nothing should stand between us and our relationship with God. It's as if our debt has been completely paid off, but we still live and strive as if we have this large debt under our name. If you are free, then live in freedom. The burden of unforgiveness can weigh us down and prevent us from living a free and victorious life in Christ.

### Allow Jesus to Heal

Do not forget, "The righteous cry out, and the Lord hears, And delivers them out of all their troubles. The Lord is near to those who have a broken heart, And saves such as have a contrite spirit" (Psalm 34:17-18). Due to an unhealed past, it's not going to be easy to forgive those who wronged us and let go of the past hurt by surrendering and starting to trust God. It might not happen quickly, but it's possible with God's help if we allow God to do a work in our heart.

Unresolved past hurts might have hardened our hearts and created deep inward struggles that we're not willing to let go of or share with others. Maybe we don't share everything with others, because we feel like some things are too personal, and if we do, we will not be received well. There's fear of attempts at receiving resolution that could potentially backfire if we decide to expose ourselves and be vulnerable. We fear receiving mockery, condemnation, and judgment instead of help. But Jesus will never take advantage of our vulnerability. We should not feel ashamed to tell Jesus about our problems. It's our responsibility to let Jesus deal with our past hurts if we want them to be resolved.

If we ask Him to free us from the burden of the past, He

will do so. Jesus is really interested in restoring us. He will come through and help us with our needs, even though it might take some time for full restoration to occur. One of the reasons why Jesus desires to free us from the heaviness and burdens of the past is the fact that He wants us to live a free and victorious life, because He loves us. Another reason why Jesus wants to take away our pain and the burdens and hurt of the past is that, while we still have them, we won't have complete freedom and experience His love the way He wants us to.

God doesn't want us to dwell on regrets of our past failures and shortcomings, to live in discouragement and despair. We can be healed by God, but it involves our agreement for His intervention and our willingness to allow Him to work in us and help us to let go of our past.

God desires that our lives are free of guilt and condemnation. It takes a leap of faith to believe in Jesus enough to allow Him to set us free from our past. It all starts with humbling ourselves before God as He frees us and removes the heaviness of the past. Jesus will heal us from the past negative experiences so that our past will not influence our present no matter how difficult or horrible it was. He will continue to work on our character to restore us in a gradual process and lift us up as we walk with Him. Part of freedom from the broken past happens immediately during the born-again process and part happens through a gradual process that includes change in our unrefined character that God continually works on to restore us into the image of His Son, Jesus Christ. It might not be easy, and it will take some time for the healing process.

We won't be able to resolve the past by trying to act as if it never happened or as if it hasn't had an impact on us. Bottling it all inside and hiding it won't help us in a relationship with Jesus. The more time we spend with God, the more He will restore our brokenness and fulfill the lack of love that we might have. And from receiving His love, we in return can reciprocate love to others.

When we meditate on His Word and love being connected to Him, then He will change our character little by little, not because we ask Him but just because it's the effect of spending time with Him. We can pray, "Jesus, please heal me of all the past hurt and heal my wounds."

Instead of humbling themselves before God and admitting they need His assistance, a proud person chooses to continue to suffer the consequences of their broken past. Pride is so important to them that they would rather suffer from the consequences of the past than to humble themselves before God. A prideful individual doesn't want to acknowledge that only Jesus and a relationship with Him can resolve their issues from the past. They try to manage their pain in their own strength but without success.

Humble yourself and pray: "God, I trust You, and I surrender to You. You know who hurt me and what keeps hurting me inside. Please treat my wounds and heal them. I want to be whole by remaining in You. I want to be set free from the past and begin living a victorious life. I know that You're the only one who is capable of helping me. Every time a painful memory from my past comes to mind, I want to run to You so that it doesn't drag me back and force me to relive it."

### Pain Can Lead to Jesus

Unresolved hurt can push us to isolation or it can push us into the arms of Jesus. Unhealed wounds from the past can change how we view God and make us hesitant to connect with Him. We may mistakenly think, based on our past experiences and a lack of love from others, that God the Father is not genuinely interested in spending time with us. We place a limit in our minds on how much God can reveal Himself to us. Our understanding of God prevents us from fully reaching out to Him. There is no limit to how much we can know God through personal experience.

Difficulties reveal to us that nothing can substitute for Jesus in our lives. Our problems help us by highlighting our dependence on God. The existence of problems entices us to rely on and seek after Him. God, out of His mercy, desires to help us when we don't even deserve His help. Nobody and nothing else can help us as much as He can. Jesus is asking, "Do you want to be helped?"

God desires that we bring our problems to Him in humility and say, "I can't solve this on my own. Please help me!" We have to realize that our lives fully depend on God. Knowing this gives us peace if we're in right standing with Him through a continuous relationship.

When we encounter difficulties in life, we need to focus on Jesus. If we have tensions or misunderstandings with others, we focus on Jesus. If we're feeling down, we focus on Jesus.

God uses difficult situations in life to encourage us to reach out to Him and seek Him—to run to Him, to cling closer to Him in our relationship, and to ask Him for guidance. Explain your situation to Him so that you can receive His peace and experience His love.

God uses the negative experiences that have happened to us in the past to lead us to a solution that is hidden in Christ. God allowed us to go through the difficulties that we have encountered so that we would run to Him. If we had never gone through the agony and pain that we did, our character would have never been refined to where we are now. So don't look back and don't dwell on the past. We shouldn't have regrets about our past since it led us closer to Jesus and a relationship with Him. "Let us therefore come boldly to the throne of grace, that we may obtain mercy and find grace to help in time of need" (Hebrews 4:16).

The pain from the past can lead us to get closer to God and form a relationship with Him, or the sufferings can make us feel as if God is not just, since the situation was allowed to happen, and we can end up blaming God and getting bitter at Him.

## The Key of Forgiveness

It's quite clear: we are called to forgive. "And be kind to one another, tenderhearted, forgiving one another, even as God in Christ forgave you" (Ephesians 4:32). And, "Whenever you stand praying, if you have anything against anyone, forgive him, that your Father in heaven may also forgive you your trespasses" (Mark 11:25).

Our relationship with God can be directly impacted by the unhealed hurt we've experienced from others in the past. Built up pride prevents us from forgiving our offenders. We feel like the person who has hurt us doesn't deserve our forgiveness for what he or she has done to us. But God is waiting for us to forgive our debtors—those who have offended or hurt us in some way.

Forgiveness involves letting go of grudges, bitterness, and offense. It's not easy to forgive others for all the injustice that has been done against us, but if we keep on holding grudges against someone, it means we haven't completely forgiven them. Unforgiveness is a sin, which is why forgiving others is necessary before we can fully restore and resume our relationship with God. If we continue in unforgiveness, we will experience anger and hatred toward those who have hurt us, and this will even affect our relationship with others who haven't wronged us. Unforgiveness toward others who have hurt us correlates to God's unforgiveness toward us: "For if you forgive men their trespasses, your heavenly Father will also forgive you. But if you do not forgive men their trespasses, neither will your Father forgive your trespasses" (Matthew 6:14-15).

We, ourselves, can remember how many times we have wronged or hurt others and God didn't discipline us right away, and instead gave us time to repent. Make a decision to forgive people even if they don't deserve it. When we forgive our offenders, this doesn't mean they're automatically forgiven by God. They still need to ask God for forgiveness for hurting us, and if possible, they should ask us for forgiveness, as well. Without forgiving those who have wronged us, we won't be able to continue a healthy fellowship with Jesus as God intended it to be.

Those who have hurt us, or are currently hurting us, are actually upsetting God with their actions. And knowing this, we will have compassion toward them, because their wrongful actions await God's judgment. Understanding this and not wanting them to be punished, we would be driven to pray for God to grant them a repentant heart.

God teaches us how to love others around us by exercising love, care, mercy, compassion, and empathy toward those who don't deserve it. The most important thing that God did for us was to forgive us our sins when we repented, and He continues to sanctify us throughout our lives. We need to forgive, even if it's not easy. We can pray this prayer to God: "Please bring every situation to mind where someone hurt me and I forgot to forgive them. I forgive everyone who has ever hurt me in the past. I ask You to show me any unforgiveness that I am still holding onto. Please give me strength to forgive others."

It's important to recognize that everyone has been hurt and that some are still hurting from their past experiences. We will encounter someone who lashes out, is rude, hateful, angry, and unloving toward us, or tries to provoke us by mocking us or putting us down. Those who are rude to us, angry at us, or prideful reveal that they're still in the hurting stage and haven't dealt with their past by allowing Jesus to mend them and heal them with His love.

Because sin in their life causes them pain, it hardened their hearts, making it difficult to love God and others. Faced with a choice, they can choose to humbly surrender to God and find healing, or remain trapped in their pain.

Their actions and deeds show they may be feeling distant from God and struggling to see themselves as God sees them. That unresolved past hurt keeps them away from God, resulting in a lack of true fellowship with Him.

Jesus taught, "Therefore if you bring your gift to the altar, and there remember that your brother has something against you, leave your gift there before the altar, and go your way. First be reconciled to your brother, and then come and offer your gift" (Matthew 5:23–24).

We need to learn to forgive and ask for forgiveness of those whom we have wronged. Unforgiveness eats away at us, and therefore, it needs to be resolved before we can be completely healed from the past.

When we walk with God and experience His love, remembering His love for us helps us when we are in difficult situations with others or are attacked by them. We need to make a decision to practice love, kindness, compassion, and patience toward them. This, in turn, can be something that God can use to heal them later down the road with. We can pray for them by asking God how we can be used to help this person. We can also ask Him to soften their heart toward God and surrender to Him through humility.

God doesn't want problems from the past or present to limit our relationship with Him. He wants to help us solve our problems so we can have the best relationship possible. Don't let what has happened to you in the past be a stumbling block in your fellowship with God.

Even though God has already forgiven you, the past can try to drag you back into a defeated mindset. You can still continue to unearth skeletons that were long dead and buried. If we asked God for forgiveness and He truly granted it, we must learn to forgive ourselves and let go of the past. Then we can walk in freedom and approach God with confidence.

## Seeing People Through His Eyes

The way we view ourselves can directly affect how we interact with others. If we know God and see ourselves through His eyes, then we will treat others the way that He wants us to. Without walking in God's love, we will see others in a distorted way. If we follow Him, we won't respond to wrongdoings of others in a fleshly way.

When we walk closely with God, we will discern the actions of others, see them as He sees them, and forgive their offense instead of retaliating against them.

We need to be more concerned with their reconciliation toward God than their reconciliation with us, because their relationship with God is way more important than their relationship with us. We will see them through His eyes only if we abide in Him, and we will pray that God softens their hearts and turns them from their wicked ways toward Himself so that they can re-establish their relationship with Him. God extends great love and compassion toward our souls when He forgives us, and we can also extend love, compassion, and kindness toward others when we forgive them for offending us.

By seeing people through God's eyes, we will have compassion for those who have hurt us or have offended us in any way. If someone who doesn't know God offends us, we understand that they act sinfully because they love sin and they don't understand the consequences of their actions. Similarly, if a born-again believer offends us, we remember that they're still a child of God who hurt us due to not being vigilant at the moment and are not abiding in Him. In both situations, the love for them compels us to pray for them and forgive them. Humility is needed in our relationship with Jesus, and it's also needed to forgive others. The true meaning of forgiveness is to treat others as if they had never hurt you.

Ask God to give you the strength to forgive people right away and to surrender the situation to Him. When offense happens, we should run to Him, explain the situation, pour our heart out before Him, and receive peace from Him. We can always rely on Jesus, the One in whom we put our trust.

## Peace, Joy, and Love

Spending more time with Jesus can resolve our problems. Simply knowing the Lord and spending quality time in His presence brings peace. It's not like God is promising us a rational, logical solution to our problem in order for us to feel at ease. We have peace regardless, just because we are walking in the ways of the Lord.

At times, we try to focus on our life's circumstances and problems and how to solve them, rather than focusing on our relationship with God and how God can solve them. Many of our problems come from the fact that we don't follow Jesus as closely as He wants us to. He will take care of our needs and issues as we walk with Him through life.

Many of our problems happen because we don't spend enough time with Jesus and because we pay more attention to other things, situations, or people rather than Jesus. When we direct our attention away from Him, we are expressing that Jesus is not enough to help us and that we must go elsewhere for our answers.

Problems, challenges, and difficulties are simply meant to direct our attention to God and bring us closer to Him. God is watching over us. What decisions will we make when we face difficult situations in life? He is testing our hearts. Will we seek Him first or continue to be discouraged by the circumstances, dwelling on them and allowing the challenges that come our way to break us? When we are in pain, are we willing to die to ourselves and follow Him no matter what? Only those for whom Jesus is the closest friend and for whom He is the ultimate satisfaction will have peace, joy, and love abiding amidst these difficult circumstances. A relationship with God removes doubt regarding the problems we face and what God is doing in our lives.

Do we really love Jesus? Is Jesus our living water, bread of life, light of the world, the way, the truth, the vine, the door, the good Shepherd, the resurrection, and the life? Our actions in life during difficult times reveal the answer to these questions.

God wants us to have real, lasting peace, joy, and love and it will only be possible by abiding in Him. "These things I have spoken to you, that in Me you may have peace" (John 16:33). There will be hardships, trials, tests, and tribulations in our lives even after we are set free from past hurt. They are to test our faith and help us become more Christlike. God allows difficulties to happen in life for our own good. The pressure and heat purify us if we allow God to do His work. God doesn't want us to be miserable when He puts us through these tribulations. He wants to demolish our strongholds, continue working on our sanctification, and make us practice submitting our flesh to Him to increase our faith.

This is evidenced by the words of the apostle Peter: "In this you greatly rejoice, though now for a little while, if need be, you have been grieved by various trials, that the genuineness of your faith, being much more precious than gold that perishes, though it is tested by fire, may be found to praise, honor, and glory at the revelation of Jesus Christ" (1 Peter 1:6-7).

## God Eliminates Burdens

The Bible instructs, "Cast your burden on the Lord, And He shall sustain you; He shall never permit the righteous to be moved" (Psalm 55:22). Are you tired of relying on your own strength and abilities to hold everything together in your life? If you are not willing to give it all to Jesus and fully surrender your problems to Him, you will continue to carry them on your own.

Jesus died to carry our burdens. He went to great lengths, enduring agony and pain, in order to free us from our sins. Why are you trying to carry your burdens when you were never meant to carry them in the first place? Are you carrying feelings of abandonment, neglect, rejection, anger, anxiety, depression, or suicidal thoughts? Open yourself up to Jesus in prayer and give it all to Him. Share your heart with Him and He will free you from your addictions, your strongholds, your burdens, and your sins. He is well aware of what is going on in your life.

Many of our problems can be fixed by spending time with God and finding peace in His presence. Instead of worrying about the things that bother you, the things that you can't change or don't know how to improve, run to Jesus every time and let Him give you peace in His presence.

If you encounter any situation in life, just remember that the most important thing is to meditate on Him, keep your gaze on Him, and focus on His presence.

When issues arise, address them straight away by telling God about them in prayer. Experience His comfort and love, and pray until peace comes back. Peace comes from knowing the Lord and spending time in His presence. It's not like God is saying, "I will give you a logical solution to the problem, and then you'll have peace." We will have peace regardless, just because we are walking in the ways of the Lord.

When we take our gaze away from Him and start focusing on problems, worries, and anxiety, then fear creeps in and tries to take hold of us. Fear and anxiety magnify the problem more than it actually is and we feel powerless to do anything about it.

When we spend time with God, He guides us, uplifts us, and encourages us when we go through challenging periods in our lives. He gives us the strength we need for the day ahead and the power to get through any difficulty we may face.

When we're in relationship with God, He will guide us and reveal the things that He wants to change in us. He will change the things that we cannot change. His desire is for us to be transformed into the image of His Son, Jesus Christ, throughout our lives.

A person needs a personal encounter with God and to experience His love in fullness by becoming a child of God through a born-again process. This sets them on the path to gradually receiving healing from their past. Only this can resolve their spiritual problems and heal their past hurts. Then at this point, God can start His work in their lives by healing all their brokenness. He will show them how He sees them, eliminating and releasing them from condemnation, false self-accusations, low self-esteem, and so on.

Jesus offers freedom from oppression of evil spirits. All that is needed is our permission and desire to be set free. We usually know what we need to be free and delivered from. If you feel like the enemy attacks you and causes oppression in any area of your life, and this prevents you from living free and victorious, then find a born-again believer to pray for you. Repent and renounce any sins and addictions before God.

God is able to free us from the chains and bondage of darkness. It's necessary, as a person cannot continuously live in sin or with emotional burdens and simultaneously have a healthy relationship with God.

We can't be regularly sad, scared, or worried and have a good relationship with God at the same time. God doesn't want us to live defeated and powerless, struggling with sin and addictions. There's no way a person who is born again and has a relationship with God would fail to live an ongoing victorious life. Nor would they fail to overcome their sinful lifestyle. Something from our past can hold us back from fully perceiving God's love. Once we permit Jesus to work in our lives and our past, He will keep setting us free as long as we let Him. He wants to deliver us from our painful past so that our relationship with Him is healthy.

Jesus will not ignore our problems or fail to address them. If the person has a relationship with Jesus, they would ask Him in prayer to set them free from any burden they have, and He will.

Let's ask ourselves honestly if we have freedom in our lives from mental, emotional, and spiritual burdens. Do we have any of the following: defeated mentality, complaining, being sad about life's circumstances, having insecurities, self-hatred, hopelessness, emptiness, having low self-esteem, feeling unworthy, self-condemnation, rejection in life, self-doubt, betrayal, having a broken heart, feeling not good enough, having a lack of love, or oppression?

If we are constantly blaming ourselves or others, it's a sign that something is seriously off. It's a sign that our trust in God is off-base when we constantly deal with things like frustration, discouragement, despair, doubt, rejection, resentment, unforgiveness, anger, pain, hurt, depression, pride, guilt, hate, worries, fear, stress, and anxiety.

Those who know God will not be affected too deeply by external circumstances no matter how big those circumstances are. Since their trust is in God, He will carry them through it all. God wants us to have the completeness and fullness of Christ, and it's possible in a close relationship with Him.

We were meant to live a complete and satisfying life with Jesus in freedom. Every born-again believer who has a relationship with Jesus will have the fruit of the Spirit: "But the fruit of the Spirit is love, joy, peace, longsuffering, kindness, goodness, faithfulness, gentleness, self-control" (Galatians 5:22-23).

We can't give ourselves complete peace and rest the way Jesus can. In Matthew 11:28, Jesus said, "Come to Me, all you who labor and are heavy laden, and I will give you rest." In John's gospel, He also promised, "Peace I leave with you, My peace I give to you; not as the world gives do I give to you. Let not your heart be troubled, neither let it be afraid" (John 14:27).

If we're being honest with ourselves, then we already know if we're living in freedom or not. We're unable to live in peace if we're constantly finding ourselves depressed, having anxiety, or feeling lonely. We can't have rest if we're continuously in a worried or angry state. If we distance ourselves from Jesus by not meditating on Him throughout the day, then we distance ourselves from His rest and His peace. It's impossible to find peace without the Prince of Peace.

Jesus is the truth. When we know Him through a relationship, then He gives us freedom in any area of our life where we don't feel completely free (see John 8:32). He can set us free from any addiction or burden, big or small.

As born-again believers and followers of Jesus Christ, we will continue to experience love, joy, and peace as long as we continue in pursuing a relationship with God. Nothing will take our joy and pleasure in our relationship with Him away from us. Love, joy, and peace do not come and go and return only when we are in fellowship with Jesus. They don't go away once we finish fellowshipping with Him, but they remain with us throughout the day.

God is more interested than we are in our freedom from things that obstruct our relationship with Him. He wants to release us from our past or present bondage.

## CHAPTER TWELVE

# The Outside Influence

*Do not be deceived: "Evil company corrupts good habits."*
(1 Corinthians 15:33)

OUR RELATIONSHIP WITH God leads to not just thinking about Him throughout the day but also speaking of Him. When we speak with others, we can't help but mention God in our conversations because He is number one in our lives. When we talk to others, we should have discernment regarding the things that are being discussed. Are they truthful? Are they positive? Are they edifying?

Paul instructed, "Whatever things are true, whatever things are noble, whatever things are just, whatever things are pure, whatever things are lovely, whatever things are of good report, if there is any virtue and if there is anything praiseworthy—meditate on these things" (Philippians 4:8).

There comes a time when we have to interact with those who don't love God above all else in their lives, those who are not fully dedicated to living for God, or those who haven't experienced Him in their lives. They live by the flesh, are dictated by their fleshly desires, and are interested in worldly values and topics that this world finds appealing. All fleshly desires are unsatisfying to our spiritual being and can be harmful to our spiritual life. By overly engaging in those kinds of conversations, we unintentionally steer our focus away from thinking about God and set it on worldly, fleshly things.

If someone asks you, "How are things going? What's new in your life?" what are they really asking? Are they interested in knowing about your spiritual life? Or are they only interested in knowing the details of your job, business, family, newest vacation, what you did during the week, or how you spend your weekends? The person who doesn't have a healthy relationship with God will not be interested in your spiritual life.

> *Remind them of these things, charging them before the Lord not to strive about words to no profit, to the ruin of the hearers. Be diligent to present yourself approved to God, a worker who does not need to be ashamed, rightly dividing the word of truth. But shun profane and idle babblings, for they will increase to more ungodliness.* (2 Timothy 2:14-16)

If the person doesn't have an adequate relationship with Jesus, they won't experience life with Him or the pleasure of having fellowship, so they will end up sharing with others anything and everything except God and life with Him. Since God is not their main focus, they will be only curious about the details of other people's lives, in general, and will be interested in sharing information they have heard from others. This doesn't seem sinful, but at the same time, there's nothing spiritual in those conversations. It doesn't edify, and the conversation feels empty if God is never mentioned.

Everything and everyone around us either pulls us closer in relationship with Jesus or distracts us and pushes us away from

God. If we don't recognize those who can potentially influence us negatively, then our spiritual life could be affected and cause damage to our relationship with Jesus. It's really important for us to gauge the content of our conversation in our relationships with other people for our own spiritual well-being.

Those who don't have a strong relationship with Jesus reveal it through their speech and actions. We contemplate and talk about what is interesting and important to us and what we love. Ask yourself if those in your network have your best interests in mind. Are they genuinely interested in your spiritual well-being? How do you know if they are or are not? Are the people in your life helping you to become closer to Jesus and encouraging you to seek Him more, or do they steer you away from Him and don't really care if you maintain fellowship with Him?

Ask yourself, "What topics or hobbies are my friends interested in the most? Do they have a real relationship with Jesus, and are they assisting and motivating me to grow in my relationship with God, as well? Or are they not really interested in following Jesus and, therefore, diverting my attention elsewhere?"

If they're not interested in Christ, they will be interested in something else. They will talk about what interests them and you will have to engage in those topics even if you personally are not interested in them. You will be involuntarily steered to meditate on those topics which will prevent you from meditating on God. They enjoy having non-spiritually edifying conversations about life, and when conversation about God comes up, it's usually merely superficial. When you try to ask them about their practical life with God, you don't receive feedback about their personal walk with God, like how they experience God, how they receive revelations from Him, or how they enjoy spending time in fellowship with Him. Their decision to reject the fellowship offer from Jesus means they also wouldn't want your behavior to remind them that they need to seek God. It's okay to interact with people on different topics, but when others start to influence us in a negative way, that's where the line is drawn in favor of our relationship with Jesus.

Not all those we associate with will understand us as we grow in our knowledge of Jesus. When a person professes to be a believer but doesn't live a real spiritual life and has no relationship with Jesus, which means life with Jesus is not important to them, then speaking with them about spiritual values will be burdensome and they will be bored. They will try to switch to other topics that are closer to their heart.

We can try to engage in conversation regarding God only so many times. But if the person isn't showing interest, then there's no point in pushing the truth on them if they don't want it. They do not seek a relationship with God and certainly will not understand it, because their spiritual eyes are blind and their spiritual ears are deaf, at least for now. But those who desire Jesus and pursue a relationship with God will be interested in talking about your experience with Jesus.

Even people who are closest to us might not have a close, healthy relationship with Jesus. And whether they want it or not, they will unintentionally or intentionally discourage us from walking closely with Him. Pray for wisdom on what to do to prevent being negatively influenced by others.

Ask God for discernment in how to limit your time with people so that they don't drag you into fruitless conversations. It's better for us to not surround ourselves with those whose influence can make our love for God grow cold. Why make it harder for ourselves to follow Jesus? You can try to influence others in a positive way, but if you notice that they are the ones who are influencing you in a negative way, make a decision in favor of your spiritual growth with Jesus. Anything that gets in the way of our relationship with Jesus or hinders that relationship is worth removing from our life.

If you want to grow spiritually, then seek those who walk with God, because they will encourage you to grow deeper in your relationship with Jesus. Even though we may not always choose our associates, this doesn't mean we should isolate ourselves from those who may not be in the right stance with God. In fact, these interactions can provide opportunities to discuss if they're open to accept the truth of God. We can only help them openly if they want to be helped. If they have hardened their hearts toward the truth or are pretending to be in a relationship with God, then we have to be more vigilant that they won't influence us while we lovingly intercede for their soul. We can pray that God would soften their heart to accept the truth.

We can pray for God to open the eyes of those in our circles who don't know Him or have lost their passion for Him, revealing the importance of a relationship with God.

It's one thing to be amongst unbelievers in places such as work, school, and college, where we have to interact with those who don't know God. But it's quite another to go and be in the company of those who claim to be born-again, Bible-believing followers of Jesus, who profess to love God and enjoy fellowship with Him and pretend to have an intimate relationship with Him, but whose words and actions speak otherwise. They don't show interest in talking about Him like He is their best friend and don't provide evidence that they have a healthy relationship with Him. With their behavior, they reveal that they're not seeking fellowship with God on a daily basis but prefer worldly values and what their flesh desires. They lose interest when others share their life and encounters with God, because they prefer to seek affirmation of their lifestyle through like-minded individuals.

When believers gather together and don't talk about God and life with Him, something is wrong with that picture. You feel drained and spiritually depleted when you're in the company of those who pretend to love God and have a relationship with Him but unable to engage in conversation about deep spiritual topics that are so important to you. That's because they're actually not experiencing walking with God in their lives.

Connect with those who will not distract you from seeking God, those that are seeking God themselves, and those that will motivate you to run after Him. Find someone to whom you can be accountable regarding your walk with God, those that will pray and have Bible study with you.

### The Fear of Man

We either walk before God or before people, but it can't be both. We're either pleasing God or pleasing people. "The fear of man brings a snare, but whoever trusts in the Lord shall be safe" (Proverbs 29:25). The first step toward pleasing God starts by maintaining a consistent relationship with Him. Your relationship with God gives you the assurance and feedback that your life and actions are pleasing to Him. If we dwell on Him and have fellowship with Him, nothing will disappoint us. God says, "I, even I, am He who comforts you. Who are you that you should be afraid of a man who will die, and of the son of a man who will be made like grass?" (Isaiah 51:12).

If we do not first do God's will by developing a relationship with Him, we will do our own will or the will of others. Are we walking before God or before men? If we walk before men, then we have a fear of men, but if we walk before God, we have fear of God. If we don't seek and receive validation from God, then we will seek validation and approval of man.

If we value men over God, then we function out of fear of man. Our flesh will remind us that we have a reputation, status, and position to uphold. People respect us for our reputation, so we have to meet their expectations. The flesh will remind us that we didn't invest into our reputation to just simply lose it, and our dignity is very important. We get upset when someone offends us, because we care about our self-image. We will be pressured to uphold our reputation that we have with them, even if deep inside, we want to live in freedom as God had intended for us. This makes us a slave to other people's opinions. We can always analyze ourselves: Where does my loyalty lie? Am I willing to disobey God just to please men?

People's opinions are a trap that keeps us from acting freely and being ourselves. God knows who we really are. Do we want to anger God, knowing that He will be upset if we walk before men instead of Him?

There is always pressure to fall in line with what society thinks is the norm, what's acceptable and current. Fear of man influences us to conform to people around us and be subject to the opinions, words, and actions of others. The desire to fit in and be accepted by others, to gain their approval, will prevent us from standing for the truth of God. We're constantly pressured and compelled to follow the crowd, to follow others, and to imitate them. In order to feel accepted by people who are close to us, and by society as a whole, we have the temptation to compromise on our relationship and stance with God if we want to be liked and accepted. The wrong mindset is to try to find compromise between what God says is the truth and other people's opinions on what is important in life.

When we're in a close relationship with God, we'll live for His approval and not anyone else's. First and foremost, we are accountable to God for our own decisions. Don't live as if your life depends on the opinions of people around you. Live your life like it depends on God's opinion of you, because it does.

We can only see our true condition as God sees it by being in a relationship with Him. Without a relationship with Jesus, we measure ourselves by our own or other people's criteria. The reason why we seek approval and act a certain way around people is because we don't have an adequate relationship with Him and we don't know God like we should.

Do you value more what God says about you or what people say about you? Are you subject to doubt, fear, worry, or influence from people, or are you subject to obedience to God? Submit to God, not to your flesh, feelings, or the reality around you. There's a need to jump through so many hoops just to accommodate people and their standards.

If we value people over God, we will try hard to get acknowledgement, reassurance, recognition, and approval from others. Fear of man leads to compromises on the truth and living and acting contrary to God's ways just to be like others around us. Accommodating people leads to avoiding offending them and pointing out the truth regarding their sinful lifestyle.

A relationship with God, the feeling of His presence, and the knowledge of His approval empower us to overcome the fear of man's evaluation. The fear of God is encased in obedience to Him. The more we grow in our trust in God, the less we'll care about men's opinion when it contradicts the will of God. If we ask God in prayer, He will remove our fear of men, but it may take some time until we learn to fully walk before God.

When we are confident in our relationship with God, we don't have to worry about what other people think of us. We know Him intimately and experience His love, knowing we can trust Him no matter what happens, because we are devoted to Him.

Fear of man makes us measure success by what people consider to be successful. They measure others by their job, business, house, car, clothing, restaurants, vacations, etc. In contrast, this is different from how God measures success. His measurement is our relationship with Him, our holiness, righteousness, fear of God, love of God, humility, servanthood, generosity, and so on. It is very tempting to live for the approval of men, especially if we have gotten used to doing it for so long.

We need to ask ourselves if we're free from others' opinions about ourselves. Because if we're not, then this hinders our relationship with Jesus. We would question what Jesus would tell us, by thinking, "How would people react to this? How will they perceive this action?" If we're not anchored in Christ, then we will be trying to please others at the expense of obeying Jesus.

Don't focus on how people perceive you if you're in the right stance with God. If God approves of your actions and you treat people with love, then don't worry and don't overthink how people evaluate you and your actions. We need to get to the point where we don't care what people will think, because we care about what God thinks. It's way more important to uphold your reputation with God than with people. Don't let people's opinion of you entice you to disobey God. Don't let people stand between you and your relationship with God.

We might have lived pleasing others for so long that it becomes difficult for us to break out of that state, but with the help of God it is possible. Fear of man usually doesn't disappear overnight. It's a gradual process where God works in us to remove the fear, piece by piece.

### Changed View of Others

John wrote, "If someone says, 'I love God,' and hates his brother, he is a liar; for he who does not love his brother whom he has seen, how can he love God whom he has not seen?" (1 John 4:20). In truth, we can't have a real, normal relationship with Jesus and a bad relationship with the people around us. A relationship with Jesus will permeate every aspect of our lives, including all the other relationships we have with others.

Our relationship with God determines the way we interact with those around us. It gives us a new lens by which we see people. The closer individuals get to God, the closer they become to each other. If a person made a decision not to pursue God's love or be in a real relationship with God, then they're unable to express God's love toward others. They can't see others as God sees them. Through our own personal experience of God, the perception of His love changes the way we look at Him, ourselves, other people, and life itself. The more time we spend in fellowship with God, the more we continue to understand and experience His love, and as a result, our received love will be expressed to others.

The heart of servitude is not based on another person's performance or because they have done something worthy of service. It's done out of love and because it's the right thing to do before God. When we walk with Jesus, we will take on God's traits, which will show through as love, care, compassion, patience, long-suffering, graciousness, gentleness, forgiveness, mercy, humility, kindness, and generosity.

# CHAPTER THIRTEEN

# Evangelizing

*How then shall they call on Him in whom they have not believed? And how shall they believe in Him of whom they have not heard? And how shall they hear without a preacher?*
(Romans 10:14)

IF WE'RE IN any kind of a relationship, we talk about it with others. It's only natural to do so. What is the reason that you would be ashamed to share about any of your relationships that you have? If we're not sharing about Jesus with others, then we need to ask ourselves why we feel ashamed about sharing Him? Why are we ashamed to present Jesus, who loves us more than anyone, who died on the cross for us, and who changed our life? If our relationship with Jesus is the most important one to us, why wouldn't we share it with others? Wouldn't you want people to also have the same life-changing experience through an ongoing relationship with God as you do now?

There's a tendency to think that everything that has to do with God in our life is considered too personal and is not meant to be shared or discussed much since it's a sensitive subject; that faith should be personal and kept confidential in life, not to be shared with others because everyone has their own beliefs. But if you have the truth, why would you hide it from others, not telling them that they can have a relationship with God just like you do? Is there something shameful about it? If you love others, why wouldn't you want the best for them, which is to know God?

Is it because it is not encouraged by others to express one's personal relationship with God? We could have the attitude that says, "My spiritual life is too personal. I don't need to share it with others. Only if people ask about my walk with God, then I will share." This type of mindset is not based on biblical teachings. Your spiritual life is a light that needs to be presented to this world so that others can find Jesus, too. Are we that afraid of not being accepted by others or to be offended by the potential reaction of those with whom we need to share God? Or are we afraid to offend others with the truth of God? If we have a relationship with Jesus, then we'll have confidence to talk about Him with others. If we don't have an ongoing devoted personal relationship with God, it will be easy for us to compromise by not sharing Jesus with them. If my spiritual life is not important to me, why would I be interested in talking about it with others? But if it's most important, why would I hide it?

We can be so much more concerned about the well-being of our relationship with others that we decide to withhold the truth from them. We would rather enjoy our relationship with them then give them a chance to get closer to God. We might even think how this will impact *us* if we tell them about God and share the gospel with them. What will they think of me if I share how God changed my life and how I experience life with God? They might distance themselves from me, and I don't want the possibility of ruining my relationship with them, never mind that their relationship with God is non-existent or ruined at the moment.

Jesus warned, "But whoever denies Me before men, him I will also deny before My Father who is in heaven" (Matthew 10:33). By being ashamed of Jesus in front of others, we're willing to compromise on what's most important in our lives. We don't want our family, friends, classmates, co-workers, neighbors to look down on us, humiliate us, or turn their backs on us. If we don't have real conviction of what we believe through a personal relationship with Jesus, of course we'll be timid and hesitant to talk about Him with others around us. What can we offer to them if we haven't been transformed by experiencing Jesus in our life? Nothing more than dead religious words devoid of practical, life-giving power. Do you really have convictions about what you believe? If yes, then turn your belief into action.

If you're not in a real, continuous relationship with God, you won't be able to share the heart of God with others. We get strong convictions, unshakeable faith, and overwhelming desire to share the gospel because of our relationship with God. If we know God, we would talk and share about Him and our encounters with Him with others. We wouldn't be able to contain the joy and excitement of knowing Him and how He works in our lives, leading and guiding us in different circumstances. We wouldn't be able to hide our life experience of living and walking with God from others. It wouldn't be burdensome for us to reveal our relationship with Him to others. If we live for Him, we will talk about Him. The more we know God, the deeper our desire to share Him with others becomes. One indicator that we know God is that we talk with others about our life with Him. Why would you be shy, intimidated, or afraid to talk about the God who is the most valuable person in your life?

Real love for others is revealed by sharing the truth with them that can save them from the wrath of God. Share with others how you know God and how you have experienced God in your life. When we're satisfied with God, then we will tell others how they also can enjoy God and a relationship with Him. No one needs to motivate us to tell others about Him. It will become natural.

When we set our priorities straight and start living for God, we will see incredible things happen in our lives. When we live for God, people notice, and they are attracted to the Jesus that they see in us. When people see Jesus in us, they want what we have. If you love reading God's Word, you will love sharing God's Word with others around you. Of course we need to have discernment and wisdom when and how to share the gospel especially in the workplace. The truth is, as we live for Jesus, we start to look like Jesus. In that place, we are able to represent Him to the world around us. The lost world is not looking for a dead religion to grab onto. They are looking for a fresh, life-giving exchange where they can know God, be known by God, and make Him known to the world around them. Don't run from this mandate; run to it.

### Representing Jesus

Our relationship with Jesus will influence the decisions that we make. We can truly *represent* Jesus if we have a relationship with Him. The way we talk about Jesus, how much we love Him, how much we value Him as our best friend, how much we enjoy His presence, how He speaks to us, and the revelations we receive from Him all reflect the experience we have in fellowship with Christ. Our relationship with God reveals itself through our testimony and how we talk about His amazing attributes, character, and revelations in such a way that others will be interested in knowing Him in the same way. People want to see those who live their lives with Jesus rather than just talk about it.

Our lives speak of Him without words. Our transformed life is a testimony to His presence in it. When we have a relationship with Jesus, we don't always need to tell others about it for them to see it. The fruit of our lives will reveal to others that we have a relationship with Him, instead of us telling them. Prove with your actions that you walk closely with Jesus, that you obey Him, and that He is your best friend. It's far easier to exaggerate the quality of the relationship we have with Jesus than to actually cultivate that quality of relationship with Him. Actions speak louder than words. Our changed character, our renewed mind, and our walk in the Spirit will speak louder than our words can ever say regarding our relationship with God.

Serving others can include introducing them to Jesus, witnessing their freedom from sin, addictions, and emotional burdens, and witness their new life in Christ.

Rather than being concerned about offending someone, we need to be more concerned about not hiding the truth that could set them free. The most important thing in life is whether or not one walks with God and has a genuine relationship with Him.

We can often get so caught up in trying to help others with the problems and issues they face that we can easily overlook the main root of the problem, which lies in God's absence or a poor relationship with Him. We should address the real problem at its source, which is the inadequate condition of their relationship with God. Once their relationship gets restored, other problems will get resolved, as well. The fruit of an inadequate relationship are expressed in pride, disobedience, selfish ambitions, and so forth.

CHAPTER FOURTEEN

# Relationship vs. Religion

*These people honor me with their lips, but their hearts are far from me.* (Mark 7:6)

NOTE THIS DAUNTING warning from Jesus: "Not everyone who says to Me, 'Lord, Lord,' shall enter the kingdom of heaven, but he who does the will of My Father in heaven. Many will say to Me in that day, 'Lord, Lord, have we not prophesied in Your name, cast out demons in Your name, and done many wonders in Your name?' And then I will declare to them, 'I never knew you; depart from Me, you who practice lawlessness!'" (Matthew 7:21-23). The truth is, God didn't create you to go to a church building for two hours each Sunday and live the rest of the week however you feel like. God wants a relationship with you seven days a week, not just two hours a week. What is often called "church" is just a building where believers gather. Each individual disciple of Jesus is actually the temple of God.

Quoting the Old Testament, Paul reminded the Corinthians, "For you are the temple of the living God. As God has said: 'I will dwell in them and walk among them. I will be their God, And they shall be My people'" (2 Corinthians 6:16).

Christianity is not just a religion; it is a lifestyle with Jesus. Jesus said, "Come and follow Me"—not a religion. Rather than performing a set of rules and obligations for Him, God desires companionship with us, for us to know Him intimately. Jesus draws people to Himself, but religion pushes people away. Man-made traditions try to complicate the truth.

We should follow the path of Jesus and not simply follow the crowd. Jesus emphasized the importance of having a personal relationship with God rather than adhering to mere religious practices, as He was against empty religious formalities.

We can either trust God above all else or place our trust in a denomination, religion, or people. If we trust someone more than God, we will follow their words instead of obeying God's commands. This is a severe issue. "Cursed *is* the man who trusts in man" (Jeremiah 17:5).

The idea of knowing religion but not knowing God has been around for a long, long time. Jesus called it out in His day, saying, "These people draw near to Me with their mouth, and honor Me with their lips, but their heart is far from Me. And in vain they worship Me, teaching as doctrines the commandments of men" (Matthew 15:8-9).

God doesn't care about our religion; He cares about our relationship with Him. We will not find God in religion, but we will find Him through a personal relationship. It has to be sought out and searched for individually. A relationship with God can begin in the church when a person gets born again, but it must be maintained in the secret room. The church can be a place where a relationship with God is formed, but the church will not maintain your relationship with Jesus for you. Yes, sermons and teachings can be beneficial to your relationship with God, but actual relationship has to be maintained alone with God in your praying closet.

The relationship with Jesus is not limited to just a Sunday morning church service. Church time shouldn't substitute for our personal time with Jesus. Don't rely on the church for your personal relationship with God. A relationship is a personal bond between two individuals. Don't rely on the church to supply all your spiritual needs. We must have a close relationship with God and sustain our spiritual life by abiding in Him. The church of Christ is not a building. The building can serve as a meeting place for born-again believers. The gathering of the saints, who are the church of Christ, can occur at any place. The most important thing is to have God's presence where believers gather. Without God's presence, it becomes a formal religious experience.

Where the spirit of the Lord is, there is freedom, including freedom from religiosity. We are connected spiritually with God if we are in God, not through associating with a certain denomination. The main thing is getting born again, and that happens when one gets adopted into the family of God.

It's a challenge not to complicate the simplicity of truth. Sometimes we become too smart for our own good. Our experience and knowledge can become a stumbling block that keeps us from having that childlike simplicity that makes it possible to have a relationship with God.

## The Dead Religion

*Woe to you, scribes and Pharisees, hypocrites! For you are like whitewashed tombs which indeed appear beautiful outwardly, but inside are full of dead men's bones and all uncleanness.* (Matthew 23:27)

Our spirit wants to connect with God in the relationship that it was designed to have. Our spirit is always looking for a way to know God more and be closer to Him, to know God's truth, not just man-made traditions about God that people have made up. We long for a real relationship with the Creator of the universe.

Unfortunately the presence of God is often suppressed in a religious setting.

People seek God and a relationship with Him, expecting to find Him in church buildings. Drawn to the promise of life with Jesus and its transformative power, many find Jesus and experience born-again process. However, some may encounter a greater focus on rituals and traditions than they anticipated. They desire a life with a living God through a relationship rather than simply playing Christianity. Their expectations are that every church member is a born-again, Bible-believing follower of Jesus, but instead they encounter religious practices, sets of rules, and religious conduct and behavior. They meet church attendees who are not born again and witness ungodly behavior from them. Seeing all of this, they become disappointed due to lack of misrepresentation of Jesus by the church goers.

Some people experienced emotional pain due to the mistreatment they endured from others within the church. They became discouraged with the church system and with God because people misrepresented Him with their lives and behaviors. They weren't taught or explained the biblical truth of getting born again in order to start a relationship with Him. Some became disappointed, got offended, and left the church, while others remained in the church and joined the behavior of lukewarm Christians and settled to be just like them while having no relationship with God. They remain offended while continuing to go to church. Deep down inside, they have wounds caused by others which only Jesus can heal, if they let Him.

Religion by itself is dead, but a relationship with Jesus gives us life. Religion is rule-based: do this, don't do that. But God created us for the main purpose of having a relationship with Him, not to follow a set of instructions or to perform a set of rules with dos and don'ts. Religious experience leads to a program with participants who go through the motions of formalities to please the attendees of the church with engaging content. The experience of a relationship with God is totally different from the experience of man-made traditions.

Man-made requirements and regulations make it harder to follow Jesus, because we have to accommodate the rules and guidelines that the leadership of the church puts in place in addition to God's Word. People try to limit God by introducing man-made traditions that everyone should follow as opposed to being guided by the Holy Spirit. Don't follow a religion; follow Jesus.

People will let you down, but Jesus will never betray you! Without a continuous relationship, one can go through the motions and do everything that a typical Christian does but still fail at pleasing God.

We can't put our full trust in the church as our primary source of nourishment for our personal relationship with God. Unfortunately, many churches are led by made-up programs that restrict the power and drown out the activity of the Holy Spirit, which prevent Him from moving. The Holy Spirit is waiting for freedom of movement to allow Him to act.

People sometimes believe frequent church attendance, participation in programs, and involvement in ministries indicate a genuine relationship with God. However, simply fulfilling man-made traditions doesn't guarantee a good standing with Jesus. God does not want you to simply follow a set of rules and laws to please Him. He doesn't want us to seek Him out of obligation. He wants us to seek Him out of love, affection, and a desire for Him. Without a personal relationship, attending church becomes a stale and tedious tradition.

We will get disappointed with religion, but Jesus will never disappoint us, so don't reject Jesus based on your failed religious experience in the church system.

Religion tries to make people look as if they are holy and righteous, having an outward appearance of godliness. Religion forces people to focus most of their attention on the outward appearance, which makes people care more about how they look on the outside rather than how their inward spiritual life and relationship with Jesus is. Some people influenced by religion believe their good relationships with others translate to a good standing with God. Often misconception is to prioritize the approval of others over what truly matters: God's perspective.

Religious tradition causes one to be concerned with what others may say or think of them and how they will be accepted, while disregarding God's approval. We often forget that God looks at the heart, not at the outward appearance. In a relationship, the person strives to please God and does not prioritize the opinions of others over God's. We either conform to man-made traditions or to God's truth: "having a form of godliness but denying its power. And from such people turn away" (2 Timothy 3:5).

## Man-made Traditions Harm Relationship

Many people in church have grown accustomed to the traditions of a church service and may be unaware that they became complacent in their walk with God because it happened so gradually. Religious atmosphere makes it easy to become comfortable and stay on the same level, imitating others instead of growing in relationship with Jesus.

By attending and participating in the church service, it's easy to feel like we're pleasing God without the need to interact with the Holy Spirit on a daily basis. If we accept what is being taught from the pulpit without having personal discernment from God, we run the risk of compromising the truth of God's Word. Some value their denomination or local church higher than God's Word, and they interpret God's Word through the prism of the teachings of the denomination or church. As a result, they interpret God's truth in a distorted way. Once you have a relationship with Jesus, you will be able to discern the truth from deception when it's being preached in the church.

Remember the words of Jesus: "If you abide in My word, you are My disciples indeed. And you shall know the truth, and the truth shall make you free" (John 8:31-32). It's difficult to realize that when you spend time with religious people, you can unwittingly begin to accept men's traditions as the truth.

Some blindly trust everything that is said in the church without any discernment, because they don't walk closely with God. It is difficult for someone who has been taught their entire life that something is biblically correct, when in fact, it was just misinterpreted from the Word of God. In the absence of direct revelation from God, they have no way of knowing if what they are being taught is true. Without a relationship with God, anything a pastor, preacher, or teacher says is accepted as biblical truth.

It's so important to be vigilant about what is being preached so that deception doesn't creep in and cause damage to our spiritual life and our walk with Jesus. We need to have confidence in our standing with God and have firm, unwavering faith in our relationship with Him.

Man-made traditions try to provide tangible good works that can be observed, measured, and compared, as if those good works can offset the lack of a personal relationship with Jesus. We can mistakenly focus on external things like appearance and good works to compensate for a weak relationship with Jesus, judging others who don't meet our standards. By having our own standard and comparing our spiritual lives with others, we get a false sense of how God sees us. Everyone needs to have a unique, individual relationship with Jesus. Don't measure yourself against others.

Are we witnessing God's truth being preached or is it watered-down truth mixed in with man's interpretation of God's Word? Religious filters and prejudice distort our view of God, hindering a personal relationship with Him.

Religious structure is performance-based and focuses on Christian duties, functions, obligations, and behaviors based on church statues. Influence of man-made traditions includes legalism, which is strict obedience and compliance with church law and commandments. It also has a strong emphasis on good works and righteous deeds, while ignoring the importance of a personal relationship with Jesus. Religion uses man-made efforts, which are implemented in order to try to please God. It has a tendency to twist Scripture to suit its own agenda. Religion is walking before men. A relationship is walking before God. Do we follow a certain denomination or do we follow Jesus? It's important to ask ourselves if the local church that we attend helps us in our walk with Jesus.

If we fall for the influence of religious traditions, then we're deceived and look at the truth through our religious glasses. We may tend to view God solely through the lens of how preachers present Him in sermons, limiting our ability to discern His true nature and restrict our understanding of God. God wants to take away those filters of knowing about Him because He wants to reveal to us who He really is. Those filters prevent us from knowing Him personally.

If we base our relationship with Jesus on a Sunday morning experience in church, then there's something wrong with our relationship. Some people who attend church regularly might find comfort in the traditions and formalities of the service. They go through the motions and are quite content of playing Christianity. They're faking being a Christian and just play a role as an actor who attends church and pretends to walk with God.

Even if you have experienced hurt from religious traditions or religious churchgoers, remember that God is not a religion or what people perceive Him to be.

## Lost Churchgoers

As we've discussed from the start of the book, we have a God-shaped void that only God can fill. Many were invited to join church but haven't been shown the steps to repentance and being born again in order to get right with God. After a while, some of them left the church, yearning for a personal relationship with Jesus rather than just following a religious system. A religious system cannot fill the God-shaped emptiness that only God can.

Those who put their faith in others will often fall away after being offended. When believers in church struggle with sin, their consciousness prompts them to repent and get right with God. They notice that others who sin in church don't desire to be free from their own sin and end up ignoring it in their own lives. They live as if everything is fine and there's no need for repentance. When those searching for help observe this, their expectations get shattered, and they often lose their faith. They become disappointed and discouraged, which can lead them to become upset at God, as if it's God's fault that someone misled them and broke their trust. Some reject Jesus based on bad experiences with religious people. Since they weren't fully grounded in God, there's a risk for them to get offended and fall away.

It's natural to want to see real-life examples of those who can show us what a relationship with Jesus looks like. We want to see those who accurately represent Jesus so we can imitate their walk with Him. While this can be good, God's ultimate desire is that we believe and trust Him in our relationship. He Himself wants to be our role model and an example that we can follow. Put your full trust in Christ and follow Him, not people.

We have to realize that just because someone attends church doesn't mean they're born-again, Bible-believing follower of Jesus who has relationship with God and is interested in maintaining and growing that relationship. Just because some talk about having a relationship with God, doesn't mean they necessarily have one. Having an external imitation of godliness and piety can hide the internal condition of wickedness.

What is my experience when I attend church? Is the truth being preached in the church I'm attending? Do I receive spiritual nourishment through church service and ministry? Does the church put emphasis on explaining the biblically born-again process, how to get born again? Does the church focus on teaching about the practical relationship with Jesus? Pray to Jesus and ask Him regarding what is being preached and taught from the pulpit to show you what is man's interpretation of the truth and what is the actual biblical truth.

Do you come to enjoy hearing a nice teaching and worship with others, or do you really connect and enjoy God's presence just like you do at home in your alone time with God? The difference between being called a child of God and actually being a child of God is having a relationship with Him.

Those who don't have a relationship with God and don't desire to reconcile with Him will not completely benefit from attending church. Of course, there is always the possibility that during the service, God will encounter them and the Holy Spirit will touch their hearts, leading them to repentance and reconciliation with Him. Sermons in the church primarily benefit those who seek God at home, those who love reading His Word, and those who spend time alone in fellowship with Him. They will get revelations from God's Word, and they will put into practice what they heard. They will enjoy God's presence in church just as they do at home. It also helps those who feel the need to establish a relationship with God or re-establish a once healthy relationship with God.

If the person doesn't read and obey what God commands in the Bible in their home, then there's little chance that they will put to practice the Word of God that they hear from the pulpit on Sundays.

The most important thing is walking with God and meditating on Him and His Word from Monday to Sunday. Then attending church will benefit that person, because God will provide a revelation from the sermon and they will dwell on it and apply it as they already have been doing throughout the week.

There are believers in the church who have a relationship with Jesus, but sadly it's lacking. Their love for God grew cold over time, which caused them to have a half-hearted devotion to Him. They're not fully committed to paying the price of following Him. They may be struggling with sin, preoccupied with the busyness of life, or have an unresolved past that they can't let go of. They think they're good with God because they also find time to pray and read the Bible, but their prayers and Bible readings are just religious formalities. It's on each individual's consciousness to get right with God and remain close to Him. When believers attend church services, if they are living in sin, if they're chasing after the world and are preoccupied by vanity or the cares of life, they are closed off to God's Word, because they live in an unrepentant state. They need to humbly come clean before God and receive forgiveness and a new start.

Not everyone who attends church is in the body of Christ. Attending church does not automatically result in a relationship with Jesus. There are those who used to have a relationship with God but no longer do. Maybe they got carried away and started to live for their selfish ambitions and became preoccupied with the things of the world. For some, their church ministry got in the way of their relationship with Jesus.

God is patiently waiting on those who resist Him to turn back to Him. God, out of His mercy, takes time to reveal Himself to those who are in bondage of sin, because He wants them to be free and to know Him personally for who He is.

God desires our full commitment. There are those in the church who have a heavy burden in their lives and want to receive freedom and get close to God. They are stuck and can't find a way out of their problems. They need someone to help them receive freedom through Christ in order to reconcile their relationship with Him.

A number of churchgoers find meaning and purpose in following the established traditions, church rules and regulations rather than the Word of God and the voice of the Holy Spirit. They claim to be Christ followers, but with their actions, they demonstrate that they do not have a relationship with God and do not obey Him. These church goers are confident that they have a relationship with Jesus, because they jump through all the religious hoops that man-made traditions have established in their church setting.

Church culture can hinder our relationship with Jesus, because it compels us to adhere to people's standards of what's considered a normal Christian life according to the criteria chosen by the majority in the church. Those who care more about accommodating to religious practices instead of focusing to please Jesus with their lives, become trapped in a religious traditions which hurt them through this self-deception. They're not fully walking in the truth, which they think they are. If we don't have a personal relationship with God, we can simply claim to follow Jesus the way we're taught in the church.

Do believers in the church typically support each other's spiritual well-being? Have you been asked, "How is your relationship with God? Do you have any struggles in your spiritual life? Is there anything you need prayer for? Would you like to meet up for coffee and talk things over? Would you like to have a Bible study together? In what way can I help you continue to grow spiritually?" Just maybe this doesn't happen as often as it *should*. But the Bible encourages us as members of the body of Christ to take care of one another's needs.

Isn't our spiritual life more important than our physical life? Those who prioritize their own spiritual life and walk with God will also care for our spiritual well-being. However, if someone doesn't walk right with God, why would they care about our walk with Him? Their focus may naturally center around various aspects of our lives, including family, work, business, hobbies, and plans.

The first and foremost reason why we gather with the church is to worship and praise God, receive revelation from Him, and then to spiritually edify, encourage, and uplift one another. We come together to give and receive spiritual nourishment through fellowship with fellow believers.

What motivates us to attend church? There are many reasons why people attend church. If a believer has the mindset of "I have to go to church because that is what believers do on Sunday" or "it has become a part of my Sunday routine and I've gotten used to going to church on Sundays" or "I want to see my friends and family to catch up with them," then those are wrong reasons. The right motive should be, "I want to encounter God's presence, receive revelation from God through others, and worship Him with the body of Christ."

When we come to church on Sunday morning, God knows how we lived the previous week. People might know us partially, but God knows our character, our thoughts, our words, and our deeds. He doesn't want us to play an actor in the church environment while living a double life away from the public view. Having a relationship with God makes us aware that He sees us all the time and that will prompt us to walk before Him instead of walking before others.

God will keep calling and drawing us back to a loving relationship with Him, to our first love for Him. There are those in the church who will respond to His loving call by repenting and changing their ways, while others will ignore His voice, harden their hearts, and continue to play religion on Sunday. Those who respond to His call will be liberated from dead religion and will wake up to a living relationship.

Our spiritual life and growth are our obligation. We're the ones responsible for allowing God to nourish and grow us spiritually in the right community of believers. Ask God to reveal to you where He wants you to be and show you those who have a relationship with Him. There's no perfect church, but that doesn't mean that in those churches we can't receive support in our walk with God.

If you really value your spiritual walk with God, then it's good to ask God to show you if you are in the right place for your spiritual growth. You can even pray, "Lord, show me where I need to be. Show me the church where I can grow spiritually, be edified, and get a deep revelation about You and the biblical truth. Let me find true believers who obey You and follow the truth of Your Word."

He will reveal this to you. He will lead you to a community of believers where you can grow and be nourished spiritually. The place where the biblical truth of God's Word and the divinity of Jesus Christ is being preached.

## A True Church

A church also needs to have the manifestation of the gifts of the Holy Spirit. A church that recognizes the importance of Christ-centeredness and teaches the importance of being born again. It's essential that the church explains how to be born again according to the Bible, which includes faith, repentance, water baptism, and baptism in the Holy Spirit. A church that addresses the needs of newly born-again believers on how to fully experience life with Jesus by living in holiness and righteousness in daily obedience to God's Word. A church that acknowledges the importance of personal fellowship with God and encourages individuals to seek God on their own.

The church that addresses core biblical truths such as love for God, love for others, sin, repentance, forgiveness, mercy, grace, Christ's sacrifice, salvation, redemption, God's justice, righteousness, holiness, picking up your cross and dying to self daily, abiding in Christ, following Jesus, renewing your mind, living by faith, being led by the Holy Spirit, sharing the gospel with others through outreach and evangelism, resisting the enemy, hell, judgment day, and eternity.

The goal of the church is to impact the lives of those who are in the body of Christ by meeting their spiritual needs. Of course, it doesn't mean that we put the responsibility for our spiritual growth on the believers in the congregation. The responsibility for our spiritual stance before God is ours. We have to have personal interest and seek spiritual growth in our alone time with God.

## The Four Types of Churchgoers

Most churches have four types of attendees:
- Those who are not born again and have never established a personal relationship with God.
- Those who were born again and once had a relationship with God but no longer do.
- Those who are born again and follow Jesus, but at the same time, constantly struggle in their walk with Him because they're easily given into sin.
- And then there are those who are born again, walk with God, and have a healthy personal relationship with Him. They overcome sin and sinful temptations, are filled with the Holy Spirit, and hunger for more of God in their lives.

Some churches are concerned with the question, how can we become more seeker-friendly? How do we attract more people so that they will want to attend and join the church? Where do we need to put effort to make the church more appealing and comfortable to the attendees? Instead of being focused on how we can attract more people, the question should be, how can we attract the presence of the Holy Spirit?

It's so easy to forget to give priority to God and allow the service to revolve around Him. We need to remember that if we do what pleases God, it will attract His presence and His glory, giving Him the freedom to do what He wants and touch people's hearts during the service. The wrong focus is on making church services and programs appealing and comfortable for listeners and avoiding addressing deep spiritual issues that get in the way of people's relationship with Jesus. To become more popular, a number of churches try to accommodate people's desires. They provide a fun and entertaining environment instead of addressing sin, holiness, and God's justice. They preach a light-hearted sermon that doesn't offend sinners or point out their sin. They don't reveal or go deep into explaining the fear of God or the severe consequences for loving sin by staying in it.

The result is a body of believers who experience great comfort with no change. The comfort will prevent them from seeking Jesus with all their hearts. They struggle with living a holy life and repeatedly succumb to sin, because they just went through the motions of being born again without fully comprehending the biblical significance of what becoming a born-again child of God means. They saw it as merely a symbol. Some believers may not have received a full explanation of the concept of being born again as presented in the Bible which is a transformative process of becoming a new creation, which frees one from the power and grasp of sin. Due to Jesus' victory over sin, they now acquire the strength to overcome sin.

It's important to find additional spiritual support outside the church walls. Find support from and get in contact with real, genuine believers in the church who have a relationship with Jesus and who can personally help you with your spiritual needs by checking up on you and keeping you accountable in your journey with Christ. Those who can actually help you keep a healthy relationship with Jesus during the week.

It's important to find and join a home fellowship prayer group or Bible study where we can grow spiritually and be edified amongst those who have a relationship with Jesus and who are interested in helping us continue in our walk with Him. This would be a place where believers can meet up together with other believers to pray for each other's needs, exchange revelations given by God, worship together, and encourage one another to continue walking with Christ. A place where you can edify one another and have Bible studies. It's important not to become isolated. Find someone who can assist you in your spiritual journey with God.

### Ministry Doesn't Define Relationship

Success in ministry does not automatically mean success in relationship with God. History shows plenty of examples of ministers of God who were diligently walking with the Lord and had a real relationship with Him, which led them to have success in ministry. Their relationship with God was obvious and seen through His presence in their ministry, and they received recognition from people. Their ministry grew in popularity, and so did the demand for them to devote their time to it. In this way, they had to compromise their fellowship time in favor of their ministry. This led them to lose the guidance of God in their lives while they still continued with their ministry in their own experience and effort. Their ministry fell apart, or they fell into sin and became exposed. Their success became their downfall. They could never have thought that their successful ministry, which raised them up in the public eye, would overcome them and become a temptation to reduce time spent with the Lord and grow distant toward Him.

This could happen to anyone if we're not careful and mindful of the importance of upholding our love and fellowship with God. It's important to ask God to reveal anything hindering our relationship with Him or starting to slowly pull us away from Him. We must strive to keep our eyes on God and never take our fellowship with Him for granted, no matter what heights we reach in ministry. Ministry achievements do not guarantee a healthy relationship with God.

Our spiritual walk is more important than our ministry! A relationship can survive without a ministry, but a ministry can't survive without a relationship. For God, having close fellowship with us is more important than what we can offer Him.

If we're not careful, then our ministry can actually become detrimental to our spiritual walk with God. If we have time for ministry during the day but have no time to spend with God, then our ministry becomes our idol. Ministry has the potential to distract us and lead us away from a relationship with God, but a relationship with God will always lead to ministry.

When we walk according to God's commandments and have a loving relationship with Him, He will show what ministry we need to be involved in, and He will bless the ministry, because He is the one who directed us to start that ministry. We have to remember that the purpose of our ministry is to glorify His name only. The ministry accomplishes His will and not ours. The success of the ministry can lead to recognition, popularity, influence, power, and money, and any of these can put us in a position to be tempted to focus on them and distance ourselves away from a relationship with Jesus. The success of a growing ministry necessitates investing more and more time in its upkeep, which increases the risk of becoming so preoccupied that we could neglect our relationship with Him. It's understandable that a thriving ministry often requires dedicated effort. However, it's important to prioritize personal fellowship with God alongside the ministry's needs to avoid overlooking our connection with God. Our minds can be preoccupied so much with ministry that we talk more about it with others than about God and our experience with Him.

Everything, including ministry, that keeps us from praying and reading the Bible regularly needs to be taken out of our lives. God will never tell us to do something at the cost of our fellowship time with Him.

### Compensating

Some prioritize ministry over intimacy in their response to Jesus' call to fellowship. Their unspoken belief might be that serving in ministry also helps their relationship with God, but this actually masks a deeper yearning for selfish ambition through external validation. In this, we fall into the trap of thinking that what we do *for* God pleases Him more than spending time *with* Him. Without Jesus guiding us, we may end up choosing a ministry based on our own skills and preferences, rather than seeking what He wants us to do. Do you think God will be pleased with our serving in the ministry in this way? A relationship with Jesus leads to a God-ordained ministry.

Without a strong foundation in their relationship with God, some may seek fulfillment through extensive involvement in church ministries. This can sometimes create an impression of closeness to God based on activity rather than genuine connection. This kind of ministry will not be pleasing to God. If we only focus solely on their ministry we can get false impression regarding their stance with God. They're more concerned about their status and reputation in the eyes of men than in the eyes of God. Sometimes ministry is the driving force to compensate for the lack of their fellowship with God.

These believers ignore His voice and continue to walk before men while being involved in ministry. They promote themselves to gain more popularity and seek the approval of men rather than seeking God's. They have no interest in working on and maintaining their relationship with Jesus, because they have grown lukewarm toward Him and have lost their first love. They desire to have a platform in order to be seen and have influence over others instead of walking in obedience and humility before God and allowing the Holy Spirit to do His work through them in the ministry. God continues to remind them, through their consciousness, to repent and get right with Him and walk before Him; to re-establish a real, loving relationship with Him; and to value time with Him over their ministry.

Even the success of a God-ordained ministry can make us become prideful and have it become all about us. Ministry is not about us; it's not supposed to be self-promotion, but its purpose is to represent God. If the ministry does become about us, then it has become our idol. Are you willing to lay down your ministry if God says so in order to do something else for Him? Would you be saddened if He redirected you to another ministry? God is testing you if your heart got attached to the ministry more than to God, who initially gave you that ministry. Is the ministry taking center stage in your life while God has moved to the sidelines?

When we spend time with God, our main goal can be to get

words and revelations from God so that we can then share them with others. We might not be as interested in receiving personal revelations from God for our own lives as we are in receiving them for others so that we can get recognition for our ministry. This is not the purpose of fellowship that God has intended for us to have. Our main focus in our alone time with God is just to be in His presence solely for Him. The ministry can't keep going and be deemed successful without a genuine personal relationship based on real love for Jesus.

> *Every branch in Me that does not bear fruit He takes away; and every branch that bears fruit He prunes, that it may bear more fruit.* (John 15:2)

The vine sustains the branch's life by providing the branch with its sap as a life source. The sap from the vine enables the branch not only to maintain life but also to produce fruit. A branch's life is way more important than its ability to produce fruit. The nutrients that the branch receives from the vine are far more important than the fruit that it bears. Fruit is just a by-product of receiving nutrients.

A branch can survive without fruit, but it can't survive without the sap from the vine. A branch can't produce fruit unless it receives nutrients from the vine. The branch that doesn't bear fruit doesn't receive the sap of the tree. By remaining in Christ, we give Jesus the ability to work through us and bear fruit in the ministry. Everyone who isn't connected to Jesus through a personal relationship isn't bearing the fruit that pleases God. Every branch that bears fruit abides in Christ and is capable of bearing fruit through a relationship with Him. Additionally, God prunes the branches of those who remain in Christ and produce fruit so that they can produce even more fruit. Relationships drive ministry, not the other way around.

We can't serve Jesus through ministry the way He meant for us if we don't know His will. And His will is revealed through personal fellowship with Him. It's just like in the family. What we do for our loved ones is way less important than our relationship with them. Ministry is just a by-product, a fruit of our life with God. As a result and outcome of that relationship, He leads us and works through us so we can bear fruit.

Everything we accomplish successfully, according to God's standard, comes out of our relationship with Jesus, and He helps us accomplish what He sends us out to do. As long as the relationship grows, the ministry will be fruitful according to God, regardless of the value people put on it. The success of the ministry comes from our relationship with God, not the approval of men. Only love will compel us to readily accept what Jesus wants us to do and perform this with gratitude. It will be burdensome to perform God's will without a relationship with Him. The most important thing is to follow His voice and to adhere to His instructions. He is the one who sends us on a mission for a specific task.

Ministry shouldn't take our focus away from the one we serve. Ministry to God will not replace a relationship with God. Some believers claim they're all sold out for Jesus, but they're actually all sold out for ministry. People's identities can be in their ministry rather than in Christ. They live for ministry and are obsessed with it. They serve others, taking part in church activities while not spending time with Jesus due to shortage of time. Their ministry can even look successful on the outside even if they live in continuous sin or have a shallow relationship with Jesus. God is testing us to see if He remains more important to us than our call to ministry.

Only if we have a relationship with Him and receive ongoing guidance from Him can we carry out God's ministry in His way. What He desires is to have loving fellowship with His children who can also do service for Him. It's our love for God and gratitude for Him that motivates us to please Him and do what He desires. If you only do things for God but don't have an ongoing relationship with Him, then your work for God is in vain. The goal is not to just stay busy being overly focused and preoccupied with ministry, trying to accomplish as much as possible; on the contrary, it's about having that relationship with Jesus and then doing what He tells us during our alone time with Him.

The wrong approach to ministry is, "I perform this service ministry to earn God's favor." The right motive to perform ministry is out of gratitude and love for Him, not in order to earn God's favor or focus on a reward in heaven. The love of a grateful heart reveals the heart of a child toward a heavenly Father. A ministry without a relationship with Jesus is guided by selfish ambitions. The ministry that we do, that is approved by God, can only be achieved by spending time with Him.

Jesus said, "And a slave does not abide in the house forever, but a son abides forever" (John 8:35). Our status of being His sons and daughters is greater than the status of us being a servant, and this mentality should drive our ministry.

Outside of Christ, good works are works of self-righteousness. To people, our good works might seem good at face value, but God knows our standing before Him, whether we abide in Christ or not.

He examines the motives of our heart for doing ministry and whether our hearts are entirely dedicated to Him. Is your ministry God-driven? Ask yourself, "Am I working for the ministry or am I working for God?"

It's easy to neglect and put aside spending time with God where no one can see us and appreciate what we do. It seems much more productive to do ministry for God in the public view and to receive validation from others.

If we prefer to do service for God rather than spend time with Him, then this would lead to a relationship based on performance. Instead, God wants us to prioritize meeting with Him over the service we can do for Him. In God's eyes, our time spent in our prayer room is way more important than our ministry for

Him. Focus more on your relationship with God. Come often before Him with your attention on Him.

## Relationship Continues on for Eternity

We can't have salvation without relationship, and we can't have relationship without salvation. Salvation and relationship are intertwined; one cannot exist without the other. How do we go through the process of justification, sanctification, and glorification? Being saved starts here on earth, but sanctification is a lifelong process. It's very important to understand that once we're born again, God continuously sanctifies us with His Word. Paul wrote, "[God] who has saved us and called us with a holy calling, not according to our works, but according to His own purpose and grace which was given to us in Christ Jesus before time began" (2 Timothy 1:9). So, we are saved. At the same time, though, we are *being* saved and *we will* be saved. "For the message of the cross is foolishness to those who are perishing, but to us who *are being saved* it is the power of God" (1 Corinthians 1:18, emphasis added).

Salvation is an ongoing process that starts with being free from the penalty of sin. It's being free from sin, not just qualifying to get into heaven. It's a walk, not merely crossing the line. It's a journey, not just a destination.

Salvation takes a lifetime to complete. It begins with justification (freedom from the penalty of sin), then it continues with sanctification (freedom from the power of sin), and finally is completed in glorification (freedom from the presence of sin).

In the New Testament, the verb "to save" is used in past, present, and future tenses—we have been saved, we are being saved, and we will be saved. Once we're born again, we receive freedom from sin. Throughout life, God continues to sanctify us—with our cooperation. In the afterlife, those who were saved will be permanently separated from the presence of sin; this separation is called glorification. "He has delivered us from such a deadly peril, and he will deliver us again. On him we have set our hope that he will continue to deliver us" (2 Corinthians 1:10).

Make no mistake, salvation is a journey. You have not signed up for a mere rescue mission, but a wonderful, long road ahead. The Bible is replete with passages on this: "But he who endures to the end shall be saved" (Matthew 24:13); "Therefore consider the goodness and severity of God: on those who fell, severity; but toward you, goodness, if you continue in His goodness. Otherwise you also will be cut off" (Romans 11:22); "I have fought the good fight, I have finished the race, I have kept the faith" (2 Timothy 4:7); "Therefore, brethren, be even more diligent to make your call and election sure, for if you do these things you will never stumble" (2 Peter 1:10); "Keep yourselves in the love of God, looking for the mercy of our Lord Jesus Christ unto eternal life" (Jude 1:21); "He who overcomes shall be clothed in white garments, and I will not blot out his name from the Book of Life; but I will confess his name before My Father and before His angels" (Revelation 3:5).

Some want to do the bare minimum in order to be saved and have their salvation secured, so they're focusing only on crossing the line. God's Word says that salvation is a continuous process in which we must work hard to walk in holiness and righteousness with God. This requires our involvement and God's involvement and our cooperation throughout our lifetime in order to finish life in holiness. During the sanctification process, God works to transform us into the image of His Son, Jesus Christ.

It's crucial that we continue to walk in salvation and work out our salvation instead of doubting our salvation when we fall into sin. We just need to repent and ask God for forgiveness. It's important to understand that we're saved and that we're being saved, which is an ongoing process. We can't live in willful, continuous, and perpetual sin all the time. To continue in willful sin is to make a mockery of Christ's sacrifice.

After being born again, it's crucial to continue asking God

for forgiveness and working out our salvation as we continue to walk in the light. "Work out your own salvation with fear and trembling" (Philippians 2:12).

Believer's life thrives on a growing relationship with Jesus, fostered by actively opening our hearts and sharing our experiences with Him. The Bride who knows Him intimately awaits Jesus' return.

# Appendix

*Suggested Scripture Reading on Keeping the Faith until the End*

You will be hated by everyone because of me, but the one who stands firm to the end will be saved. (Matthew 10:22)

Jesus answered: "Watch out that no one deceives you. For many will come in my name, claiming, 'I am the Messiah,' and will deceive many." (Matthew 24:4)

Who then is the faithful and wise servant, whom the master has put in charge of the servants in his household to give them their food at the proper time? It will be good for that servant whose master finds him doing so when he returns. Truly I tell you, he will put him in charge of all his possessions. But suppose that servant is wicked and says to himself, "My master is staying away a long time," and he then begins to beat his fellow servants and to eat and drink with drunkards. The master of that servant will come on a day when he does not expect him and at an hour he is not aware of. He will cut him to pieces and assign him a place with the hypocrites, where there will be weeping and gnashing of teeth. (Matthew 24:45-51)

And then many will be offended, will betray one another, and will hate one another. Then many false prophets will rise up and deceive many. And because lawlessness will abound, the love of many will grow cold. But he who endures to the end shall be saved. (Matthew 24:10-13)

Afterward the other virgins came also, saying, "Lord, Lord, open to us!" But he answered and said, "Assuredly, I say to you, I do not know you." Watch therefore, for you know neither the day nor the hour in which the Son of Man is coming. (Matthew 25:11-13)

And you will be hated by all for My name's sake. But he who endures to the end shall be saved. (Mark 13:13)

And everyone who competes for the prize is temperate in all things. Now they do it to obtain a perishable crown, but we for an imperishable crown. Therefore I run thus: not with uncertainty. Thus I fight: not as one who beats the air. But I discipline my body and bring it into subjection, lest, when I have preached to others, I myself should become disqualified. (1 Corinthians 9:25-27)

Now all these things happened to them as examples, and they were written for our admonition, upon whom the ends of the ages have come. Therefore let him who thinks he stands take heed lest he fall. (1 Corinthians 10:11-12)

And you, who once were alienated and enemies in your mind by wicked works, yet now He has reconciled in the body of His flesh through death, to present you holy, and blameless, and above reproach in His sight—if indeed you continue in the faith, grounded and steadfast, and are not moved away from the hope of the gospel which you heard. (Colossians 1:21-23)

For if we died with Him, We shall also live with Him. If we endure, We shall also reign with Him. If we deny Him, He also will deny us. (2 Timothy 2:11-12)

But Christ as a Son over His own house, whose house we are if we hold fast the confidence and the rejoicing of the hope firm to the end. (Hebrews 3:6)

Blessed is the man who endures temptation; for when he has been approved, he will receive the crown of life which the Lord has promised to those who love Him. (James 1:12)

For if, after they have escaped the pollutions of the world through the knowledge of the Lord and Savior Jesus Christ, they are again entangled in them and overcome, the latter end is worse for them than the beginning. For it would have been better for them not to have known the way of righteousness, than having known it, to turn from. (2 Peter 2:20-21)

Therefore let that abide in you which you heard from the beginning. If what you heard from the beginning abides in you, you also will abide in the Son and in the Father. And this is the promise that He has promised us—eternal life. (1 John 2:24-25)

Do not fear any of those things which you are about to suffer. Indeed, the devil is about to throw some of you into prison, that you may be tested, and you will have tribulation ten days. Be faithful until death, and I will give you the crown of life. "He who has an ear, let him hear what the Spirit says to the churches. He who overcomes shall not be hurt by the second death." (Revelation 2:10-11)

ANDREY BOYNETSKIY is involved in evangelizing with his wife, Elena, in the US and Australia. He has a passion to represent Jesus and assist others in their journey towards reconciling with God in order to establish a meaningful relationship with Him. Andrey was fascinated with this significant topic of a relationship with God for many years. Years later, he had the opportunity to write a book on this very topic.

Thank you for taking the time to read this book. I hope it provided valuable insights into your personal walk with God and helped draw you closer to Him. If you feel led to support our ministry in spreading the gospel, you can contribute through PayPal, Wise, or Cash App. Your support helps us continue this important work of reaching more souls with the truth. Our desire is for more people to come to know how to reconcile with God and begin a loving relationship with Him. Together, we can make an eternal impact.

- PayPal: andruha2010@gmail.com
- CashApp: $ElenaBoynetskiy
- Wise: https://wise.com/pay/me/elenab494

For questions, comments, or to share your thoughts please feel free to reach out to me at: *createdforrelationship@gmail.com*

# Citations

1. Pawson, David. "The Normal Christian Birth." DavidPawson.org. David Pawson Ministry CIO, 2021. https://www.davidpawson.org/resources/series/the-normal-christian-birth
2. Brown, Aaron D'Anthony. "How Do Christians Actually 'Die to Self'?" Christianity.com. April 22, 2021. https://www.christianity.com/wiki/bible/how-do-christians-die-to-self.html
3. Got Questions. "What does the Bible mean by 'dying to self'?" GotQuestions.org. Accessed 2023. https://www.gotquestions.org/dying-to-self.html
4. Kauflin, Jordan. "What Does It Really Mean to Take Up Your Cross and Follow Jesus?" Truth For Life Blog. November 29, 2022. https://blog.truthforlife.org/what-does-it-really-mean-to-take-up-your-cross-and-follow-jesus

# Chapter Study Questions

### Chapter 1

1. How does trying to fill the "God-shaped hole" affect our search for fulfillment, and what consequences arise from pursuing alternatives to satisfy this void?
2. How does our freedom of choice impact our decision to reconcile with God, and what are the repercussions of neglecting this choice?
3. How does this aligning of your personal desires with God's intentions impact a fulfilling life in union with God?

### Chapter 2

1. What is the difference between spiritual death and being "made alive with Christ"? How does this transformation affect one's relationship with God?
2. What is the interconnection between belief, repentance, water baptism, and baptism in the Holy Spirit in the process of becoming born again?
3. How does the Holy Spirit's presence and guidance contribute to a transformed life after the born-again experience?

### Chapter 3

1. How does Scripture illustrate that being born again empowers believers to overcome sin, despite still facing temptation?
2. What strategies does the Bible offer for navigating the ongoing conflict between the old sinful nature and the new life in Christ? How does this inner battle affect daily living for believers?
3. How can believers unintentionally distance themselves from God even after salvation? What practical steps does Scripture suggest to maintain intimacy with God and resist falling into sinful habits or thoughts?

### Chapter 4

1. How does Scripture portray the correlation between our lives' "fruit" and our relationship with God?
2. How does our visible relationship with God impact those around us? Consider the influence of our speech, priorities, and interactions on revealing our devotion to God in daily life.
3. How should believers approach receiving and responding to correction, both from God and trusted individuals, to continually refine their spiritual growth?

### Chapter 5

1. What key aspects define a healthy relationship, and how do they relate to our connection with God?
2. How does our innate need for love and acceptance impact our quest for relationships, especially our longing for a connection with God?
3. How does God's love address past hurts and fulfill our emotional needs?

## Chapter 6

1. What obstructs our connection with God, and how do selfishness, pride, past hurt, and worldly temptations contribute to this barrier?
2. How do worldly desires and blessings sometimes distract us from nurturing a genuine relationship with Jesus?
3. How can we identify and address idols that hinder our spiritual growth and connection with God? What defines idolatry in our lives, and how does it impact our relationship with Jesus?

## Chapter 7

1. How does discipline shape our consistency in connecting with God? How can we redirect these qualities to prioritize our relationship with Him?
2. What defines a sincere pursuit of God versus a half-hearted approach? How can we evaluate our commitment to fostering a genuine relationship with Jesus?
3. Why is wholehearted devotion crucial in seeking God? How do distractions and worldly desires hinder our efforts to maintain a faithful relationship with Him?

## Chapter 8

1. What characterizes the "secret place" in our relationship with God throughout our daily routine?
2. Why is undivided attention vital in our communion with God? How does reducing distractions during our alone time with Him impact our connection?
3. How can we incorporate ongoing meditation on God throughout each day?

## Chapter 9

1. What prayer forms are discussed in this chapter and how do they deepen our bond with God?
2. How does keeping prayer simple contribute to a more profound relationship with God? Why prioritize sincerity, humility, and honesty in prayer instead of elaborate expressions?
3. How does turning to God in worship and meditation reshape our perspective and reliance on Him?

## Chapter 10

1. What role does the Bible play in revealing God's character and guiding our lives?
2. Why is it essential to regard the Bible as the ultimate truth and foundation in life?
3. How does regular interaction with the Bible foster spiritual growth? What steps can we take to ensure our relationship with God through His Word keeps growing and evolving?

## Chapter 11

1. How does past hurt hinder our connection with God's love and relationships with others?
2. What steps help heal the brokenness caused by past experiences and pain from others?
3. How does blame stop spiritual growth and hinder deep relationships with God?

## Chapter 12

1. How does our daily conversation impact our relationship with God, and how can it either draw us closer or distract us from Him?

2. What warning signs in our interactions signal a potential negative influence on our spiritual growth and relationship with Jesus?
3. Why is it essential to discern the influence of those around us in terms of our spiritual walk, and how can we navigate relationships that may hinder our relationship with God?

## Chapter 13

1. What might make us hesitant to share our relationship with Jesus?
2. How does personal experience with Jesus impact your ability to openly share your faith?
3. How do our transformed lives serve as evidence of our relationship with Jesus, and how does it influence others' perception of our faith?

## Chapter 14

1. How does seeking a relationship with Jesus differ from religious adherence?
2. What challenges emerge when people expect to find a genuine connection with God within religious structures, and how might disappointment in these contexts affect their perception of God?
3. How does religion prioritize outward appearances and traditions over a personal relationship with Jesus?

# Index

## A

anxiety
  anxious 88, 182, 185, 204, 212, 226, 227, 229

## B

bitter
  bitterness 221
breakthrough 78, 178, 196, 201

## C

character 12, 19, 73, 105, 114, 124, 134, 173, 182, 188, 191, 193, 194, 200, 218, 219, 220, 244, 245, 259, 284
community 169, 186, 260
confess
  confession 48, 63, 64, 65, 66, 104, 171, 270

## D

deliver
  deliverance 183

## E

eternity 9, 22, 23, 44, 91, 143

## F

faith 32, 273
fear 11, 41, 88, 91, 94, 115, 117, 124, 174, 182, 183, 204, 206, 208, 209, 210, 212, 214, 217, 227, 229, 236, 237, 238, 239, 261, 270, 275
forgive 63, 65, 66, 67, 76, 77, 78, 79, 184, 185, 200, 217, 221, 222, 223, 224

## G

grace 13, 17, 38, 51, 53, 56, 61, 62, 67, 69, 70, 82, 84, 182, 186, 209, 220, 269

# H

Holy Spirit  17, 19, 23, 31, 32, 34, 36, 38, 39, 40, 41, 42, 43, 45, 51, 65, 142, 152, 153, 159, 164, 179, 181, 186, 187, 188, 189, 190, 194, 205, 251, 252, 256, 260, 261, 265, 281
hope  13, 23, 43, 56, 111, 151, 194, 269, 275

# I

inherit
  inheritance  190

# J

jealous
  jealousy  138, 152
joy  44, 55, 96, 97, 112, 157, 171, 172, 182, 190, 205, 215, 225, 226, 229, 230, 243

# K

knowledge
  knowing  16, 18, 42, 46, 47, 50, 52, 55, 72, 95, 99, 106, 149, 155, 174, 194, 197, 200, 201, 210, 234, 249, 275

# L

love  12, 13, 14, 15, 16, 17, 18, 19, 20, 21, 23, 24, 26, 27, 30, 37, 43, 48, 58, 59, 61, 62, 63, 64, 65, 68, 73, 74, 75, 76, 77, 78, 79, 87, 88, 89, 90, 91, 92, 93, 94, 95, 96, 97, 98, 99, 100, 101, 102, 103, 104, 107, 109, 110, 111, 112, 113, 115, 116, 122, 127, 128, 131, 133, 134, 135, 136, 137, 138, 139, 151, 152, 153, 154, 157, 163, 164, 170, 171, 172, 173, 174, 175, 176, 178, 184, 185, 186, 190, 198, 199, 202, 206, 207, 211, 212, 213, 214, 218, 219, 220, 222, 223, 224, 225, 226, 227, 228, 229, 230, 231, 233, 234, 235, 238, 239, 240, 242, 244, 251, 256, 259, 263, 265, 266, 267, 268, 270, 274, 275, 282, 284

# M

memory  164, 219
mind  21, 23, 30, 32, 33, 34, 43, 54, 56, 57, 61, 66, 73, 90, 91, 93, 94, 108, 110, 123, 124, 152, 154, 156, 159, 163, 164, 173, 184, 188, 189, 191, 193, 202, 219, 222, 233, 242, 245, 275

## N

newness
  new 36, 69

## O

obey
  obedience ii, 16, 25, 26, 28, 30, 76, 82, 90, 109, 114, 119, 130, 146, 158, 171, 176, 177, 180, 181, 184, 188, 196, 203, 208, 216, 217, 218, 226, 228, 235, 265, 266, 267, 270

## P

perseverance 105, 127, 189
persistence 105, 127, 189
prayer 105, 127, 189

## R

repent
  repentance 21, 28, 32, 34, 59, 62, 63, 66, 75, 77, 79, 142, 184, 185, 189, 200, 221, 255, 265, 270

## S

salvation 9, 10, 14, 18, 20, 31, 32, 34, 39, 42, 44, 50, 53, 62, 171, 176, 186, 188, 269, 270, 282
sin 9, 11, 14, 17, 18, 19, 23, 27, 29, 30, 31, 33, 34, 35, 36, 37, 38, 39, 40, 42, 43, 44, 45, 51, 52, 53, 54, 55, 56, 57, 58, 59, 60, 61, 62, 63, 64, 65, 66, 67, 68, 69, 70, 76, 77, 80, 82, 85, 89, 103, 104, 112, 123, 171, 182, 184, 185, 189, 206, 207, 209, 211, 212, 213, 217, 221, 228, 255, 256, 257, 261, 262, 263, 267, 269, 270, 282
surrender 25, 47, 75, 81, 101, 108, 109, 130, 170, 176, 181, 219, 223, 224, 226

## T

testimony 244
tongue 188, 244
trauma 48

## U

understanding  ii, 14, 19, 26, 33, 46, 47, 48, 83, 95, 102, 124, 156, 157, 174, 180, 181, 194, 197, 201, 208, 209, 219

## W

work
  works  ii, 16, 25, 26, 28, 30, 76, 82, 90, 109, 114, 119, 130, 146, 158, 171, 176, 177, 180, 181, 184, 188, 196, 203, 208, 216, 217, 218, 226, 228, 235, 265, 266, 267, 270

## Y

yearn  25, 78, 94

For bulk order information, contact *Tall Pine Books*
*www.TallPineBooks.com*